Committees and Commissions in India
1975

Concepts in Communication
Informatics & Librarianship-49

General Editor : **S.P. Agrawal**

Committees and Commissions in India 1975

Volume 13

A Concept's Project

Compiled by a team of professionals
under the auspice of
VIRENDRA KUMAR

CONCEPT PUBLISHING COMPANY, NEW DELHI 110059

ISBN 81-7022-482-9 (Vol. 13)

First Published 1993

Published and Printed by
Ashok Kumar Mittal
Concept Publishing Company
A/15-16, Commercial Block, Mohan Garden
NEW DELHI 110059 (India)

Lasertypeset by
Printing Express
H-13, Bali Nagar
NEW DELHI 110015

GENERAL EDITOR'S INTRODUCTION

In the context of the changing world, the role of the government – be it at central, state or local level – is becoming more prevasive in the modern society. Everyday, it has to encounter new problems and face new issues which demand quite a new thinking and novel strategies to overcome them. Thus, the increasing role of the government in every sphere of people's life has broadened its functions and responsibilities tremendously and enlarged its activities to such an extent that the government machinery of its own can hardly manage its affairs. Moreover, its functions are becoming more complicated and complex requiring the assistance of outside specialists, technocrats and specialized agencies.

In view of this, the modern government has to set-up committees and commissions and working or study groups on various problems and issue from time to time. In the light of the recommendations of these committees and commissions, the government takes decisions on key issues and problems. Often the government is obliged to seek the assistance of a committee to evaluate some of its schemes in operation so that on the basis of the evaluation reports of the committee, it may either continue, modify or scrap the on-going schemes. In other words, the committees or commissions, etc., exercise a great deal of pivotal force in shaping the policies and programmes of the government and for this purpose submit a large number of reports.

In these volumes of *Committees and Commissions in India*, now being published under the *Concepts in Communication Informatics and Librarianship (CICIL)* series, an attempt has been made to cover the period from 1974 onwards. The volumes include the vital data about only those reports of the committees and commissions which have been constituted by the Central Government. We have made every endeavour to include the digest of all the important reports on various vital issues of great importance and on major areas of national development.

We have also an ambitious plan to publish the digests of the important reports of the committees and commissions appointed by different state governments, the semi-government organisations and the learned bodies as also the reports published during the period of the British Government.

The publication has been brought out under the guidance of Shri Virendra Kumar, specialist in his own right with vast experience of working in Government Documents Section in the Central Secretariat Library and having the privilege of the blessings of Dr. S.R. Ranganathan – the father of Indian Library Science. I also put on record the collaborative help provided by Shri M.W.K. Sherwani.

We are sure that this compilation will prove a very useful reference tool for researchers, serious students and scholars of the public administration and political science, administrators, policy-makers, educationists and historians.

S.P. AGRAWAL

PREFACE

This volume of *Committees and Commissions in India* attempts to understand the activities of the various Committees and Commissions during the period 1974.

A 'Commission' is a governmental agency created to perform a particular function such as special investigations or on governmental regulations of business. It is appointed mainly when it is thought that a matter involves some financial questions. There are other reasons for which a Commission is appointed, e.g., in matters pertaining to welfare of the State and its citizens and or improving the efficiency in an administration. The status of a 'Committee' is also the same as that of a 'Commission', but it does not possess as wide powers as are enjoyed by a Commission and has to limit itself to specific work assigned to it under its terms of reference. While arriving at decisions in the form of recommendations, a Commission or Committee ensures that such decisions are representative of interests of various types of people and also a safeguard against abuse of power.

A Committee or a Commission comprises a Chairman, the Members and Member Secretary (sometimes there is also an Assistant Secretary). In some cases, there are even One-man Commissions and the enquiry in such Commissions is entrusted to an Officer-on-Special Duty.

The Chairman of a Commission is a person well-versed mostly in legal matters and is often a retired judge of a High Court or the Supreme Court of India. Occasionally, a Member of Parliament is also appointed as the Chairman of a Commission. On the other hand, the Chairman of the Committee is mostly a specialist in the subject of the Committee. He can be a Leader or a Convenor also, if he heads a Panel, a Study Group or a Delegation, etc.

The Members of a Commission, Committee, Panel, Study Group etc., are specialists in their respective fields and provide valuable guidance to the Commission or the Committee in making recommendations.

The Member-Secretary or Secretary is generally nominated from among the experienced officials who have the requisite competent knowledge of the subject on which the Commission or the Committee is appointed.

Committees and Commissions in India provides in chronological order vital information about Committees and Commissions appointed by the Government from time to time. Information for each Committee or Commission is presented in a compact form in four parts, namely; Constitution; Appointment; Terms of Reference and Recommendations.

CONTENTS

1

RAILWAY ACCIDENT INVESTIGATION REPORT ON DERAILMENT OF 59 UP KAMRUP EXPRESS BETWEEN NEW JALPAIGURI AND AMBARI FALAKATA STATIONS OF NORTH-EAST FRONTIER RAILWAY AT ABOUT 11.35 HOURS ON 26TH FEBRUARY, 1975

March 1–3, 1975[1]

One Man Commission Shri J.Y. Marathe, Additional Commissioner of Railway Safety, North-Eastern Circle, Gorakhpur.

Officers Present Shri G. Bhattacharjya; A.K. Chatterjee; Shri S. Ponnuswamy; Shri Srikant Sharma

Appointment

The Commission was constituted under Rule 4 of the Railway Board's Notification No. 59/TTV/42/1 dated the 11th April, 1966.

Terms of Reference

To inquire into the derailment of 59 UP Kamrup Express between New Jalpaiguri and Ambari Falakata Stations of Northeast Frontier Railway at about 11.35 hours on 26 February, 1975.

Conclusions

35. *Cause*: On full consideration of the factual material and circumstantial evidence, I have come to the conclusion that the derailment of 59 Up Kamrup Express at km. 7/13-14 between New Jal-

---

1. Ministry of Tourism and Civil Aviation (Commission of Railway Safety) Government of India, New Delhi, 1986, i + 14 p.

paiguri and Ambari Falakata stations on the New Jalpaiguri-New Bongaigaon B.G. Section of Northeast Frontier Railway at about 11.35 hours on 26-2-75 was due to buckline of track occasioned by excessive creep and jamming of joints.

36. *Responsibility*:

36.1 The Permanent Way Inspector-I, New Jalpaiguri, B.K. Nandy is responsible for this accident. In assessing the gravity of his offence, the remarks made in paras 32 and 33 may, however, be taken into consideration.

> [Shri B.K. Nandy, 54 years of age joined Railway Service as a Gangman on 16-4-38 and after working his way through the posts of Keyman, Mate and Head Mate, was promoted as APWI (Assistant Permanent Way Inspector) on 8-11-51. He was promoted as PWI, Grade Rs. 250-380 (AS) on 28-7-59, as PWI, Grade Rs. 335-485 (AS) on 17-10-63 and as PWI, Grade Rs. 450-575 (AS) on 24-4-70 and is working in that capacity at present.
> He had no punishment in the past.]

36.2 A certain amount of blame lies on the Assistant Engineer/New Jalpaiguri, Mr. N. Tirupatayya for slack supervision and not ensuring that the work of pulling back the creep, though sanctioned in October, 1974 was carried out by the PWI in time.

37. *Relief Measures*: The relief measures were prompt and satisfactory.

Recommendations

38. Although there are standing instructions that as soon as six or more continuous joints become jammed or there is a creep in excess of 150 mm, creep adjustment work should be done, these instructions were found to have been ignored by the Permanent Way Inspector. The Assistant Engineer and the Divisional Engineer who frequently trolley over the section, did not seem to have bothered about non-adjustment of the creep in time which was the heaviest in km. 7, although labour was sanctioned for that purpose since October 1974. The machinery for ensuring that the standing instructions are complied with in time, needs to be tightened up.

39. In certain locations, if Fair-V or Fair-T anchors are not found to be fully successful in arresting the creep, it is suggested that 40 to 60 per cent of sleepers may be provided with Anti-Creep Bearing Plates. Improved track maintenance at these locations and steps to avoid the causes which lead to creep as mentioned in Para 638(b)—W.W. Manual should also be taken and would need hardly any emphasis.

40. In km. 7 and 8 between New Jalpaiguri and Ambari Falakata, it was seen that there was differential creep on the two right rails, the rail having moved ahead by 39″ and the left rail by 22″. The differential creep was obviously the result of fittings on one rail being more loose than on the other. As such creep leads to staggering of joints and sleepers going out of square, more and proper attention should be given to ensure that the fittings are uniformly tight on both the rails.

41. There was a mixture of soft wood and hard wood sleepers in the track between New Jalpaiguri and Ambari Falakata. This is against the standing instructions contained in para 647(b) of W.W. Manual. Mixing of the two types of sleepers affects the track modulus and the running is not satisfactory. It may, therefore, be ensured that as far as possible, the two types of sleepers are not mixed up in the track.

42. The general slackness in maintenance of track and its poor condition on the Northeast Frontier Railway have been commented upon on a number of occasions in the past and this brings a bad name to the entire Civil Engineering Department of the Railway. Some effective steps to improve the state of affairs are urgently called for.

43. There are standing instructions that on Mail and Express Trains, speed recorders should be provided in addition to the speedometers. On the day in question, however, no speed recorder was found to have been provided in the VDO Speed Indicator on the Engine of 59 Up Kamrup Express. When a recorder is inserted in a speedometer the fact is mentioned in a separate register kept in the Loco Foreman's Office. It was, however, seen that this register had entries only up to 6-2-75 and thereafter the register was blank. The machinery ensuring that the speed recorders are always inserted needs to be tightened up.

44. It was understood during the inquiry that the speed recorders recovered from the Mail and Express Trains are merely kept in a bunch and are checked at random by the AME (Assistant Mechanical Engineer) and if he finds that any driver has exceeded

speed anywhere, a Warning is issued to that driver. This does not seem to be adequate and it is considered that there should be a proper system of examining each recorder and taking action against the defaulting driver wherever necessary. This will also ensure a post check whether a recorder was provided on every train or not.

45. There was no vacuum gauge provided in the Guard's Van even on an important train, like Kamrup Express. It also came out in the evidence that on 50 per cent of Mail and Express Trains gauges are not provided. In the absence of a gauge, the Guard is likely to forget checking of the vacuum and the extent to which it is created and this may lead to unsafe working. Necessary measures may be taken to ensure that in all Mail and express Trains, vacuum gauges are invariably provided in the Guard's van.

46. There are standing instructions that the Control should give a time signal at 17.00 hours everyday, to all stations to adjust their clocks. It was, however, understood that this time signal is not being regularly given and sometimes it is not given because the Control lines are out of order. Adjustment of time at all stations and of all operating staff is a matter of vital importance and it may be ensured that time signals are given regularly by the Control of 17.00 hours.

47. At New Jalpaiguri station there are no clocks in the station office and the block cabins on either side and the station staff depend on their own watches. This is not a satisfactory arrangement and proper clocks should be proved in the Assistant Station Master's Office as well as in the Cabins.

48. When a train enters a block section, the information about the train entering the section is given by beats on the Block Instrument to the station ahead which in turn acknowledges this information also by beats on the Block Instrument. Sometimes when the Station Master in the station ahead is busy and does not acknowledge the information, the same is again and again conveyed by the original station by beats till it is acknowledged by the station ahead. It is only when the information is acknowledged that the time seen in the clock is recorded in the Train Register of the station ahead which likely to be quite different from the actual time, the train entered the section. It is suggested that in addition to conveying this information by beats, the same should also be conveyed by the block telephone repeating the time the train entered the section so that the timings recorded will be accurate. For this purpose, a suitable subsidiary rule under G.R. 335 may be provided.

Railway Board's Comments on Various Parts of the Report

Railway Board's O.M. No. 75/Safety (A&R)Y7Y5 dt. 25-11-75

Para 38: Necessary action has been taken by the railway administration.

Para 39: 75 per cent of sleepers have been provided with Fair-V Anchors. M.S.CANTED bearing plates have also been provided in the existing track.

Para 40 Necessary action has been taken by the railway administration.

Para 41: Efforts will be made by the railways that as far as possible two types of sleepers are not mixed up.

Para 42: The general standard of maintenance on the B.G. section of the N.F. Railway is comparable with any other B.G. main line sections. Constant attention will also be paid to continue the good maintenance practices.

Paras 43 and 44: Railway Administration has been asked vide Board's letter No. 73M (M & P) 467/3 dated 26-9-1975 to adhere to the CRS's observations furnished in his Note forwarded under this letter No. RS. 22—T(4)/75 dated 1-9-1975.

Para 45: Northeast Frontier Railways as well as Eastern Railway have confirmed that no passenger or express train is running with defective or deficient vacuum gauges. All other Railways have also been advised suitably in this regard.

Paras 46 and 47: Necessary action has been taken by the railway administration.

Para 48: Necessary instructions on the subject have been issued to Railways vide Railway Board's circular No. 75/Safety (A&R)/29/14 dated 21-11-76.

RAILWAY ACCIDENT INVESTIGATION REPORT ON DERAILMENT OF 365 UP SEALDAH-LALGOLA PASSENGER TRAIN AT THE UP FACING POINTS OF BIRNAGAR STATION AT 89/14-16 ON SEALDAH-LALGOLA SECTION OF EASTERN RAILWAY AT ABOUT 16.23 HOURS ON 26TH MARCH, 1975[1]

One Man Commission Shri S.K. Mojumdar, Additional Commissioner of Railway Safety, Eastern Circle, Calcutta.

Officers Present Shri R.K. Basu; Shri N. Basak; Shri S.K. Julka; Shri R.R. Ghosh.

Appointment

The Commission was constituted under Rule 4 of the Statutory Investigation into Railway Accidents Rule, 1973 issued by the Ministry of Tourism and Civil Aviation vide their Notification No. RS 13.T(8)/71 dated 19th April, 1973.

Terms of Reference

To enquire into the derailment of 365 Up Sealdah-Lalgola Passenger Train at the up facing points of Birnagar Station at 89/14-16 on Sealdah-Lalgola section of Eastern Railway at about 16.23 hours on 26th March, 1975.

---

1. Ministry of Tourism and Civil Aviation (Commission of Railway Safety), Government of India, New Delhi, 1986, (i) + 10 p.

Conclusions

23. After full consideration of all facts, material and circumstantial evidence I have reached the conclusion that the derailment of 365 Up Sealdah-Lalgola Passenger at the Up facing points of Birnagar Station on Sealdah-Lalgola Section of Eastern Railway at 16.23 hours on 26-3-75 was caused by mismanipulation of the facing points under the train. This was possible as the levers of the Up Home signal and the lock bar of the facing points were normalised just before the train engine came over the lock bar.

24. *Responsibility*: Shuntman, Sri Ramjit Kahar (working as Leverman), is held responsible for the above accident in putting back the Up Home signal to 'On' and unlocking the facing points in the face of an approaching train before it had completely passed the signal and changing over the points before the train had come to a stand. He has thus violated General Rule 36(c) and Subsidiary Rule 36(c)(i). He has also failed to record ASM's Private Number for the line nomination and to give his own Private Number to the Assistant Station Master in confirmation of his having set and locked the route for 365 Up. In addition he failed to record the ASM's Private Number for the confirmation of the pulling of slide for the Up Main Home signal as well as its cancellation and changing the slide to that for Down Loop Home signal as alleged by him. He has thus violated the instructions contained in para 5(b)(ii) of the Station Working Rules for Birnagar.

25. *Service particulars*: Sri Ramjit Kahar, aged 31½ years, read up to Class V, was appointed as Gateman on 18-9-67 and promoted as Shuntman on 21-1-70. He had no punishment.

26. *Relief measures*: The injured passengers were promptly removed to the nearest hospital at Birnagar from where they were transferred to the Sub-divisional Hospital at Ranaghat. The Railway Medical team also reached the site by the medical van of Ranaghat and looked after the injured passengers in the hospital. Relief measures are considered satisfactory.

Recommendations

27. It is distressing to note that the procedure laid down in the Station Working Rules regarding exchange of Private Numbers are being flagrantly disregarded. As indicated in para 11 and the Note of

the report, the practice of not exchanging Private Numbers simultaneously for the various transactions and transmitting of instructions, has become a regular feature at the station. The numbers are recorded subsequently at the close of a shift, which nullifies the very purpose for which the procedure has been introduced and most of the Station Operating Staff appeared to be liable to blame in this regard. The checks by supervisory staff as well as officers have also been ineffective in detecting and stopping this practice. The Station Master, Sri P.R. Bhowmick is blameworthy for lack of supervision and not insisting on the correct procedure being followed in train working.

28. Another serious irregularity observed was that a Shuntman was being frequently deputed to work as Leverman in the Cabin without his having undergone any training for this work nor having a competency certificate in this category. I was informed that: "there is no Leave Reserve Leverman Grade II in the Sealdah Division, for Cabinman Grade, II and Leverman Grade I, instead Relieving Pointsmen have been provided. Pointsmen and Shuntmen have the same initial training course. Due to acute shortage of Relieving Pointsmen, Relieving Shuntman Sri Ramjit Kahar had to be utilised by the Relief Arrangements. Clerk, Sealdah, at the Birnagar Cabin from 24-3-75." At the inquiry Sri Kahar also complained that the Station Working Rules had not been explained to him when he signed the Assurance Register. He had not been tested by the Traffic Inspector on the Leverman's duty and had been trained only as a Shuntman. This is a highly undesirable state of affairs as no competency certificate indicating that he had been tested as Leverman could be produced before me. It is recommended that staff who have not been tested and whose competency has not been certified, must not be deputed to work as Leverman in a Cabin even in short relieving arrangements. Whenever such staff are posted at a station they should be tested by the Traffic Inspector of the section in the categories in which they have been trained and the test certificate must be available at the station for check by supervising officials. At present the competency certificates are maintained in the headquarters as such, verification on the spot is not possible and irregularities of the type indicated above continue without being brought to light. Necessary steps may also be taken to ensure that the Station Working Rules are fully explained to the staff by the Station Master before taking their signature in the Assurance Register.

29. There was no vacuum gauge in the brake van of 365 Up nor did the guard have one with him. Such a deficiency used to be an exception in earlier days but has now become the rule more so in the branch line sections and calls for Railway Board's attention.

Railway Board's Comments on Various Parts of the Report

Para 27: Instructions already exist that in order to avoid multiple exchange of private numbers between the Station Master and the Cabin, it would be sufficient of only one private number is exchanged for the entire transaction consisting of nomination of line and releasing of SM's control on the Home Signal, but the exchange should take place only prior to the release of SM's control over the signal, i.e., at the end of the transaction. These instructions have been reiterated to the railways.

Para 28: Necessary action had been taken by the railway administration. Suitable instructions have also been issued to the railways vide letter No. E(NG) I-76PMI/36 dated 27-3-1976.

Para 29 : Suitable action has been taken by the railway administration.

3

UNIVERSITY GRANTS COMMISSION, SECOND REVIEW COMMITTEE ON SOCIAL WORK EDUCATION IN INDIA 1975 – REPORT[1]

Convenor Dr. (Miss) Armaity S. Desai

Members Dr. A.B. Bose; Prof. S. Dasgupta; Prof. K.D. Gangrade; Dr. J.N. Kaul; Dr. K.V. Sridharan

Co-opted Members Mr. S.R. Mohsini; Dr. K.G. Krishnamoorthy.

Appointment

A review of social work education under university auspices became imperative because of the rapid addition of training programmes in social work in the 1960s and the early 1970s, a majority of which were in the university framework. Many universities recognised departments in affiliated colleges or they affiliated single-faculty colleges for both under-graduate and post-graduate social work education. Some universities either establish their own departments, or created teaching facilities for social work in department already existing such as sociology.

While this expansion of Social Work education was taking place, the universities had no means for establishing standards for professional education. The criteria for establishing such standards were required to be related to the type of administrative structure necessary for professional education within the university framework; the type of linkage with the university; the staffing and grant-in-aid patterns. The standards were also related to the educational programme the syllabi, field work, and research.

The Association of the Schools of Social Work in India (ASSWI)

---

1. New Delhi, University Grants Commission 1980, 239 p.

had established minimum standards in 1961, but they were not periodically reviewed and upgraded. The first Review Committee had also set up certain criteria, but these were not enforced, and probably were not even known to the universities which affiliated the colleges of social work or established their own teaching departments.

There is no authority in social work education for the enforcement of standards, or for the recognition of equivalence. Newly established institutions tend to borrow existing syllabi without questioning their stability for the region in which they are established. The syllabi have never been reviewed as a whole since the late fifties and the early sixties although, periodically the ASSWI has addressed itself to some areas of the contents. Hence, it was necessary to review them for relevance in the present context of national development.

The First Review Committee for Social Work Education in India was appointed by the University Grants Commission in 1960. Since no subsequent review of Social Work education had been taken, a Second Review Committee was appointed by the Panel on Social Work of the University Grants Commission at its meeting on April 28, 1975.

Terms of Reference

1. Undertake a critical review of the existing programmes of social work education, including courses, field work and research:

(a) The scope of the review covers education at the doctoral, post-graduate, under-graduate and para-professional levels in colleges and departments of social work, and social work offered as an optional subject in departments other than social work.

(b) They will be examined especially from the point of view of their relevance to the needs of the country.

(c) The outgrowth of such examination may be the development of norms for education in social work, at each of these levels, in order to facilitate the establishment of equivalence.

2. Suggest changes that may be introduced with a view to making these programmes more meaningful and relevant.

3. Suggest ways and means of effecting these changes.

4. Study the procedural problems of the colleges and depart-

ments of social work within their respective universities.

5. Study the funding pattern.
6. Examine the role of the colleges and departments of Social Work in implementing the National Service Scheme, and suggest ways in which they could help effectively in accomplishing the objectives of the scheme.
7. Any other matters arising out of the above terms of reference.

Contents

Preface; Acknowledgements; Introduction; A Historical Review and a Future Perspective; Some Facts about Social Work Education: The Current Scene; Programme of Professional Education: Some General Considerations; Specifics of the Curricular related at the Para-Professional and the Bachelor's Levels; Specifics of the Curricular related to Education at the Master's Degree and Advanced Levels; Organisation of Social Work Education; Institutions for Social Work Education and the National Service Scheme; Summary of the Findings of the Second Review Committee for Social Work Education of the University Grants Commission; Summary of the Recommendations of the Second Review Committee for Social Work Education of the University Grants Commission; Appendix A, B and C; Index.

Findings

Introduction

The UGC appointed the first review committee for social work education in 1960 and the present committee in 1975. This report has been prepared with the perspective in view that any profession must review its past and must look ahead to its future so that it may be able to equip its educands for practice.

The issues faced by this Committee are:

1. The need to ensure a systematic development of social work in terms of its geographical distribution, and affiliation to recognised boards of education and universities.
2. The need to provide a holistic framework for the development

of a ladder programme of education where there are several termination points related to job functions in the country, but, at the same time, also relate each phase of education to the next, so that there are no dead-end training programmes and no dead-end jobs.

3. The need to develop standards, the means by which institutions could be assisted to develop and to maintain such standards; and the identification of structures for enforcement of standards.
4. The need to relate output of trained manpower to employment opportunities, to examine the problems of recruitment of trained social workers, and to make social work training at various levels as a requirement for different levels of identified job positions in the community; the problems of pay scales, personnel requirements, and promotions for attracting suitable candidates in the profession, and, therefore, the quality of manpower available to man its services; and the need for increasingly recruiting students from those levels of society which, in fact, it seeks to serve and influence.
5. Closely related to the type of manpower which is attracted to the profession, is the need to examine the question of the type of teachers, their qualifications and practice experience, and on-going development of their knowledge and skills as teachers and practitioners.
6. The need to increase effectiveness of the profession dependent on the quality of preparation of its practitioners. The factors which determine adequacy of preparation, and, which therefore, require a thorough examination, are the courses and their relevance to the social realities, the need to develop a conceptual and operational design of field work, the examination system, extension services and research, and the development of interdisciplinary character with a holistic view of man and its consequent implications for practice skills and the nature of service delivery.
7. The need to shift the emphasis from remedial to developmental functions in the training of social workers, and to widen it from a narrow urban to a wider rural and tribal base to meet the needs of the majority in our population.
8. The need to examine the question of the institution's relative autonomy, and its relationships to existing academic structures

in order to make it possible for institutions to be responsive to the changing realities and to participate in and promote change.

9. Lastly, the need to provide for an organisational structure which will assure the development of social work education, including the development of practice skills and research.

While the major issues facing the profession are outlined above, their sequential arrangement does not connote order of priority. In fact, a major problem of the profession lies with the governmental and non-governmental employing agencies. They also need to develop adequate personnel policies and salary structure. There is very little possibility for the profession to attract suitable candidates unless the employing agencies identify relevant tasks for which qualification in social work is regarded as necessary. Designing a relevant curriculum, or developing suitable educational administrative structures is dependent on the definitions and descriptions of the tasks of the personnel in the agencies. Only then the investment will be commensurate to the quality of the desired manpower.

The above issues identified by the Committee, encompass its terms of reference which include:

1. Review critically the existing programmes of social work education—including courses, field work and research—in relation to education at the doctoral, post-graduate, undergraduate and para-professional levels; their relevance to the needs of the country; and the development of norms at each level to facilitate the establishment of equivalence.
2. Suggest changes with a view to making these programmes more meaningful and relevant, and ways of effecting these changes.
3. Study and suggest changes or modifications in such administrative matters as procedural problems, funding patterns, and relationship to the various academic structures in their respective universities.

   Examine the present role of institutions for social work education in relation to the National Service Scheme, and suggest ways in which they could help, effectively, in accomplishing the objectives of this scheme.

The Committee sought to obtain the views and suggestions from a wide spectrum of persons—educators, university administrators, students and practitioners. With this objective in view, the committee met one representative from each institution for social work education in one of three regional meetings, to cover all the institutions. At every regional meeting, the Committee took the opportunity of visiting the institutions to discuss the specific problems; it met the students of their representatives and university administrators, including the vice-chancellors. The Committee also met representatives of the Indian Association of Trained Social Workers. A survey was also undertaken, and responses obtained from 33 out of 35 existing institutions. Eventually, the Committee decided to delete one of these institutions from its total count because its primary emphasis, from the very first year, was on labour welfare and personnel management. Institutions of the latter type were wholly excluded from the study.

8.1.0.0. SOME FACTS ABOUT INSTITUTIONS FOR SOCIAL WORK EDUCATION: TRENDS AND PROBLEMS

8.1.1.0. A PROFILE OF THE INSTITUTIONS

8.1.1.1. Programmes

There were 34 institutions for social work education. Of these, 11 offered the Ph.D. (one additionally had a D.Litt.), 28 offered the master's degree, of which 5 also had a bachelor's degree programme. Of the two institutions that offered a post-graduate diploma of two years' duration, one was affiliated to a university and the other was a private institution. In addition, there were 5 other bachelor's degree programmes which did not offer a master's degree. Additionally, one offered a B.A. degree, wherein, social work was a compulsory subject with other options and students were placed for field work. Excluding this B.A. programme, there were only 10 bachelor's programmes and 30 institutions at the post-graduate level. There are 3 one-year post-graduate diploma courses (one offered by an university), and four certificate courses of one-year duration at the post SSC level in these 34 institutions.

8.1.1.2. Location (2.2.3.0.)

While Maharashtra (8) and Tamil Nadu (6) had a cluster of institutions, there were none in states in the extreme north and east, such as Punjab, Jammu and Kashmir, and the Himalayas and the north-eastern hill-states. The four states in the south had 14 out of 34 institutions. Twenty-six, out of 28 locations, were in urban areas. Thus, rural and tribal areas remained grossly underserved. There were only four institutions with a rural bias.

8.1.1.3. Organisational Pattern

a. *Affiliation* (2.1.2.0.)

These institutions showed six types of pattern of affiliation to universities. This resulted in varying degrees of autonomy and budgetary allocations, with far reaching implications on their functioning. All, except the institution, were affiliated to universities. Two institutions were in central universities, three were in deemed universities. Twenty-one institutions were located in state universities—12 were single-faculty colleges, 9 located in multi-faculty colleges, and only 7 are departments of state universities (one of the latter was constituted as a Faculty of Social Work). Twenty-two, out of 34 institutions, were under private managements.

b. *Organisational Pattern* (6.3.1.1. and 6.3.1.2.)

The problem of autonomy of professional education for social work within the university framework, came up for discussion in regional and committee meetings. As long as an institution was constituted as a department within a college or a university and placed on a par with other departments, problems were likely to arise for a professional training programme which has distinctly different requirements. There was also the problem of placing social work under a different discipline such as sociology. None of these arrangements were satisfactory. They affected the programme adversely as differential inputs were not recognised. It is, therefore, necessary to study the manner in which other professional courses in the university such as medicine, law and business are constituted with their separate Faculties. Furthermore, Faculty affiliation affected the degree both in its nomenclature and in the imposition of academic regulations on social work such as a set pattern of marks and the evaluation system.

c. *Board of Studies* (6.3.1.4.)

Not in all cases was a séparate Board of Studies constituted for social work. A body which has very important academic functions such as the development of syllabi, and appointment of examiners in its own discipline, should therefore be constituted to persons drawn from that specific discipline and knowledgeable in its subject matter. This is obviously not possible when Board members are drawn from disciplines other than social work. In some cases it was found that the Chairman of the Board of Studies in social work was not from that profession. Such a person could never give professional direction to the work of the Board.

8.1.1.2. **Lack of Designated Centres of Advanced Studies** (6.3.1.5.)

Social work education has no institution of advanced studies. None of the existing programmes are recognised for their areas of expertise. Whether it is for faculty improvement, the development of teaching materials or for testing educational/training models and developing relevant publications, such institutions are required.

8.1.2.0. STUDENTS

8.1.2.1. **Enrolment and Graduation** (2.2.1.0.)

Complete information in respect of the master's and bachelor's degree levels in the institutions was not available. However, in spite of the limitations and gaps in the data, it is observed that the average enrolment went up from 24.5 in 1970-71 to 31 in 1974-75. With drop-outs and failures, wastage and stagnation in social work education is estimated at about 15 per cent. The total enrolment for five years for 23 institutions (master's degree) was 2,875 and the total number that graduated was 2,407 giving a percentage of 83 of successful candidates. The total enrolment in the bachelor's programmes, for the same five year period, was 426 and the number graduated was 361, giving 84 per cent who passed. The drop-out rate in certificate courses ranged from 27 to 44 per cent.

The figures show a very limited output of front-line workers at the para-professional and bachelor's levels. Between the bachelor's and the master's programmes, the total number of students graduating is estimated to be no more than 800, or 900 at the most. Of these, the bachelors' level graduates would be less than 150.

8.1.2.2. **Sex Ratio in Enrolment** (2.2.2.0.)

Enrolment of men was 1,977 as against 898 women in the last five years for the MSW programme. Enrolment for female students was thus 45 per cent. The same trend was visible in the BSW, diploma and certificate courses. Enrolment figures for labour welfare showed a heavy bias towards male students..And, even in subjects related to social work, the trend is the same (15 per cent of women in 1974-75). There were 3 institutions, of which one, at the master's level, as exclusively for men (Madras), and there were two which were exclusively for women, one at the master's level (Madras) and one at the bachelor's level (Nagpur).

8.1.2.3. **Availability of Seats and Actual Enrolment** (2.2.3.0.)

Before 1970-71, a majority of the institutions enrolled less than 30 students. By 1973-74, less than half had such low cnrolment. By 1974-75, three institutions enrolled 51 to 60 students, and four 61, whereas, only three institutions enrolled less than 20 students. Most of the institutions functioned at their actual capacity. A few (mostly bachelor's) were underutilised (altogether, between 5 and 8 institutions in the last 5 years at the bachelor's and master's levels). About 4 enrolled more than their actual capacity.

8.1.2.4. **Students from Scheduled Castes and Tribes** (2.2.4.0.)

The bulk of the enrolment of students from the scheduled castes and tribes was in the bachelor's programme—because of a major contribution made by three institutions in Nagpur, where 95 to 99 per cent of enrolment was of scheduled caste students on government scholarships. Also, in Gujarat Vidyapeeth, 60 per cent of the students were from the scheduled tribes, 30 per cent from the scheduled castes, and only 10 per cent from other communities. Enrolment of the scheduled caste/tribe students for the master's programme in the last 5 years, was only per cent. The general stagnation rate of these students in the MSW programme was 16 to 23 per cent while it was only 6 per cent for the other students.

8.1.2.5. **Students' Fees/Scholarships** (6.2.4.3.)

The fees paid by students were related to the general fee structure of university education, especially in the liberal arts faculty. The fee bears no relationship to the higher costs of social work education primarily because the nature of training involves a low ratio of students to faculty of at least 10:1. Fees probably do not exceed 20 per cent of the budget, and in some cases may be only between a fifth and a tenth.

However, the cost of social work education for the student is very high, because, unlike liberal arts/science students, he incurs additional, and considerable expenditure on such items as transport to and from field work placements, visits connected with his field work assignments, typing of the research project, camps and study tours.

For 16 institutions at the master's level, from the available information, such consolidated costs worked out from Rs. 1,000 to Rs. 1,400 and more (for items such as tuition, library fees, examination fees, students' union fees, camp expenses, research project, and caution money). The highest consolidated cost of education was Rs. 3,350 in one deemed university, while the third highest was Rs. 1,680 in a private institution which subsequently became affiliated to a university. Generally, the costs were higher in older institutions. Actual tuition fees ranged from the class interval of Rs. 300 to Rs. 400 to that of Rs. 900 to Rs. 1,000. There was a scatter between the entire range with 10 institutions costing the students Rs. 600 or less, and 7 institutions over Rs. 700.

The fee structure of under-graduate education was less heavy. A majority of the colleges charged between Rs. 200 and Rs. 300 as tuition fees. The financial cost of research project was also non-existent for most institutions at this level of training. However, expenditure on field work, camps/study ours, library, students' union and examinations fees remained.

Because of the high cost of social work education and the full-time nature of the programme—which does not allow for part-time work, external/private study, or correspondence courses—it is necessary to locate funds, which will assist students from groups with economic disabilities to enrol in the programme. It was found that between 1973-74 and 1974-75, 1,594 (50 per cent) were able to obtain some type of aid, mostly for tuition fees. The bulk of the scholarships (1,380) were from the government for the various eligible groups. The students from the scheduled castes and tribes (a majority of whom were concentrated in the three institutions in Nagpur and one in Ahmedabad, largely at the BSW level) were the largest recipients. The economically backward students, whose parents earned less than Rs. 1,800, were next. University and UGC scholarships helped only 94 students, while the institutions assisted about 61 from their own resources, and private funding assisted another 31 students. Female students received 38 per cent of the total number of scholarships awarded. (They constitute 45 per cent in the student population.)

8.1.3.0. PERSONNEL

8.1.3.1. Faculty

a. *Faculty Positions* (6.1.1.1.)

The total number of faculties in the 33 institutions which sent in their questionnaires, was 356. Of these, 284 were full-time and 72 served part-time. The male/female distribution for full-time faculty, was 49 and 23 respectively. The majority of the teachers were lecturers. There were 27 positions of professors, of which, only 3 were held by women. The senior positions—professors, readers and senior lecturers—accounted for only 23 per cent of the teaching faculty.

b. *Faculty Size and Workload* (6.1.1.2.)

Institutions established before 1950 had more than 11 faculty members. Of the 14 institutions established prior to 1960, 7 had between 11 and 15 and one had as many as 25 faculty. Among institutions established after 1960, only one had a faculty size of about 15, 12 had between 6 and 10, and 7 had less than five. Departments of state universities and affiliated colleges did not have enough faculty members. It was difficult to obtain visiting lecturers for inter-disciplinary subjects because honoraria for TA/DA were not sanctioned.

The work-load of faculty in institutions for social work education, includes class-room teaching, guidance of research projects/term paper; field instruction and liaison with fieldwork agencies; administration of field service activities and projects run by the institution; administrative responsibilities in the institution; conducting research; development of teaching materials; extension lectures; short-term courses and seminars; attendance at conferences, reading papers, participation and responsibility in professional organisations; consultation; writing papers, monographs, reports, books, editorship.

At the regional meetings, work-load emerged as the single most problematic area for the faculty. Most universities blindly equated the work-load in terms of lecture hours only thus equating social work teachers with those of other disciplines, without giving recognition to the other teaching responsibilities, such as field instruction, a substantial component, and non-teaching work which contributes to the total academic programme and field extension activities in the community.

c. *Faculty Qualifications* (6.1.1.3.)

A majority of the 323 faculty (n-356), from whom information was obtained, had only one degree at the master's level—124 in social work and 54 in other subjects. About 65 per cent of the faculty had a degree in social work, while others were drawn from social sciences and personnel management. Twenty-two per cent had an additional master's degree in a subject other than social work. Only 56 had Ph.D. and one had a D.Litt. Only 17, out of 34 institutions, had faculty with Ph.D. degrees, majority of which had 3 such persons or less. It is obvious that a majority of these post-graduate institutions have very few faculty with degree beyond the master's resulting in the lack of development of research.

d. *Relevance of Subjects to Degree Obtained* (6.1.1.4.)

A majority of the teachers handled social work/social science subjects relevant to their degrees. Eighteen teachers had social work degrees and taught social science subjects, and 7 teachers had social science degrees but taught social work subjects. We do not favour this for obvious academic reasons.

e. *Teaching/Professional Practice Experience* (6.1.1.5.)

The largest number of teachers (102 out of 356) had between 2 to 5 years of teaching experience—both among social work and social science teachers. The next group (74) in order of experience, had between 6 and 10 years. Only 71 teachers out of 356, had taught for more than 10 years. This explains why fewer positions in the higher academic categories were filled. It also brings out the need for systematic faculty development programmes in these institutions.

Only 54 teachers were stated to be in direct practice; of them, 13 were in clinical practice and 10 in community work, while 31 teachers, unfortunately, did not state the nature of their practice. In view of the fact that social work faculty teach subjects which have practice implications, it is very necessary to examine the means by which faculty can have on-going field practice experience.

f. *Need for Additional Faculty* (6.1.1.6.)

Lack of finances to attract suitable faculty was the single major factor, cited by 15 institutions for not filling needed positions. Nine other institutions said such persons were actually not available. Two institutions felt that their location was a hindrance to attracting competent faculty. Persuading the university to permit specialised persons from other disciplines/ professions, as visiting lecturers, was another difficulty. Persons with Ph.D., could not be found by these institutions to conform to the UGC requirements. The total number required was 72, of whom, 55 were needed for full-time work, 11 part-time and 6 as visiting lectures. A majority required social work faculty for field instruction and class teaching. The lack of adequate number of faculty over-loads those in position and leads to a deterioration in the quality of the training.

g. *Faculty Development* (6.1.1.7.)

As a majority of faculty had little teaching experience and even less practice experience, the need for faculty development was voiced persistently by participating institutions at regional meetings. This merits serious consideration. Implementation of any newly designed curriculum will be inadequate without properly developed faculty. Teaching techniques also need to be improved.

h. *Faculty Exchange; Exchange of Faculty and Practitioners/ Administrators/Policy makers; Special Lectureships by Eminent Social Work Professionals* (6.1.1.8.)

The lack of experienced faculty, is further aggravated by the absence of faculty exchange between institutions (it is not done even when they are located in the same area). We need to infuse stimulation and bring in the knowledge and skills of experienced educators, practitioners, administrators and policy-makers in the training programme, especially in view of the relative inexperience of faculty.

i. *Faculty Recruitment and Promotions* (6.1.1.9.)

In their first appointments, there is a need to place greater emphasis on practice experience of faculty rather than on academic credits. In promotion to the Readers' and Professors' posts, adequate emphasis is not given to contributions to practice. In keeping with other social science disciplines, there is a tendency to place greater emphasis on publications and research. This trend will eventually undermine the importance of practice in the profession.

j. *Faculty Selection Committees* (6.1.1.10)

These are not always established in a way that standards of social work education will be safeguarded. It is necessary to consider the manner in which such committees should be constituted.

8.1.3.2. **Library Staff** (6.1.2.0.)

The position in relation to the library staff is related to the size of the library. In several institutions, the library is managed by designated faculty and students. This position is very unsatisfactory from the point of view of students.

8.1.3.3. **Administrative Staff** (6.1.3.0.)

The type of staff employed included office superintendent, assistant, accountant, clerks, stenographers, and support staff such as the cleaning persons, peons, watchmen, gardeners and drivers. The highest number employed in any one institution was 32. Nine institutions had less than 5 persons in their administrative staff, 11 had 6 to 10, 4 had 11 to 20, and 3 had 21 and above.

One institution had no administrative staff and 2 shared it with the main college office. Five did not respond to this item and it may be concluded that they may not have had any administrative staff, making such institutions a total of eight out of 34. The bulk of the rest (26 institutions) had 10 or less people on their staff and the model category was only 5 or less. Lack of administrative staff, especially typists, has adverse effects on the training programme in which considerable documentation of field records and case studies has to be prepared. Where indigenous teaching materials are lacking, the role of the institution in preparing necessary teaching materials, which have relevance to local conditions, situations and events, is very important.

8.1.4.0. CONTINUING EDUCATION, RESEARCH, PUBLICATIONS AND EXTENSION FACILITIES

8.1.4.1. **Continuing Education** (2.4.1.0.)

These institutions have several continuing education activities. In the last 5 years, 23 institutions reported that they conducted short-term courses and seminars. In a majority of these courses, the duration was one to two weeks. The participants for these courses included staff from various institutions of social welfare and defence and the National Service Scheme, trained social workers, students and labour welfare officers. The organisation of these courses is on an *ad hoc* basis and lacks a systematic plan to provide in-service training, staff development, and continuing education programmes to various groups such as policy-makers, administrators, educators, reseachers, practitioners and volunteers.

8.1.4.2. **Research** (2.4.2.0.)

About 18 institutions undertook research studies, ranging from 1 to 5, in the last 10 years. Four institutions had studies ranging from 6 to 10. The oldest institution in the country had 88 studies. The paucity of studies is due to the emphasis on practice, rather than the development of the knowledge base, a considerable expenditure of time on students' field work, a lack of adequate staff (time and/or expertise), and inadequate finances to provide a continuing core unit. The Planning, Research, Evaluation and Monitoring Division of the Department of Social Welfare, Government of India, is making commendable efforts to stimulate research in these institutions through the funds made available by the Planning Commission.

8.1.4.3. **Publications** (2.4.3.0.)

Of the 34 institutions, 14 had no publications to their credit. A majority of the remaining had a very small number of publications and teaching materials except in the case of two institutions, which had over 31 such publications. Those in the regional languages were negligible. The need for educational materials, which had relevance for India, was stressed considerably at regional meetings. This area of concern needs our urgent attention.

8.1.4.4. **Field Service Project** (2.4.4.0.)

Of the 34 institutions, 17 had field service project and a majority were community centres in urban areas. Balwadis, nutrition and health projects were organised in the community centres, as well as outside of them, as specific projects. Family welfare, including foster care and adoption, and school social work, were also reported. Very few projects had a cost of Rs. 5,000 or less. The mode was in the category of Rs. 21,000 to Rs. 40,000 and four projects cost over a lakh of rupees. That as many as half the number of institutions have reported these projects, and tried to raise the necessary amounts through donations or government schemes, shows the importance attached by these educational institutions to the development of practice and to training for practice. This necessary investment was considerable, bearing on the necessary training infrastructure for social work education.

8.1.5.0. LIBRARY (2.5.0.0.)

About a third (12) had less than 2,000 books. Eighteen had over 3,000 books. A majority of the institutions, established prior to 1960, had over 3,000 volumes; while those established after 1960, had comparatively more institutions with less than 2,000 books. Again, state university institutions had a poor showing with 11 out of 27 having less than 2,000 volumes. The situation with regard to library holdings today is very poor. Some institutions do not have a separate library as they share existing facilities and budgets of the multi-faculty college or the university. Social work, with a smaller enrolment, is likely to be alloted a low priority in the acquisition of books.

8.1.6.0. CAMPUS FACILITIES (2.6.0.0.)

8.1.6.1. Institutional Premises (2.6.1.0.)

Twenty-nine institutions were housed in their own buildings, 4 were rented and one did not specify. A majority had only 2 or 3 classrooms and 2 rooms for administrative purposes. Fifteen institutions had six or more faculty rooms, while the rest had less than six. With individual requirements for field instructions and research, the number of faculty rooms, individually allotted, is poor. The number of classrooms available is also meagre especially if programmes, at other educational levels, are to be introduced.

8.1.6.2. Hostel Facilities (2.6.2.0.)

A majority of hostels and 40 or less seats. There were 13 hostels for men and 11 or women. However, 4 hostels for women accommodated less than 10 persons in each. The present hostels facilities will be found limited in the event of multi-level programmes being introduced.

8.1.6.3. Faculty Housing (2.6.3.0.)

Sixteen institutions provided housing while 14 provided none. Only 2 provided it to most of their faculty. Among institutions established before 1960, a majority provided such housing. In contrast, among the institutions established after 1960, a majority did not provide with such housing. Among state supported institutions, over 50 per cent provided no housing,and all of them were single-faculty, affiliated colleges.

8.1.7.0. FUNDS (6.2.0.0.)

A major factor in the organisational problems of these institutions, was the availability of funds—especially to employ an adequate number of faculty, to provide better library facility and infrastructure support such as the administrative staff. All, except one institution (33), are now a part of the university. Public expenditure on social work education has thus increased. However, the pattern of funding and the actual financial support received varied, depending upon the relationship of the institution to the university : whether an institution was an affiliated college or an university department, or whether it was a state or a central university. The operating ministry for single-faculty, affiliated colleges also differed. In some cases, the institutions may be under the Ministry of Education, and in others, the Ministry of Social Welfare. The percentage of budget sanctioned varied from 33 to 90 per cent (6.2.1.0.)

Out of 23 institutions, there were 20 with budgets of less than Rs. 2,00,000 in 1972-73 and there were 15 such institutions by 1974-75. The expenditure rose from year to year and reflected the increased costs. A majority of the institutions, which had expenditures over Rs. 1,50,000, were those established before 1960. Those with budgets of less than Rs. 1,50,000, were generally those established after 1960. They generally had small enrolments and greater difficulty in ensuring an adequate flow of funds to support the programme. (6.2.2.0)

Eight institutions had deficits ranging from Rs. 20,000 to Rs. 40,000 and 10 others had deficits below Rs. 20,000. Two institutions had a deficit of over Rs. 1,00,000 for 1973 and 1974. Without adequate outlay on funds, both at the central and state levels, the institutions cannot ensure either an adequate quality or quantity of social welfare manpower. (6.2.3.0)

8.1.8.0. ORGANISATIONS ASSOCIATED WITH SOCIAL WORK EDUCATION

8.1.8.1. Areas of Concern for the Development of Social Work Education

The major areas of concern for the development of social work education are to:

a. Ensure a systematic development of social work education in terms of its geographical distribution and affiliation to recognised boards of education and universities.

b. Provide a holistic framework for the development of a ladder education programme of education with several termination points related to job-functions in the country, and to relate each phase of education to the next, so that there are no dead-end training programmes and no dead-end-jobs.
c. Develop syllabi which are under constant review for relevance and which provide a career ladder from one academic level to the next.
d. Develop field work and field service projects.
e. Publish books/case studies related to social work/social welfare/social development for all academic levels from the para-professional upwards.
f. Develop teaching materials for social work education at all academic levels.
g. Develop research expertise and funding of research projects.
h. Provide stable funding sources related to the cost of social work education.
i. Specify the relationship of these institutions to their affiliating organisations to ensure responsiveness of social work education to the realities.
j. Relate man-power training to existing job positions, and identify job positions which require professional training and specify them as social work positions.
k. Develop the role of social work education in NSS programmes.

For such development we need to identify organisational structures for effecting change, development and stability in growth. The following two sections deal with this problem in terms of existing and the required organisational structures.

8.1.8.1.a. *The University Grants Commission* (6.4.2.1.)

The UGC has had a Panel on Social Work Education on the same lines as has been done for other disciplines. This matter is noted with satisfaction. Adequate staff will, however, be required to carry on the activities of the Panel for the development of social work education.

The criteria and policies of UGC schemes do not suit the small professional programmes where enrolment is small and controlled by various factors which do not generally affect the general arts and science colleges. Hence, the UGC Schemes require suitable modification.

8.1.8.1.b. *The Department of Social Welfare, Government of India* (6.4.2.2.)

It is a matter of considerable satisfaction that the Department of Social Welfare has constituted a separate Division for Planning, Research, Evaluation and Monitoring (PREM). A professional person has also been appointed as its first Director. This is likely to have far reaching implications in raising professional practice. The work of this Division in the field of sponsorship of research studies and compilation of statistics, with the necessary support of the Planning Commission, has considerably improved the position in regard to data availability. The utility of these functions, especially for teaching, planning and implementation of programmes, cannot be overemphasized.

However, the Department does not have a well-defined programme for training and development of manpower in social welfare. The establishment of a Training Cell within PREM, for the development of social work education, might plug this lacuna. Its present functions involve some aspects of social work education. Those functions which are dealt with by other departments/sections, could be transferred to this Department. This need is felt because the Department is concerned with social work education at the paraprofessional level as well as at the degree levels where maintenance grants are not channelled through the UGC. It has an important role to play in assessing the manpower needs of social welfare and designing suitable training programmes to meet such manpower needs.

8.1.8.1.c. *Planning Commission* (6.4.2.3.)

The Planning Commission has a very important role to play in the formulation of policies and programmes and in the utilisation of research relating to social welfare and social work. However, we feel the Commission could play a much bigger role in social work education with regard to its funding. The Planning Commission, at present, does not appropriate special funds for this purpose at the degree level to enable the Ministry of Social Welfare to function as the operating ministry for educational programmes in social work. This gap is acutely felt especially by institutions which do not receive their maintenance grants from the UGC.

8.1.8.1.d. *Association of Schools of Social Work in India (ASSWI)* (6.4.2.4.)

Only 12 out of 26 master's degree courses (and 2-year post-graduate diploma courses) which were surveyed, stated that they had such membership. At that time, the Constitution did not permit affiliation to the courses at the bachelor's level. It has, now, been suitably amended. While the Association is composed of "schools of social work", only 5 out of 34 retain that appellation today. The Association's name is a legacy of American and British education in India, and needs to be changed to "Association for Social Work Education in India".

The Association has performed very important functions, since its establishment in 1959, in organising seminars for staff development and in publishing their proceedings. It has worked on syllabi and periodically reviewed some course content. It has also attempted to establish standards but being an association by voluntary affiliation, it has not been possible to review institutions periodically and to enforce standards.

8.1.9.0. *Need for the Establishment of A Council for Social Work Education* (6.4.3.0.)

As indicated above, there are 4 organisations which have overlapping concerns for institutions providing social work education. It is very necessary to develop a structure which will have joint planning, funding, and programming functions to upgrade social work education and to maintain standards at all levels—from the para-professional to advanced levels of training. It would lead to a more rational utilisation of manpower and resources.

8.1.10.0. *Need for Setting Up Independent Review Committees* (6.4.4.0.)

There is an urgent need for these committees because of the varying levels of the quality of education, the facilities available, management-faculty relations and other factors so vital to the maintenance of standards in social work education. Standards cannot be maintained without periodic intervention of review committees and it is likely that certain circumstances in institutions can also lead to variations in achievement of standards.

8.2.0.0. MULTI-LEVEL PROGRAMMES OF PROFESSIONAL EDUCATION

8.2.1.0. A CRITIQUE OF THE PRESENT CURRICULA (3.1.7.0., 4.1.1.0., 4.2.1.0., 5.1.1.0., 5.2.1.0., 5.3.1.0.)

Our curricula are derived from the residual/remedial/rehabilitative model of practice borrowed largely from the west—mainly the U.S.A. For example, a majority of our curricula place emphasis on social and individual problems of pathology rather than on the problems of the individual and society in the context of poverty and development. The curricula similarly show an urban than a rural bias, derived as they are, from a western, technologically oriented society. There is a concentration of curricula at the master's degree level when what we need in India actually are large numbers of lower level workers.

Field work faces another set of problems when it comes to recognizing it as a valid component of the professional curriculum. Universities do not sanction adequate number of faculty, for this, because they do not take into consideration the amount of time spent on field instruction by each faculty responsible for it and the proportion of the educational time spent by the student on this activity. There is also a lack of involvement of agencies in the students' training. The agencies are poorly developed and do not provide adequate opportunities for the student's learning. The design of field work is not adequately spelled out and field instructors do not have the advantage of syllabi to back them as the class-room instructors have with them. There is a lack of linkage between class-room theory and field practice. Expected hours of field work also vary.

We question the prescription of a research project as compulsory for all students at the master's level, in terms of students' competence and utilisation of research skills on his job. The heavy demand on faculty time which compulsory research makes is not commensurate to actual outcome in preparing research personnel for the profession. There is also a need to move away from studies which only describe a problem, to research which tests the validity of our knowledge, as also to alternative strategies of intervention and administrative arrangements for service delivery or evaluation of practice.

The following is a critique of programmes at each level.

8.2.1.1. Para-professional/Auxiliary Training Programmes (4.1.1.0.)

Since independence in 1947, there has been a rapid growth in the delivery of services, both in the developmental and welfare sectors. There were only 5 institutions providing social work education before 1950, and 9 more were added in the entire decade of the fifties. As a result, much of the initiative for preparation and training of para-professional workers was undertaken by the government or given over to existing institutions for rural reconstruction such as the Kasturba Memorial Trust. The demand for instant manpower led to the development of *ad hoc* training courses of short duration. These continue to exist although it is now almost 30 years since independence. The reasons for such an *ad hoc* approach are the lack of cohesive social policy, frequent change of programmes and personnel from plan to plan; lack of identification of job positions requiring training in social work and the lack of an adequate manpower policy.

This situation has led to several deleterious effects. The training given to para-professional staff is so narrow-based that the frequent changes in plans results in unemployment of previously employed persons, further resulting inconsiderable expenditure incurred on retraining. The best candidates are not attracted. There is a lack of upward mobility because of dead-end training and jobs. Candidates are first selected and then trained. This results in huge expenditures on the protection of their salaries during training. Additionally, the provision of stipends has to be made for the duration of their training. Moreover, because such training is confined to the governmental sector, there is a lack of trained para-professional/auxiliary manpower for the voluntary sector.

8.2.1.2. Bachelor's Degree Programmes (4.2.1.0.)

There appears to be considerable ambivalence in recognising the professional focus at the bachelor's level. This is due to a lack of clarity in perceiving objectives for training at this level.

The content of the bachelor's level courses is as varied as it is stereotyped in the master's programmes. Not having any specific western models, and no associational structure for promoting interchange (the Association of Schools of Social Work in India excluded them till recently), these courses had greater scope for experimentation, and in a few cases, did rclate themselves to the local realities. Except in one institution, no linkage was planned between the bachelor's and the master's programmes—even where both existed in the same institution. The bachelor's programmes did not, therefore, affect their master's programmes in any way. Out of 9 bachelor's programmes, from which information was available, 5 were fully generic. Of these, one provided electives in an area of interest.

The order of utilisation of the settings for field work placements, reported for 1974-75, showed health and medical (68), rural (41), social defence (34) and family and child welfare (29). Unlike the master's programme, a proportionately larger number was placed in rural welfare because of 2 BSW institutions being rural in their orientation (Gujarat Vidyapeeth and Vishwa-Bharati). While most institutions had 8 to 12 hours of field work, one had as low as 4. This is hardly desirable since BSW workers mainly perform direct service functions.

Only one institution at the BSW level required its candidates to do research. At this level, the goal is to prepare persons to function in a team as investigators, coders and tabulators, rather than to prepare them as independent researchers. A research project is not, therefore, generally seen as a requirements for this stage of learning.

The BSW courses have, generally, between 1,300 and 1,500 aggregate marks based on the three-year curriculum. The papers are either less than 500 marks per year, or vary between 500 to 700, and field work is either 100 marks or less, or ranges between 101 and 200 marks.

8.2.1.3. **Master's Degree Programmes** (5.1.1.0.)

Out of 27 programmes at the master's level, only 6 were fully generic. Yet, an examination of the specialisation curricula show that they lack basic principles of curriculum organisation such a providing uniformity in the core concepts of a specialisation (which need to be included), and giving adequate weightage to the specialisation papers in the total courses undertake in the two years.

An examination of the courses offered showed that they were very stereotype, especially those offered in the first year. The majority opted for labour welfare as a specialisation rather than for social work specialisations, the latter, even when offered, were generally the traditional ones. A greater number of specialisations were included in the syllabi than were actually available at a number of institutions which catered for specialisations. The number of specialisations actually offered were: labour welfare and personnel management (16), community organisation/development (14), family and child welfare, (12), medical and psychiatric social work (10), correctional administration (10), social welfare administration (5), social research and statistics (1), and, tribal welfare and welfare of backward classes (2). A number of reasons offered by institutions for not being abie to provide more syllabi were as follows: lack of suitable staff in the concerned specialisation (9), lack of student response to the course (3), lack of funds to employ additional faculty (2), lack of employment opportunities in the specialisation (2) or low salaries.

The distribution of the total number of courses offered, in the first and second year, was very varied ranging from 5 to 10 with an average of 7. Specialisation subjects generally ranged from 1 to 3. Ten institutions offered 2 papers only, five offered 3 papers, one offered 5 papers, and one offered as many as 9 papers. Generally, one paper was offered in the first year. There was also a mistaken notion that the term connotes that all students take the same courses, or the students offer one paper in each field and this is erroneously supposed to make the course generic.

Forty-four per cent of the students in institutions offering specialisations, belonged to labour welfare and personnel management. Of the total of 1,632 students in 122 institutions which offered specialisation, the break-up by specialisation of the total enrolment in the three years of 1972, 1973, and 1974, was as follows: labour welfare/personnel management/industrial relations (727), family and child welfare (234), medical and psychiatric social work (209), correctional administration (102), rural development (93), community development, rural and urban (63), administration (58), research (55) and tribal welfare (10). We conclude from the above, that students are interested in the specialisations that carry greater salaries and benefit — viz., the labour and management settings. The choice is further titled in favour of urban than rural/tribal work; more remedial and rehabilitative than developmental and change-oriented (e.g., community, rural or tribal) activity.

The time allocated to social work methods, which are the core of practice skills, was minimal (as indicated by the number of terms in which they were taught and the marks allocated). In their enthusiasm to orient social work to new fields or activities, the institutions offered courses that were only descriptive and had no theoretical/conceptual base, or courses for which, the theoretical content could be provided in its present curriculum structure.

The majority of courses had 4 terms. Seven institutions followed the semester system. The number of weeks in a term/semester varied from 15 to 20. The time devote to course work varied from 21 periods of 45 minutes to less than 20 periods of 60 minutes.

The total number of marks for each year was 500 or less, in 15 institutions; 501 to 700 in 6; 701 to 1,000 in 2; and 1,001 to 1,300 in one. These distributions are likely to place unequal demands on students in the different institutions. For field work, most programmes allocated between 100 and 200 marks per year. A majority allocated only 100 marks for research.

8.2.2.0. SOME GENERAL CONSIDERATIONS REGARDING THE ACADEMIC PROGRAMME

8.2.2.4. Language (3.3.5.0.)

Instruction, by and large, was imparted in English, although some teaching was being given in regional languages in a few institutions. This pattern was prevalent both at the under-graduate and graduate levels.

8.2.2.7. Core Bibliographies (3.3.8.0.)

These need to be prepared for teaching at each level—paraprofessional, bachelor's and master's. We also need to evolve mechanisms for updating them. A core bibliography for the master's degree was subsequently, prepared.

8.2.2.1. Admission Procedures (3.3.1.0.)

The procedures utilised by some universities were not suitable for admission in social work education programmes where individual interviews are essential for assessment of motivation and capacity for social work. Mere academic qualification and marks, as criteria, are not adequate.

8.2.2.2. **Orientation Programme** (3.3.3.0.)

This was recognised as essential by all institutions for neophytes, because social work as a profession is unfamiliar to the new comer in terms of roles, methods used, and service delivery systems.

8.2.2.3. **Study Tours and Camps** (3.3.4.0.)

These were means for training and were recognised as essential elements of the programmes. Proper financial underwriting was required for these study tours and camps.

8.2.2.5. **Examinations** (3.3.6.0.)

The examination, at the moment, was the main method of evaluation. However, internal assessment, even partial, was utilised by some institutions. (In fact, internal assessment for field work was utilised by most institutions). Very few institutions had internal assessment also for course work.

8.2.2.6. **Part-time, External/Private Study and Correspondence Courses** (3.3.7.0.)

Concern was voiced against private/external studies, or correspondence courses, because the nature of social work education demands the development of not only knowledge, but also of skills and attitudes. However, part-time study, through the accumulation of credits, was recognised as useful, especially for those social welfare staff who have no training and for those already employed, and others who cannot devote attention to full-time studies.

8.2.3.0. RECRUITMENT RULES FOR JOBS (3.3.10.0.)

No amount of curriculum work and manpower training will have the desired effect on social welfare and development programmes in the absence of a national manpower policy for social welfare designating specific posts in the government/ voluntary sector as requiring special training in social welfare/ development at a specific level. The role of government departments and the Union/State Public Service Commission, in designating such positions, cannot be underestimated. Work needs to be taken up urgently in this matter. This was voiced at all regional meetings.

8.3.0.0. NATIONAL SERVICE SCHEME

8.3.1.0. RATIONALE (7.0.0.0)

Involving student youth in the programme of national development, has engaged the attention of the government since independence. All the Education Commission have stressed the desirability of involving youth in community work. In pursuance of this recommendation, the Government of India, Ministry of Education and Social Welfare, launched the National Service Scheme in 1969, the Gandhi Centenary year. The scheme covered 113 universities and 265,000 students in 1976-77.

8.3.2.0. RESPONSIBILITIES OF THE EDUCATIONAL INSTITUTIONS OF SOCIAL WORK FOR NSS (7.1.0.0.)

In order to meet the needs of orientation of university staff to the method of implementation of the scheme (social welfare activities of an institutional and non-institutional nature, and also to meet the needs of consultancy, and publications, the Government of India and the University Grants Commission selected various institutions for social work education to shoulder these responsibilities. The first Honorary Adviser, to the Government for NSS, was the principal of one of these institutions. In addition, two institutions, the Tata Institute of Social Sciences, and the Delhi School of Social Work, were appointed to offer consultancy services to the institutions for social work education (which were entrusted with the responsibility for NSS), to the central and state governments, and the universities. The were also expected to prepare literature on different aspects of the Scheme.

8.3.3.0. ACHIEVEMENTS (7.2.0.0.)

These institutions had so far trained 1,725 university/college teachers as NSS Programme Officers, and assisted directly in the implementation of university level NSS programmes. The content of training has been periodically revised in the light of experience and relevance to need. Their functions have included training, consultancy, research and evaluation, organisation of demonstration projects, dissemination of information, on-the-spot guidance to local units, liaison among the governmental and voluntary organizations, colleges and NSS units and rural and urban communities. The NSS units, in these institutions for social work education, are provided grants for the appointment of a full-time NSS coordinator in the Reader's scale, one stenographer and Rs. 2,000 as contingency allowance.

8.3.4.0. PROBLEMS IN IMPLEMENTATION (7.4.0.0.)

Problems in the implementation of the scheme related to transfers of trained teachers to college/ universities where there was no NSS or they already had adequately trained staff so that there was considerable wastage of trained manpower. All institutions for social work education do not have a developmental orientation. Therefore, they were unable to play an adequate role in the type of activities envisaged by NSS. The ad hoc nature of the Scheme has resulted in some reluctance on the part of institutions for social work education to take on this responsibility. The continuing investment of institutions for social work education needs to be considered.

8.4.0.0. CONCLUSION

This chapter has highlighted the findings of the Second Review Committee on Social Work Education. They were based on questionnaire responses, analyses of syllabi, discussions at three regional meetings of representatives from institutions for social work education, and on meetings with faculty, students, and administrators of some universities where the committee held its meetings. The committee also had a meeting with the representatives of the Indian Association of Trained Social Workers in Delhi. The material thus obtained, included the various factors pertaining to the infrastructure of social work education; the education programmes at various levels, their objectives, content, field work and factors related to curriculum administration; and the supporting organisations (government and voluntary) for social work education. The role of these educational institutions in the National Service Scheme was also analysed. The next chapter will summarise the recommendations based on these findings.

Recommendations

9.0.0.0. INTRODUCTION

In the introduction of the summary in Chapter 8, the tasks confronting social work education were briefly outlined. The recommendations of the Committee, as stated in this chapter, encompass these identified tasks. In the first major section we will consider organisational and administrative aspects of social work education and in the second major section we will consider the academic programmes.

9.1.0.0. INFRASTRUCTURE OF SOCIAL WORK EDUCATION: GENERAL RECOMMENDATIONS ON THE FUTURE DEVELOPMENT OF SOCIAL WORK EDUCATION

9.1.1.0. ORGANISATIONAL STRUCTURE

9.1.1.1. Distribution of Programmes at Various Levels (2.1.1.0.)

Several academic levels are suggested. They are based on the academic terminal points with related job opportunities. The need today is for frontline workers in nation-building tasks. It is, therefore, recommended that special emphasis be given to increasing training for workers at lower levels through existing institutions, or in those newly started ones in other locations which can provide the necessary experience.

(10) + 2	=	1 + 1 years at HSC level for para-professional/auxiliary training. The two years may provide such capsule courses that termination is possible at the end of each of the two years. (The gram or bal sevika training may fall into this pattern).
Bachelor's	=	3 years (Could be made into 1 + 2 years providing a point of termination at the end of the first year, e.g., for mukhya sevikas).

Master's	=	2 years.
M.Phil./Post-Master's Certificate	=	1 year to a year and a half.
Ph.D	=	To be completed within a maximum period of 5 years. (Para 21.1.0)

9.1.1.2. **Location** (2.1.3.0.)

a. Special efforts should be made to locate new institution in the extreme north and north-east, wherever there are job opportunities.

b. Because of the type of jobs available at lower and middle levels, they should be located in rural/tribal areas. This will give them the bias required for work in these areas.

c. Where there is more than one institution in a location, e.g., in a city of town, each should preferably develop distinctly different academic programmes (such as by changing the emphasis in their curricula).

d. The needs of an area, and availability of job positions, must be carefully examined before locating the institution. (Para 2.1.3.0)

9.1.1.3. **Organisational Pattern** (6.3.0.0.)

a. New programmes may be started under any auspices, provided they are accredited by the authority recommended in this report and they are a part of the pattern of social work education suggested in Para 9.1.1.1 of the Report. All programmes should fall into the educational pattern in the country—they must provide opportunities for further academic advancement, they must prepare workers already trained (and with job experiences preferably at lower levels) to higher levels (6.3.1.0.).

b. In view of the special needs and the nature of the programmes of the institutions, the First Review Committee had already emphasized the need for autonomy. The Second Review Committee strongly endorses this view. All institutions which now function as departments of universities/colleges, should become separately constituted programmes and no new programmes should be started without first according them such separate identity

(6.3.1.1.).

c. The courses should not only be instituted as separate degrees from other disciplines, but should be constituted into a separate Faculty of Social Work (6.3.1.2.).

d. They should have a separate Board of Studies which is largely made up of people in the profession—both from the institution and from outside (6.3.1.3.).

e. Examiners appointed by these Boards of Studies for the subjects of social work should be persons with professional background, whether they are academicians/practitioners/administrators/policy makers (6.3.1.3.).

9.1.1.4. **Expansion and Development**

a. Emphasis should be placed on qualitative improvement of the programmes (2.1.4.0.).

b. No new institutions should be affiliated to universities, or otherwise recognised for support, unless basic requirements (norms as stated in the this report), and infrastructure such as professional competence, academic standards, financial and organisational viability, established (2.1.4.0.).

c. Certain institutions may be selected for their particular areas of strength. Sufficient inputs must then be provided to further strengthen these areas, e.g., research, community work, social work education, or service to one of the target groups, e.g., criminology or children (6.3.1.4.).

d. The UGC has now a new programme called "Departments of Special Assistance" which may be implemented (6.3.1.4.).

9.1.2.0. STUDENTS

Enrolment in professional institutions should be based on adequate manpower planning which in turn is based on identification of society's needs, the goals to be achieved, and, the tasks for accomplishing these goals. Training should be so designed that the personnel meet the identified needs of society. Appraisal of the manpower required at all levels should be undertaken for social work personnel.

9.1.2.1. **Enrolment and Graduation (2.2.1.0.)**

a. We need to increase the facilities for training, at the bachelor's level. Similarly, training at the para-professional level needs to be instituted in these institutions for social work education. A special group must be appointed to look into the instituting of para-professional programmes on a planned basis, to cover the states and union territories. The new programmes in social work education should be started, if not for the para-professional training programme, at least at the bachelor's level and later developed to the master's degree.

b. Before para-professional and degree programmes are instituted, a dialogue needs to be initiated with the state government departments which employ social workers at levels below the master's degree (social welfare, corrections, backward class welfare, tribal welfare, rural development, labour, and home). A list of job positions in the voluntary sector needs to be prepared.

c. All *ad hoc* courses run by governmental and semi-governmental bodies should be gradually phased out. The purpose of *ad hoc* training courses is to give refresher courses or continuing education rather than as a substitute for training of manpower. Such ad hoc, short duration courses are inadequate for persons who have no professional background. (Para 2.2.1.0)

9.1.2.2. **Sex Ratio (2.2.2.0.)**

The ratio of women to men is at present 4:6. Although it can be exceeded in favour of women or even maintained as it is, it should not decrease in favour of men; for women have considerable contribution to make in this field. As special incentive scholarships may be instituted to encourage women in this profession especially at more advanced levels in places where women are not enrolled in adequate numbers.

9.1.2.3. **Students from Scheduled Castes and Tribes (2.2.4.0.)**

a. Their enrolment needs to be substantially increased. The Association of Schools of Social Work in India could consider advertising and conducting four regional centres during vacations for students who may be interested in seeking admission to these institutions. A preliminary selection could be made at such centres and a training programme—of at least six week's duration, from the middle of May to the end of June—could be organised. Thc students selected should obviously possess motivation and potential for social work, otherwise, the training will be wasted. The number of those trained will depend upon the indication of requirements given by the institutions. The students should be equipped with basic knowledge useful for entering the field of social work, and also language skills. The final selection may be made by the institution where the candidate has made an application.

b. Some new institutions require to be located in tribal areas in the north-eastern hill districts. In Madhya Pradesh, Gujarat, Rajasthan, and Maharashtra—in places with large tribal populations. The existing social work education programmes could also be strengthened to take up tribal-based work.

c. Unless social work education programmes are started at the para-professional and bachelor's levels, there will be no increase of enrolment from these groups at higher levels. Unless opportunities for training at lower levels (para-professional) is provided first to these groups, it will not be possible for them to be recruited to higher levels of education and job positions. Secondly even when scholarships for education are made available for students, their families still need them to earn as soon as they have achieved some training. The lower level training will thus open up job opportunities quite early for such students. Indeed, there is scope for such graduated in the tribal development schemes.

9.1.2.4. **Student Scholarship** (6.2.4.3.)

In view of the problems of attracting, or retaining students from the disadvantaged sections to higher education, we recommend that a further increase in scholarships be made to include maintenance grants. The grants must include both tuition and maintenance to make education possible for such students. These scholarships may be instituted at the bachelor's, master's, M.Phil., and Ph.D. levels on consideration of merit and need. Such a programme, if centrally administered, would facilitate awards on a need-cum-merit basis of all the schools. It would also provide a better means for scrutiny and selection based on the criteria laid down for such scholarships. It is also recommended that the UGC and ICSSR specially provide talent scholarship for social work students to continue from the under-graduate to the post-graduate programmes.

9.1.3.0. PERSONNEL

9.1.3.1. Faculty

a. *Faculty Positions* (6.1.1.1.)

Social work educational programmes at the degree and post-degree levels should have only three categories of positions—Professor, Reader and Lecturer. It is recommended that at least one-fourth of the positions should be those of Professors and another 25 to 33 per cent in the category of Reader. The rest, about 40 to 45 per cent, should be at the level of Lecturer. Because of the current emphasis of the UGC on college and university teachers acquiring the M.Phil. and Ph.D. degrees, a higher ratio of Professors and Readers is considered necessary. Where a new programme is started, the senior-most position should be held by someone at the level of a Professor, and failing that, a Reader.

b. *Faculty Size and Work-Load* (6.1.1.2.)

The work, requiring the presence of the teacher in the institution, should not exceed 25 hours per week and the entire work-load, including all assignments besides direct work with students, should not exceed 35 hours. No social work training programme can provide qualitatively high standards, unless standards are maintained in computing faculty work-load and teacher-student ratio. This is especially so for an educational programme in which field work is as important a component as lectures.

i. The faculty-student ratio should aim at 1:8, and should not normally go beyond 1:10 (excluding the head of the institution).
ii. A newly established programme (40 to 50 students) must have a minimum of 4 faculty (excluding the Director) all of whom (5) must hold suitable qualifications in social work.
iii. A teacher should teach no more than 3 courses on an average. He must spend only 3 to 4 class hours per week and give direct

field instruction to about 6 students, and guide 3, or, at the most 4 others, for research. In addition, he may have 2 or 3 students who have instructors in the field, but for whom he is responsible as a faculty adviser. This teaching load per week—or 3 to 4 hours of class teaching, 9 hours of field instruction, and 2 to 4 hours of research—is considered as optimum. Additionally, such teachers will carry responsibilities of an administrative nature—for staff development, or for short-term courses. It is important to give credit to faculty by allocating a certain number of hours for work done in the community in the capacity of consultant/chairmen of committees in organisations/and for providing leadership as office bearers in professional organisations or for undertaking responsibilities of a professional nature. Similarly, teachers who are involved in research should have their teaching programme (as outlined above) suitably modified.

c. *Faculty Qualifications* (6.1.1.3.)

A considerable number of faculty need to be assisted in meeting the academic attainments for higher education laid down by the UGC. A planned approach towards assisting them to obtain M.Phil./Ph.D. is required.

i. *Ph.D:* The institutions may provide leave for faculty with at least 3 years of service with them. The must obtain the Ph.D. within a specified period—such as five years—and maximum leave with pay in accordance with the faculty improvement schemes of the UGC should be granted.

ii. *M.Phil.:* Recommendations same, as above, are applicable except that the period of completion should be two to two and a half years. Leave with pay should be granted as per faculty improvement schemes of the UGC.

iii. *Additional Master's* (Multi-disciplinary emphasis): The faculty appointed in institutions for social work education should primarily consist of persons holding degrees in social work because substantial teaching is required in subjects which have professional content. However, it is very enriching for social work faculty to pursue any particular social science discipline at the master's level, which is related to the social work subject they teach. Opportunities, similar to those made for the M.Phil., should be given to faculty to work toward such an additional degree.

d. *Relevance of Subjects to Degree Obtained* (6.1.1.4.)

Social science teachers cannot give the necessary social work perspective to subjects like Indian Social Problems or Research. Such subjects should, therefore, be taught by social work teachers.

Social science should be taught by those with a post-graduate degree in that subject. It is valuable to have social scientists drawn from their respective disciplines as Visiting Lecturers. Since their primary identification is with their own discipline, they are likely to have more up to date knowledge and trends in their field. If a rich variety of social science disciplines has to be provided, it is better to associate competent persons with the programme as Visiting Lecturers because it is neither feasible to appoint so many persons on a full-time basis, nor can they be easily integrated into the full-time programme. Alternately, special incentive could be given to enable social work faculty to obtain a master's degree in a social science discipline. In all subjects taught by instructors belonging to another discipline, it is essential that one social work faculty person be also assigned to the subject. This would enable the instructor to relate to the particular content required for social work students and assist students with the integration of inter-disciplinary knowledge. It is found that the students are otherwise apt to miss the significance of such knowledge for social work. Some subjects could be better taught by the seminar rather than the lecture method where an inter-disciplinary team of teachers participates.

e. *Professional Practice/Teaching Experience* (6.1.1.5.)

Practice experience should always underpin teaching. It can be provided through the following:

i. On-going practice experience in field service projects of the institution.
ii. On-going practice experience in other governmental and voluntary programmes.
iii. Periodic exchange between faculty and practitioners/

administrators, so that each can bring a new dimension to the exchanged position. The difference in salary should be made up by UGC. Relaxation in educational qualifications should be permitted to practitioners who have made a contribution to the field. Benefits should be protected, during absence from the parent institution, including housing.

iv. For recruitment to teaching position, due regard should be paid to practice experience instead of relying exclusively on higher academic qualifications and/or only teaching experience.

v. The institution may draw on the field practitioners to do some team teaching to enrich the academic programme.

vi. New institutions should have a good proportion (at least 50 per cent) of persons with a minimum of five years of teaching experience.

f. *Need For Additional Faculty* (6.1.1.6.)

i. Little attention has been paid to the problem of recruiting faculty systematically from the practitioners. Such candidates should be given adequate opportunities by providing them necessary training for becoming academicians. And they should be placed in suitable positions. We need a national talent search and a systematic programme for recruitment and preparation of such faculty. Short courses may initially be provided to persons willing to take job leave from practice positions. Subsequently, they could be placed when a position mutually satisfactory to the employer and the recruit is found. This is a task which the Association of Schools of Social Work in India may consider as its special service to the institutions.

ii. Visiting Lectureships should be encouraged for special subjects, especially from other disciplines, and a suitable honorarium provided to the lecturers.

g. *Faculty Development* (6.1.1.7.)

Without proper faculty development, no implementation of any newly designed curriculum will be adequate. The teaching techniques need to be improved and training provided for the same. Some of the faculty development programmes are:

i. Providing leave for pursuing a higher degree, or a degree in an allied discipline, and study leave for practice experience, are the measures already cited. It is also necessary to institute a leave plan for professional growth of faculty. Such leave may be granted after six or seven years of full-time teaching. The salary must be protected, preferably by an UGC scheme which underwrites such leave. Prior to sanction, the faculty concerned must provide a plan to further his academic competence. Senior faculty could utilise the opportunity for writing, research or consultation/teaching at a newly developing institution and to carry out staff development programmes for such institutions. Interchange of faculty between institutions is a worthwhile method of providing for special expertise as well as stimulating new ideas. This could be done most easily when several institutions are in the same area and could share faculty for teaching, field instruction, research, consultation and staff development.

ii. The role played by the Association of Schools of Social Work in India in organizing regular seminars for faculty, held almost every year since the late fifties, has been widely recognized. The Association accomplishes this in spite of financial constraints. The UGC should recognize the Association for organising summer institutes as well as for undertaking longer term training (such as of newly entering faculty). Such programmes can always be offered in conjunction with social work training institutions in the universities, or with those institutions which have the necessary expertise for the type of subjects to be taught by the new faculty recruit. With the two decades of experience built up by it, the Association has the necessary expertise for promoting faculty development on a planned, annual basis.

h. *Faculty Exchange; Exchange of Faculty and Practitioners/ Administrators/Policy Makers; Special Lectureships by Eminent Social Work Professionals* (6.1.1.8.)

i. Exchange of faculty between institutions, should be considered, particularly to assist newly established programmes. Fellowships may be established by UGC for this purpose. Short-term exchanges (of less than an academic year) should be encouraged as it is much more difficult to work out programmes of longer duration.

ii. Exchange between teachers and practitioners/administrators/ policy makers should be promoted.

iii. Fellowships on the same lines as national professorships may be instituted. The institutions can then invite eminent social work persons with experience as policy makers, administrators, those in the international field, or academicians. (Such persons may include those who have retired).

i. *Faculty Recruitment and Promotions* (6.1.1.9.)

i. Equal emphasis should be given on practice experience, as on academic degrees/research, for the lecturer's posts. Paid, full-time professional practice experience is the minimum desirable.

ii. Promotions to Readers' and Professors' posts should also give due weightage to practice.

j. *Faculty Selection Committee* (6.1.1.0.)

Such committees should be composed in a manner prescribed by the university for the selection of faculty. However, it is recommended that two to three experts with professional training in the area of the faculty position to be filled, should be on these committees. Where specialisations are offered, the departmental head of the specialisation to which the faculty is being recruited, should also be present besides the Head of the institutions. The UGC Panel on Social Work Education must prepare and maintain an up-to-date list of persons considered to be subject-matter specialists, who should be invited to sit on the selection committee.

9.1.3.2. **Library Staff** (6.1.2.0.)

The library staff recommended, in proportion to the size of the library, is given below. Only the most essential minimum needs are specified here Institutions may make additional provisions:

a. *Less than 3,000 books*
1 Librarian
1 Peon

b. *3,000-5,000 books*
 1 Librarian
 1 Assistant Librarian (Professional)

c. *5,000-10,000 books*
 1 Librarian
 1 Professional Assistant
 1 Library Assistant
 1 Peon/Typist Clerk

d. *10,000-15,000 books*
 1 Librarian
 2 Library Assistants
 1 Typist Clerk
 2 Peons

e. *15,000 and above*
 Suitable additional Staff may be provided.

9.1.3.3. **Administrative Staff (6.1.3.0.)**

Administrative support is necessary for the faculty in carrying out various functions such as correspondence, report writing, paper writing, preparation of case studies and records, research, activities related to field work and community service, and the organisation of short-term courses.

The minimum staff recommended for a newly established programme (about 40 to 50 students) is as follows:

1 Office Superintendent
1 Accountant
1 Steno-typist
1 Clerk-typist
1 Filing Clerk
1 Peon

The staffing pattern above is only a nucleus and any programme that goes beyond 40 to 50 students, will need additional staff such as typists. Where the number of students is at least 70, the appointment of a Registrar or an administrative head, becomes very essential. In addition, an institution needs such support staff as cleaning staff, watchmen (3 for 24 hours), gardener (where applicable) and driver (where applicable). Institutions which run their own hostel, should have the necessary supervisory and support staff.

9.1.4.0. CONTINUING EDUCATION, RESEARCH, PUBLICATIONS AND EXTENSION FACILITIES

9.1.4.1. Continuing Education (2.4.1.0.)

To make this programme more effective, the UGC should initiate it in various states. The concerned state governments should also undertake such courses in collaboration with the training institutions. A few selected institutions could cater to the needs of a group of states and adequate finances for administrative expenses, training costs and for TA/DA for the participants could be provided. One institution in each state should be assisted in carrying out such programmes for its own area. The position of a co-ordinator of such programmes may be provided for in the budget of the institution. The profession has several needs to fulfil in such extension education especially for the following target groups for whom it should be designed.

a. A backlog of untrained staff.
b. Volunteers at the policy and planning level and field level persons.
c. Orientation on social aspects of development to policy-makers (legislators, members of parliament, corporators/zilla parishad, panchayat samiti/gram panchayat elected members); and planners (at central, state and district levels); and administrators (official and non-official).
d. Re-tool/re-orient its graduates in newly emerging theories and their practice implications.

9.1.4.2. Research (2.4.2.0.)

Research is essential in building up an indigenous base for social work education and also in developing concepts, theories and tools of measurement for social work. It could be undertaken both by the institutions and the faculty. Appropriate measures would have to be initiated separately in increasing the research output for these two types. Following are the recommendations:

a. The existing staff should be strengthened at the institutional level for enhancing research capabilities.

b. Separate budget allocations could be made for initiating major research projects on problems of national importance and areas of key interest to the profession.

c. Where such research competence is adequately built up, it is necessary to develop Research Units in the institutions by providing a continuation budget to them. Such persons include a Professor/Reader in charge of the Unit, one Research Officer, a statistician-cum-programmer and four Research Assistants. They must function as the consultative unit to other faculty who should be encouraged to undertake research.

d. To reduce the time lag between data collection and analysis, the institutions should be aided in acquiring data processing machines like calculators, punchers, sorters, tabulators, data tapes.

e. Incentives like special allowances and leave, should be offered to the faculty for research studies, or for training in research. A few institutions could be strengthened for providing regular advanced courses in research to faculty.

f. Institutions which are already bringing out periodic annotated bibliographies on books and journal articles related to social development and welfare, should be given financial support to recruit the necessary staff to continue the service to the profession.

9.1.4.3. **Publications and Teaching Materials** (2.4.3.0.)

Without the development of an indigenous base, educational programmes of social work will continue to rely heavily on western textual material. We need to give top priority for producing materials which are indigenous in their references and relevant to local situations. If a majority of the faculty members prefer to write in English, the publications can be translated later into the regional languages. Similarly, regional language publications could be translated into English.

The following suggestions pertain to the development of such indigenous literature.

a. *National Level*

The University Grants Commission, the Department of Social Welfare, the National Council for Social Work Education (proposed) may select persons and provide grants, equivalent to their salary, for a period of one year. They must be relieved from teaching responsibilities to concentrate on writing. In addition, a certain amount may be given as honorarium and at least one-third of the royalties on the books. A systematic approach to bring out such publications is required.

b. *Institutional Level*

At the institutional level, typing and mimeographing facilities should be provided.

c. *Funding Journals*

As the first step towards developing an indigenous base, existing professional journals should be subsidised by the UGC, so that the persons commissioned to write the articles can be paid. A systematic programme can thus be developed for publication of indigenous literature.

9.1.4.4. **Field Service Projects of Institutions** (2.4.4.0.)

Projects organised by training institutions need sustained inputs. Token grants would not suffice for their maintenance. These inputs include staff salaries, building and equipment, and the necessary expenditure on the services. Each of these centres should be staffed by a person as the head, who is at least at the level of a lecturer capable of directing the projects, giving field instruction and preparing teaching materials. Both the UGC and state governments need to pay special attention to the development of such infrastructure for training. The state government will benefit especially as these centres can be utilised by them for testing, demonstration and research and for pilot projects and field training of personnel.

The training institutions have always had much difficulty in raising the financial support for such field service projects. Yet, the very fact that so many of them have tried to raise the necessary finance shows the importance of such projects to the institutions. It is recommended, therefore, that such field projects be included in the budget of all training programmes as necessary expenditure (on the analogy of grants for laboratories to science colleges). Training institutions should not be put into the situation where they are compelled to raise funds — the faculty already have numerous demands on their time.

9.1.5.0. LIBRARY (2.5.0.0.)

9.1.5.1. **Newly Established Institution**

Considering the importance of a library to academic institutions for meaningful studies at the post-graduate level and for research, it is recommended that a newly established institution must start with a minimum of 1,500 volumes in the library. It must start with 2,000 books if it offers more than one programme, e.g., bachelor's and master's. In addition, the library must subscribe to at least 20 journals at the start of its establishment and gradually build up the number of such journals. The stock of books should be enhanced, within the first few years, to 10,000 volumes which include social work, social science and behavioural science subjects.

9.1.5.2. **Continuing Budgets**

For additions to the library, the minimum financial assistance suggested is Rs. 20,000 per 100 students or at least 50 major titles a year plus journals. When an under-graduate programme is added to a graduate programme, the budget should be provided for at least 800 titles a year and 40 journals.

9.1.5.3. **Library Development Grants**

Similar to the UGC pattern, five year development grants should be given to libraries of colleges which receive state government grants. We note that state institutions need special inputs, both for development grants for libraries and for enhanced expenditure on the recurring library grants.

9.1.6.0. CAMPUS FACILITIES (2.6.0.0.)

9.1.6.1. **Institutional Premises** (2.6.1.0.)

As building facilities are inadequate, it is necessary to expand them before any additional programmes, at various educational levels, are offered.

9.1.6.2. **Hostel Facilities** (2.6.2.0.)

Special UGC funding requires to be made available on a 75 per cent basis for these institutions. This is especially so for single-faculty, affiliated colleges, which could gradually build up the required minimum basic amenities. (Such colleges generally do not have share in the university students' housing).

9.1.6.3. **Faculty Housing** (2.6.3.0.)

The nature of social work professional education demands that the faculty members live on the campus. Lack of sufficient housing facilities on the campus causes organisation and administrative inconvenience. Besides, paucity of housing hampers the institutions in attracting talent from outside their location. The institutions should, therefore, be substantially aided for housing, especially the single-faculty, affiliated colleges.

9.1.7.0. FUNDS (6.2.0.0.)

Institutions which are central and deemed universities and the departments of universities, generally get UGC/State education department funds as development and maintenance grants. It is the single-faculty affiliated institutions that face the major problem of funding source. They receive very small maintenance grants and rarely any development grants. There is a large number of institutions under this pattern.

9.1.7.1. **Maintenance Grants**

It is recommended that all social work education, from para-professional to the Ph.D., should be placed under the UGC for the purpose of grants and maintenance of standards. If UGC statutes do not permit this, it is suggested that the Department of Social Welfare be the operating Department for these single-faculty, affiliated colleges. (This will be similar to the practice followed in the case of other professional institutions such as medicine and agriculture.)

Where a well established pattern of funding already exists in the state Department of Education, and is operating without difficulties, the practice should not be discontinued. The pattern suggested applies to that large majority of institutions where funding position has been generally unsatisfactory. The state level directorates of social welfare education and the Ministry of Education and Social Welfare, Government of India, should together be responsible for 90 per cent of the expenditure on the approved items, while the remainder of 10 per cent may be raised by the institution through its fees and other sources. Where the college has a good trust endowment as income, the percentage reimbursed would depend on the deficit incurred. Such sharing of costs between the state and the centre is also a recognition of the fact that several social work educational institutions serve students from many states besides their own. These grants should be made available for existing institutions, each on merit, and for new institutions after they are accredited. A lack of such a funding pattern shows little recognition of the need for developing manpower for social development and welfare.

9.1.7.2. **Development Grants**

Besides maintenance grants, the central/state government (through the operating ministries) should also make development grants available to these institutions on lines similar to those made by the UGC. The minimum strength stipulated by the UGC for an institution to qualify for the development grants, as well as grants for special schemes (book bank, student aid fund) need to be modified. The present qualifications demanded of the institutions by the UGC do not reflect the usual size of these institutions which is related to job opportunities, availability of trained faculty, financial resources, field work facilities, and other factors which are beyond the control of individual institutions. The minimum required strength should be as follows:

a. Post-graduate institutions:	50
b. Under-graduate institutions:	75
c. Institutions with an under-graduate and continuing post-graduate programme:	100

9.1.7.3. Admissible Items of Expenditure

The Committee has recommended in detail the items of expenditure which can be taken into account for purpose of grants by the state and central governments on the basis of 90 per cent of shared responsibility. In the case of institutions which are departments of their respective universities, one hundred per cent grant should be admissible for these items since the fees are collected centrally.

The admissible items of expenditure include:

a. Salaries, allowances, benefits, ex-gratia payment, and honoraria.
b. Establishment expenses, rent, taxes, maintenance and repairs; purchase and maintenance of equipment; stationery, telephone, postage, telegrams, conveyance and transport; advertisement; insurance, and such other recurring expenditures.
c. Library.
d. Field service projects.
e. Research cell.
f. Continuing education, seminars, short-term courses.
g. Faculty development.
h. Professional affiliation.
i. Subsidy for the hostel.

9.1.8.0. ORGANISATIONS ASSOCIATED WITH SOCIAL WORK EDUCATION

9.1.8.1. The University Grants Commission (6.4.2.1.)

a. *Appointment of a Full-Time Officer*

The Panel on Social Work Education should be served by a full-time officer appointed by the UGC. The person should be in the Professor's grade, and must have at least ten years of experience in social work education. He must also have held a position of some responsibility in the administration of the academic programme in his own institution. The person must be capable of gaining the confidence of the heads of institutions with whom he will directly work on the programme. The services of this person may be provided on loan by institutions for a period of three years. His work would include:

i. Convening meeting of the Panel and serving as its Secretary; convening meetings of all sub-committees appointed by the Panel, serving as the Secretary of these sub-committees and the responsibility for related matters such as implementation of decisions taken, follow up of the recommendations with concerned bodies; and finalisation and production of reports.
ii. Planning and execution of all summer seminars, short-term courses, etc., in collaboration with either the Association of Schools of Social Work in India or individual institutions.
iii. All matters pertaining to the UGC fellowships, sanction of research projects of the UGC, implementation of the UGC schemes and bringing about modifications in policy (where indicated) to suit the needs of smaller professional programmes as in social work education. Sometimes minimum requirements for grants to special projects are tied to the size of the institutions, i.e., the number of beneficiaries.
iv. Reviewing frequently the norms for professional training.
v. Planned development of publications, research, field service projects and teaching aids for social work education in collaboration with other relevant organisations such as the Association of Schools of Social Work in India and with the Training Cell proposed for the Department of Social Welfare, Government of India.
vi. Co-ordinating, as an ex-officio member, the activities of the UGC with over-all training in social work, in the major policy committees of the Association of Schools of Social Work in India and the Training Cell in the Department of Social Welfare, Government of India.
vii. Organising visits of lecturers to social work training institutions such as fields experts and national professors.

He should, therefore, be given necessary support such as a professional assistant on the level of a lecturer who can assist with correspondence and attending to all routine matters. Administrative staff such as a stenographer, a typist-clerk and a messenger should also be sanctioned.

b. *Establishment of NSS Cell in the UGC*

A permanent NSS Cell, consisting of the representatives of the social work educational institutions responsible for NSS in their universities, should be set up in the UGC. A full-time Special Officer on Duty in the Professor's scale should be in charge of the cell.

9.1.8.2. The Department of Social Welfare, Government of India (6.4.2.2.)

A separate Division for Planning, Research, Evaluation and Monitoring, created by the Department of Social Welfare, has sponsored research studies and compiled statistics, with the necessary financial support of the Planning Commission. The utility of these functions for teaching, planning and implementation of programmes, cannot be over-emphasized. The Committee, therefore, strongly recommends that this Division should be considerably strengthened and documentation of information undertaken on a large scale.

The Department should have a full-fledged Training Cell which will deal with matters related to social work education. The activity of such a Cell should encompass:

a. Planning and development of manpower for social welfare. (Work with Department of Personnel of the Government of India, the Planning Commission, the various ministries employing social workers, and employees in the voluntary sector, for a planned development of social work manpower and to relate training to job opportunities.)
b. Deployment of training institutions in non-favoured areas, e.g., backward, rural and tribal.
c. Providing equivalence and recognition to non-degree programmes.
d. Development of syllabi for non-degree programmes.
e. Development of publications and teaching aids in both English and vernacular.
f. Development of Research Cells in the training institutions and non-teaching institutions engaged in research.
g. Administration of maintenance and development grants to the under-graduate and post-graduate degree institutions affiliated to the state universities, and for non-degree training

programmes.

h. Grants to the Association of Schools of Social Work in India which would contract for execution of some of the schemes of the Cell.

The Department should recruit persons with necessary expertise for the work in the training cell. It may either draft persons from the existing training institutions and avail of their services for two or three years; or, it may employ a qualified social work educator at the senior level, with at least ten years of experience and expertise in administration of training programmes and curriculum development. He should be supported by two persons in the position of Lecturer (equivalent to Research Officer). This would assure some continuity, as well as bring fresh points of view and provide the Department expert assistance. The lien and salary of such persons, in their parent institutions, should be protected.

9.1.8.3. The Planning Commission (6.4.2.3.)

The Planning Commission has a very important role to play in the formulation of policies, programmes and the utilisation of research relating to the field of social welfare and social work. It is therefore necessary to have a person at a senior level who in association with the training institutions and the Association of Schools of Social Work in India, will be responsible for establishing appropriate policies for funding social work education. The Commission, which has hitherto played a limited role, needs to formulate an adequate scheme for the purpose of assuming such responsibility for social work education. In formulating the Five-Year Plans for the nation's social welfare sector, social work educators should be involved, both at the central and the state levels.

9.1.8.4. Association of Schools of Social Work in India (6.4.2.4.)

The Association is a voluntary, standard setting organ of the training institutions. It should be the spokesman of the social work educators and remain as a non-government organisation. It should be responsible for constant reviews of the curricula and for retraining and retooling faculty and also for preparing new faculty, for research pertaining to social work education, and for preparing teaching materials. The Association should also publish a journal devoted to educational issues and must provide the necessary leadership to the training institutions through consultancy.

We recommend that the proposed training cell in the Department of Social Welfare and the UGC, assist the association with maintenance and development grants since the Association is an essential arm for their activity with the training institutions.

9.1.9.0. ESTABLISHMENT OF A NATIONAL COUNCIL FOR SOCIAL WORK EDUCATION (6.4.3.0.)

9.1.9.1. Rationale (6.4.3.1.)

As indicated in the preceding section, there are four organisations which are involved with social work education. Each of these organisations has overlapping concerns (social work education) and addresses mainly the same audience (social work educators). Therefore, to upgrade social work education and to maintain standards, some joint planning, pattern of funding, and a programme of action are necessary. It then becomes possible to make rational use of manpower and resources. The National Council for Social Work Education may be established to achieve this goal.

The role of the Association of Schools of Social Work in India, as an executing body for some of the activities of the National Council, should be recognised. The Association could be delegated certain tasks; the necessary funds could be allocated to it. The tasks to be delegated to the ASSWI may be decided upon mutually and reviewed from time to time. The functions of the National Council are envisaged to be regulatory while that of the ASSWI to be representative.

9.1.9.2. The Council Structure (6.4.3.2.)

Such a council should be established by a joint resolution of the University Grants Commission and the Department of Social Welfare. It should essentially be autonomous and similar to other bodies created by the Government of India. The Department of Social Welfare should be the operating Department. The council should be flexible, innovative and must have a dynamic staff — it should not hamper change with bureaucratic structures.

The head of the Council should be an eminent social work educator. He should be assisted by staff who are capable of providing consultation to training institutions, preparing teaching aids and educational resource materials of use to institutions. They should also be capable of undertaking or commissioning research.

9.1.9.3. **Responsibilities (6.4.3.3.)**

a. *Programme and Faculty Development*

i. Develop educational policies and directions for relating social work education to social realities.
ii. Perform standard setting and accrediting functions.
iii. Develop an integrated programme of training from the para-professional to post-graduate level.
iv. Devise training courses to be run in collaboration with the Association of Schools of Social Work in India, and individual institutions.
v. Provide consultation to training institutions and faculty.

b. *Teaching Aids and Publications*

Promote teaching aids and resources, publications and a journal of social work education.

c. *Research*

Undertake or commission research on social work education; scrutinise all research projects and administer research grants on behalf of the Department of Social Welfare and the University Grants Commission; offer consultation services to such institutions undertaking research and develop research expertise of institutions.

d. *Funds*

Provide funding to all institutions not directly maintained by the UGC, and to advise the state government on their contribution to such training programmes. Also, to provide funds for the maintenance of the two professional associations — the Association of Schools of Social Work in India and the Indian Association of Trained Social Workers.

e. *Manpower Development*

i. Make statutory provisions for employing trained social workers in specified positions in both Government and the voluntary sectors.
ii. Develop a manpower policy in collaboration with government and private organisations, to assess the requirements for trained manpower to be prepared by the training institutions.
iii. Establish rules for recruitment.

9.1.9.4. **The Governing Board (6.4.3.4.)**

The Council should have a Governing Board which frames policies and guides its activities. It should meet at least twice a year. The Constitution of the Board is as follows:

		Number
i.	Chairman	1
ii.	Member-secretary should be the Director of the Council	1
iii.	Representatives of Professional Associations: The Association of School of Work in India — the President and the Executive Secretary (2) The Indian Association of Trained Social Workers — the President and the Executive Secretary (2)	4
iv.	Social work educators nominated by rotation	6
v.	Representatives of students by rotation	6
vi.	The Chairman of the UGC Panel on Social Work Education and the Officer in charge of social work education	2
vii.	The representative of the Planning Division of the Planning Commission	1
viii.	The representative of the Department of Social Welfare, Government of India in charge of research and training	1
ix.	Directors of Social Welfare (State/Union Territories by rotation.	5

x. Representatives of national voluntary organisations	2
xi. The Central Social Welfare Board (1)	1
xii. Representatives of higher education	2
a. Association of Vice-Chancellors (1)	
b. Inter-Collegiate Board (1)	
xiii. Nomination of eminent professional social workers (2)	2
xiv. Members of Parliament (2)	2
Total	36

The Board should be responsible for over-all policy making and standard setting. It should recommend curricular of relevance to the field realities. It should receive reports of the Director on work in progress and work executed.

9.1.9.5. **Funds**

Appropriate funding arrangements will be required to be made for the Council's functions.

9.1.10.0. **Independent Review Committees** (6.4.4.0.)

The UGC should appoint independent review committees for each of the institutions which is within the university system. The Panel on Social Work Education should name a group of persons, and this list may be utilised to appoint members of the Committee. Such Review Committees should, ultimately, be appointed by the National Council and the Review should be undertaken every five years. The institutions that do not come up to the specified norms, should be visited by the Committee every two years, and only two such terms should given in which the institutions have to meet the required standards.

9.2.0.0. RECOMMENDATIONS FOR THE PROGRAMME OF PROFESSIONAL EDUCATION

9.2.1.0. BUILDING THE SOCIAL WORK CURRICULUM (3.1.0.0.)

The focus of an educational programme is the learner while the curriculum is designed to help the learner to achieve the objectives of the educational programme. The objective of a professional curriculum is to prepare the type and quality of manpower capable of performing the tasks and functions which ultimately achieve the goals the profession has set for itself in the context of the particular society which it seeks to serve. Therefore, to recommend a social work curriculum which has relevance in the Indian context, we must first do the following:

a. State the *social realities,* and the *goals* to be achieved;
b. Relate these goals to the *tasks and functions of social workers* which will lead to their achievement.
c. It is then that the educator can define the *educational objectives as the stated behavioural outcomes,* which the student must achieve in relation to the tasks and functions for which he is being prepared.
d. Once such objectives or behavioural outcomes are specified, it is possible to select the *content* of the curriculum which will lead to the achievement of these objectives. This strategy has been elaborated in the report. It is stated here briefly because it provides the philosophical orientation, and the framework for building the curriculum as suggested in the report. Regional variation should be taken into account in developing such curricula. Only guidelines are provided in this report.

9.2.1.1. **The Social Realities** (3.1.1.0.)

Poverty and population are interrelated problems which confront us and at the interface of these problems are illiteracy; malnutrition; poor habitat (sanitation, potable water, housing, communication and accessibility to services); low productivity; unemployment; underemployment; and the disabilities resulting from social and economic inequity, and the exploitation of the vulnerable and weaker sections of our society. Growth with social justice has not been achieved and the gains of development have yet to reach the economically vulnerable sections of society. A large proportion of this population is in the rural areas and poor. These then are the social realities to which social workers must respond. And social work must design a curriculum relevant to the type of manpower required to work in these conditions.

9.2.1.2. **The Tasks** (3.1.2.0.)

The tasks of social workers are largely development but they may also be remedial. The tasks of the social workers, envisaged in relation to these social realities, are those of the catalytic agent for developing and/or modifying current policies/service/ institutional structures; educating the people to recognise their inherent capacity, for action, and, to identify the policies/institutional and socio-political structures that exploit them, or, identify structures which do not achieve social goals for all; to assist the micro-community to build its own resources through community cooperation and action which services the interests of all its groups; (giving primary emphasis to the weakest segments). The social worker has to act as the enabler, guide, teacher, advocate, broker, negotiator and sometimes as the one to lead the confrontation, when this is indicated, on behalf of the client system he must serve, especially the most vulnerable sections of our society.

In the process, social work cannot ignore the tasks which are remedial and rehabilitative for those persons whose functioning is already impaired. These tasks have been and still remain recognised by society as the specific responsibilities of the profession of social work. A lack of our recognition of these roles would place a particular hardship on persons who face the residual problems in our society such as abandonment and personal handicap. What is sought to be achieved is to rearrange our priorities so that the primary problems affecting the larger segment of our population receive greater emphasis than the residual problems.

9.2.1.3. **Functions** (3.1.3.0.)

The functions (roles) for which we envisage the preparation of social workers at different levels are as follows:

a. Delivery of services/change agent functions utilising the knowledge related to the work with communities, groups, families and individuals, as well as societal institutions, and creating new services as and where required.
b. Planning, policy development, programming and administration related to the delivery of services.
c. Monitoring, evaluation and research skills related to improve-

ment, change and development of knowledge and skills in the delivery of services.

d. Supervision, training and education of manpower required for the delivery of services.

These functions are neither hierarchical no mutually exclusive. They represent social work function in activities which may be developmental/change oriented or remedial and rehabilitative, and require knowledge and skills at varying levels of complexity. All social workers will need to engage in these functions. However, there may be greater stress on some functions than on others at various levels. For some social workers, knowledge of these functions may be necessary even when they are not exercised. Hence, curricular development at each level must be related to the preparation for these functions with the relative emphasis varying at each level of training.

9.2.1.4. **Levels of Practice and Related Job Positions** (3.1.4.0.)

A major problem today is the lack of clear recognition that certain job require expertise in social work. The job that exist today end in blind alleys, in subordinate positions and intended to support the functioning of other personnel. There is no career ladder. These are also limited opportunities for growth in the job situation and technical know-how plays only peripheral role in decision-making. In the mainstream of decision-making, either in the voluntary or in the governmental sector, formal training in social work does not receive recognition. This has affected the quality of programme planning and implementation in both the sectors. The quality of manpower attracted to the profession has also been affected. Short-term training is not a substitute for professional training. In the end, it is more expensive. If we are to relate the training to the employability of its professionals, it is recommended that the University Grants Commission, the Department of Social Welfare at the centre and the Association of Schools of Social Work in India take special steps to remedy this situation. Related to the levels of training are job-positions with the major direct practice responsibilities carried by auxiliary/para-professional workers and graduates with a bachelor's degree; middle level administrative, policy, research and teaching functions may be carried by graduates at the master's level; and higher level policy, administration, research and teaching functions by graduates at the M.Phil/Ph.D. levels, A recommendation, related to a systematic identification of such job positions, has been made separately.

9.2.1.5. Organizational Principles in Building the Curriculum (3.1.5.0.)

The focus of work should be the vulnerable sections of society. These client systems, the methodology of working with them, and the suitable service delivery systems, should be made the content of the syllabus. We must also take into consideration the fact that our target system may be other than the client system because this target system may affect or impede the functioning of the client systems, e.g., economic and political decision makers and power groups. These then are the elements to be considered in building the curriculum. Knowledge of society and organisations, of social and individual behaviour and strategies of action and change, should be the essential content of the curriculum. The approach is both integrated and holistic and based on the needs of society. The philosophical orientation of the social work syllabus with a holistic approach, is to develop an integrated body of skills to work with individuals, groups and communities; and to take a stance that is developmental/change oriented and interdisciplinary.

9.2.2.0. A CONCEPTUAL FRAMEWORK FOR SOCIAL WORK EDUCATION

9.2.2.1. The Objectives of Professional Education for Social Work (3.1.6.0.)

The components of any activity (or programme) reflect the objectives to be achieved through that activity, the content, the methodology for achieving the stated objective and the parameters within which it takes place. The Committee has stated, in considerable detail, the objectives to be achieved in training; the focus at each level of training, the major conceptual framework for the content of the curriculum and the factors related to the administration of the curriculum which provide the boundaries as well as indicate the norms for a qualitatively satisfactory training.

The objectives of the curriculum are stated in terms of behavioural outcomes, that is, the knowledge to be mastered (cognitive), the skills to be developed (psychomotor), the attitudes, values and the professional behaviour to be acquired (affective). All these objectives may be stated in behavioural terms and revised periodically with corresponding change in our curriculum objectives and professional beliefs. While the over-all objectives for professional education, especially at the bachelor's and the master's level may not differ too much, it may be recognised that specific objectives could be stated for each level. However, in the report, we have only stated the over-all objectives of training for social work. We have discussed the focus of the programme at each level but not the specific behavioural objectives or outcome at those levels.

9.2.2.2. **The Focus at Each Level of Training**

a. *Para-professional/Auxiliary Level* (4.1.3.0.)

It must train for field level tasks, should be self-contained and terminal, but also must prepare for entry into the next level. The curriculum should have core content of knowledge and skills applicable to social work practice in a wide a variety of situations requiring work with people but also providing specific knowledge and skills in a service area (e.g., multipurpose worker in urban slums or lower level institutional staff). The course should be designed to develop the attitudes and values of the profession; be geared at the post-SSC level and should be certified by higher boards of education. Lastly, it should be provided through existing institutions for social work education or in related developmental institutes such as rural/tribal institutes, rather than in the higher secondary schools or junior colleges, because of the type of infrastructure required by such training programmes.

b. *Bachelor's Level* (4.2.3.0.)

It is the first degree level. It should prepare field workers and the supervisors of para-professional/auxiliary staff or practice in situations which require knowledge and skills in the management of interpersonal relationships and community/ institutional processes. Practice would require intervention in situations which do not show an unusually problematic or pathological condition. The preparation at this level should be for specific job skills or tasks. Programme media should be emphasized, whether these are non-formal education techniques, home-management and nutrition, health, organisation and management of cooperatives, or work with youth, women and children. When engaging in change functions, the activities may be in the nature of education and developmental of awareness of the problematic situation. Problem-solving may be directed at specific situations or target groups.

c. *Master's Level* (5.1.3.0.)

It should be a second degree, assuming field level practice competence of its students. The focus at this level, should be on policy, planning, and administrative functions; research, teaching and supervisory functional, and on practice requiring considerable knowledge from allied disciplines, and a level of complexity which goes beyond the basic skills of enable and guide.

d. *M. Phil* (5.2.3.0.)

The person should preferably be recruited after his having had some practice/teaching experience. Thus, the primary focus should be on developing his knowledge, in depth and in extent, in his substantive area of practice. The focus should be on developing such skills as in the analysis and conceptualisation of knowledge skills in teaching, or skills in policy, planning administration, or research skills, or a higher order of clinical/practice related skills. The programme should provide a base for entry into the Ph.D.

e. *Ph.D.* (5.3.3.0.)

As with the graduate at the other levels, the student entering the Ph.D. should be recruited after some practice/teaching experience. The focus should be on the development of a perspective on the knowledge which is currently available to the profession. He should develop such skills as the capacity to identify gaps in knowledge/intervention strategies. This level of education should provide opportunity to utilise selectively, the knowledge from related disciplines to strengthen the professional content and the intervention strategies. The scholar should be able to contribute to the knowledge base of the profession including the intervention strategies.

9.2.2.3. **The Syllabus** (Chapters 3, 4 and 5.)

Change in the syllabus was a matter requiring immediate attention of the individual institutions for social work education and the organisations responsible for maintaining academic norms. The University Grants Commission and the Association of Schools of Social Work in India should evolve syllabi which are relevant to the current situation and which meet the regional and local needs. This change of syllabus will require a review of the courses, field work and research at each level of training.

The curricular emphasis needs to be on the developmental work and social change oriented practice. It needs to develop integrated knowledge and skills in working with people. Practitioners need to develop an understanding of behaviour whether this behaviour is an expression of an individual, a family, a group or a community. They need to develop a capacity for organising and mobilising groups and communities, to enable them in their problem-solving work and to assist the client system to obtain their share in development. It is necessary to develop in the practitioner the capacity to act as the facilitator, educator and guide. The practitioner can do this by assisting people to enter into problem-solving and by developing in them the capacity for self-understanding, and, by changing negative factors within the client system, their environment, and social structure, which affect their social functioning. The practitioner must also develop ability of helping people—individually and in groups—to cop with these factors.

a. *Courses* (3.2.2.1.)

A conceptual framework, for developing the syllabus, is given in the report. It is only a guideline for the individual curriculum framer for evolving the course content. In this summary of recommendations, we can only list the major conceptual areas for courses at the paraprofessional/auxiliary, the bachelor's and the master's levels. They are as follows:

i. Subject-matter related to professional practice and to the profession.

ii. Subject-matter related to the problems of society (social development/pathology or deviance) and the delivery of social services.
iii. Subject-matter related to society, social structure, social institutions, and social change processes and strategies.
iv. Subject-matter related to the behavioural and biological sciences.
v. Subject-matter offered as electives, and additional course offering which enlarge the scope of the student's learning, or are specific to job skills.

The degree of emphasis laid on each area above will depend on the specific goals of the curriculum at each level of learning and the type of job positions for which the students are being prepared. The number of courses offered under each of these subject areas, will therefore also vary, as well as the relative weightage to be given to different aspects of the curriculum. In the present context of social development and welfare, specialisations are not recommended, although there may be reasons for which individual institutions continue to offer them. Even when one or two or three courses in a specific area of interest, are offered, these cannot be regarded as specialisations. They are special areas of interest rather than concentrations of a depth and extent to be termed as specialisations. Electives may thus replace specialisations. This is further elaborated a little later.

At the M.Phil./Ph.D. level, courses are not particularly necessary. The students at the Master's level do not have adequate scope to read and develop analytical skills and, therefore, the M.Phil. programme should allow the greatest scope for individual study, and writing of analytical papers for presentation in seminars where peer group learning should be promoted. Also, students who reach the M.Phil./Ph.D. levels have already crystallized their interest areas and it is impossible to provide the number of courses that would be needed to encompass such a broad spectrum. Advanced courses in research methodology and statistics may be given as preparation for work on the dissertation (5.2.4.0. and 5.3.4.0.).

At all other levels, the curriculum may be organised keeping in view the objectives and the focus at each level outlined in Chapter 3 of the report. The conceptual framework of the courses is so designed that curriculum framers in different institutions, can develop their own courses utilising it as a guide to comprehensiveness. At the same time, the framework provides a basis by which individual curriculum framers can decide on the relative weightage to be given to each area including the number of courses, the number of hours and the proportion of marks to be allocated.

In view of the Committee's recommendations, it is very necessary that institutions in the same region come together for a review and should develop their particular syllabi. A Syllabus Cell, established in national bodies such as the Association of Schools of Social Work in India, will provide a mechanism for frequent review of curricula. Teaching methods and materials related to course content should also be undertaken.

The Committee has made two significant recommendations on the specialisations offered and the specialisation approach (4.3.1.0.). It is evident that for the purpose of a job, Industrial Relations/ Personnel Management require persons with relevant training. The content of training in this specialisation is on longer solely related to social work. In fact, while it can utilise some of the content of social work, it has largely developed its own identity. Labour welfare, however, continues to share greater identity with social work. Two full years of study are required to really to justice to the Industrial Relations/Personnel Management specialisation. We recommend, therefore, that even where the same institution continues to award this degree, it should be provided as a separate course of two full years, appropriately covering the vast development in that field.

The Committee gave very serious consideration to the existing pattern of specialisation in social work. We doubt whether existing social work knowledge is adequate for a field related specialist approach in social work, or whether this approach is relevant to most jobs in the field. Having stated our thinking, we are of the view that, were some institutions to retain the specialisation pattern for social work education, the number of papers in the specialisation should be at least half of the total number of papers required. The papers should cover the major problems identified, the philosophy and history of development of the field, legislation, administration, the relevant methods of social work and research in that field. In no case should two specialisations be combined unless they have some relevance and share the same theoretical framework.

b. *Field Work* (3.2.2.2.)

This was identified as another major area requiring change. We believe that the University Grants Commission and the Association of Schools of Social Work in India, will have to pay considerable attention to the question of objectives, design, content and methodology of field work. An analysis of a developmental focus in the student's field experience, in each setting, is required. The strategies of interaction for social change need to be strengthened through field practice. The student needs to be prepared for the role of change agent rather than for just the traditional remedial and rehabilitative functions. It is also necessary to evaluate the suitability of experience that traditional agency placements provide and to devise other means of learning in the field such as case studies of specific field experiments/programmes/ administrative decisions. Placements selected and the tasks assigned to the students must have significance for the students. Adequate field work opportunities should be made available. This should first be ascertained before situating a new institution in a specific location. Students should spend at least 15 hours on field work every week; in case the student takes up a research project he should give 12 hours to field work.

Concurrent field work has considerable value since the skills and attitudes develop only over a period of time. However, the students' difficulty in having one foot in the class and the other in field can be reduced considerably if they attend classes for three days consecutively, and utilise the remainder of the week for field work. It has considerable merit where field work requires the student's continuous presence, or his stay away from the institution such as in a village or in a residential programme for children or adults.

Block field work may be continued where a specific learning gain is attached to it and it is feasible. The rationale of having block field work at the end of the two years need to be reviewed. The student might probably see this as a period of disengagement, rather than re-engagement, as it comes towards the end of his learning. It is also difficult for the institution to help the student integrate this new learning that may take place, especially when block field work requires the student to stay in a location too far away from the institution. Hence it may be necessary to experiment with block field work in the middle of the academic year between October and December. The remainder of the concurrent field work time should be utilised to follow-up on the activities undertaken during the block field work.

Camps and study tours are seen as valid components of the students' field learning. We recommend them for the reasons mentioned in the report. If they are to be essential components of learning, they should be accepted as items of reimbursable expenditure in the financial grant to the institution. Institutional visits in the same location, especially as a part of the students' orientation to the field of social work at the point of entry, are also recommended. Laboratory training may also be provided especially where it has relevance to specific courses, e.g., nutrition or home-management.

It is necessary that to accord high priority for the review of field work in each institution—especially in relation to integrating the developmental emphasis. There is considerable need to define tasks and content in field learning and to make evaluation related to such content. The same mechanism suggested for the frequent review of syllabi may also be utilised for field work, since class-room courses and field work should be well integrated.

c. *Research* (3.2.2.3.)

The question of retaining the research project, as a compulsory requirement at the master's level, needs to be reviewed. This requirement does not seem to be necessary in view of the fact that most students do not themselves becomes producers of research. Instead, their ability to effectively use research needs to be strengthened. Further, analytical abilities need to be developed throughout all the courses. The *ability* to identify problems for study and to undertake a simple survey to understand a problem, or to study the effects of a programme or service, may be included in their field work experience. If need be, the hours may be increased for field work to include this exercise in lieu of research. However, such research-related activity should not take more than 20 to 25 per cent of the student's time, since the emphasis in field work is the development of social work practice skills. It is necessary, therefore, to explore the ways in which the entire curriculum and the learning experiences can be so designed as to develop the analytical and conceptual skills (which are usually enhanced through a research exercise), particularly if research become optional. We also need to emphasize a higher order of research skills for students who do opt for research. Through electives, we can offer courses in research and statistics which go beyond the minimum requirements so that we can train some persons for research in social work. This is not the same as a full specialisation in research which is not advocated at the master's level.

Further, we need to help all levels of students in recognising the need and importance of data for programme monitoring and evaluation. At the bachelor's level, we need to train persons who can be members of a research team such as investigators, coders, and tabulators, while, at the master's level the emphasis should be on developing the capacity to design and carry out research projects.

9.2.3.0. CURRICULUM ADMINISTRATION

A good educational programme includes not only the syllabi but a number of supporting factors which ensure its quality. These matters of curriculum administration may be stated to be the supporting educational norms. They include:

a. The necessary number and duration of the terms/semesters.
b. The distribution and relative weightage of time for different aspects of the curriculum such as classes, field work, laboratory work and research.
c. The allocation of marks to the various aspects of the curriculum.
d. The eligibility requirements at each stage of admission.
e. The language of instruction at each stage.

As these norms vary from stage to stage, it is not possible for us to go into the details, which are fully covered in Chapters 4 and 5. We recommend that these norms be utilised in the review of the programme of each institution and for the accreditation of these institutions by the authority suggested in this report (4.1.5.0., 4.2.5.0., 5.1.5.0., 5.2.5.0., 5.3.5.0.).

Specific mention, however, may be made of the three important matters connected with the administration of a programme:

a. Admission procedures should include the interview of individual candidates. In addition, group discussion, essay test, psychological/aptitude tests and rating scales may be utilised (3.3.1.0.0.).

b. Criteria for examinations should be increasingly internal rather than external; periodic rather than at one point in time; and they should not be the only means of assessment which should also include assignments and class participation; finally grades rather than than marks should be utilised (3.3.6.0.).

c. Part-time study should be established by the institutions which are now offering full-time courses only. Ultimately, such part-time study will make it possible for students to accumulate all the credits required by the full-time programme—albeit over a longer period. Admission, academic and assessment requirements should, however, remain the same. Persons, with family or employment obligations, will thus be able to earn the necessary credits for the degree.

d. External/private study and correspondence courses are not recommended because of the very nature of requirements of social work education. These include the use of case studies, the utilisation of practice experience and skills in classroom teaching, and the development of the necessary professional attitudes. All this can only be nurtured and assessed in a direct teacher-student situation.

e. Social work courses are not recommended as subsidiary and minor subject in universities. Wherever they are now offered, it is recommend that they may be discontinued as they cannot prepare students for social work. They only confuse the employers, all of whom are not sufficiently aware of the nature and extent of education for social work.

9.2.4.0. RECRUITMENT RULES FOR JOBS (3.3.10.0.)

The Department of Social Welfare, Government of India, should initiate the process of identifying jobs at various levels in the government and the voluntary sector at central and state levels. It should also assist in review of recruitment rules where training should be made essential to the appointment in a particular position. The Government needs a large number of social development cadres, to enlarge its scope of activities for the vulnerable sectors, in development and welfare.

9.3.0.0. RECOMMENDATIONS FOR THE NATIONAL SERVICE SCHEME (7.5.0.0.)

It is recommended that:

a. The NSS training units of the educational institutions for social work should be made permanent as the lack of permanency affects the recruitment and retention of staff and it is deleterious to the programme ultimately. Till such time as this is possible, a five-year sanction should be given instead of the present, year-to-year, extension.

b. The work of these Units should be periodically reviewed by a Standing Sub-Committee constituted by the UGC Panel on Social Work Education.

c. The grant to the NSS Units should be increased so as to enable them to undertake consultancy, demonstration and publication functions more effectively. As the programme of NSS is expanding, more institutions for social work education may be selected for establishing such units.

d. All educational institutions for social work should directly undertake the implementation of NSS in their own Universities or should at least directly associate themselves with the programme implementation/demonstration at the University level.

e. The person who is appointed in the position of Reader, should have teaching experience and where institutions have to cover several states, additional NSS Co-ordinators should be provided.

f. The University Grants Commission should constitute a permanent NSS Cell which should consist of the representatives from the institutions for social work education. It should be administered by a full-time Special Officer on Duty in the Professor's scale.

g. The representatives of these institutions should be associated with various subject panels which have been constituted by the University Grants Commission to consider the question of the integration of NSS with the curriculum and to restructure courses so as to make them responsive to the developmental needs and national goals.

h. These institutions should meet at least once a year to review their training, research, consultancy and pilot programmes and to plan future projects in the light of their experience.

9.4.0.0. CONCLUSION

A summary of the findings and the recommendations from the review of social work education has brought out some major problems:

a. The manner of location of institutions which leaves large areas underserved.
b. The lopsided development of programmes at the higher levels of training—there are very few programmes at the lower levels for direct service/front-line workers.
c. The need for change in syllabi to emphasize social change and development.
d. The need to review field work and improve its content and methodology.
e. The problems of affiliation to the university—especially with regard to the recognition of the special needs of professional education for social work.
f. And last, but not the least, is the problem of funds which make it possible to educate and prepare social workers for practice in the context of development and distributive justice.

Although the Committee was appointed by the University Grants Commission, the findings and the recommendations are of importance and relevance to the institutions for social work education, the Department of Social Welfare in the Ministry of Education and Social Welfare, Government and India, the Planning Commission and the Association of Schools of Social Work in India as well as the University Grants Commission. We believe that some of the suggestions will be examined and implemented by the relevant bodies so as to strengthen and to enable the profession of social work to make an effective contribution to national development.

4

INTER-MINISTERIAL GROUP ON FREIGHT EQUALISATION OF COMMODITIES 1975 – REPORT

June 13, 1975[1]

Chairman Shri S.S. Marathe, Chairman, Bureau of Industrial Costs & Prices, Ministy of Industrial Development, New Delhi

Members Shri V.K. Dar; Shri A.F. Couto; Dr. A.K. Sengupta; Shri Bimal Jalan; Shri K.G. Vaidya; Shri S.K. Dhar; Shri V.K. Sthannunathan; Shri M. Satyapal

Convenor Dr. Y.K. Alagh

Appointment

In response to representations received from some State Governments, particularly from the Governments of West Bengal and Tamil Nadu, regarding disadvantages suffered by textile mills in these states on account of high freights paid on raw cotton, the Ministry of Commerce constituted a Committee in 1973 to examine the proposals for introduction for a Freight Equalisation Scheme for raw cotton. In its report, the Committee indicated that after considering the various implications, it found it difficult to recommend any freight equalisation scheme for raw cotton. It, however, suggested that when the Planning Commission undertook review of the policy of equalising the prices of important commodities throughout the country in light of the observations made in the Draft Fifth Plan Document, it might also study the similar approach for raw materials for textile industry as a whole covering items such as cotton, yarn and other inputs.

The Planning Commission, accordingly, set up, in June 1975 an Inter-Ministerial Group on Frieght Equilisation of Commodities vide its notification No. 31/75 EG & P dated 13th June, 1975.

----

1. Planning Commission, Government of India, New Delhi, 1977, (i) +57 p.

Terms of Reference

1. To indicate the existing freight equalisation policies for steel, cement, fertilisers, etc.

2. To suggest the broad principles to be taken into account in the adoption of the freight equalisation policy.

3. In this background, to study the scope and feasibility of adoption of freight equalisation policy for raw cotton to encourage the dispersed and balanced development of the cotton textile industry.

Contents

Introduction; I. Consideration for Freight Equalisation; II. Analysis of Freight Equalisation Schemes; III. Freight Equalisation of Raw Cotton; IV. Transport Subsidy; Summary of Conclusions and Recommendations; Annexures from I to VIII.

Recommendations

It has been suggested in Part I of the report that in planning for industrial investments in the organised sector the following principles might be taken into account:

(i) Prices of commodities and rates for services should reflect real costs at the place of production and at the place of consumption,
(ii) Prices of homogeneous goods should be the same at the given location with regard to origin and should differ from location to location by the marginal cost of transportation,
(iii) The present discounted value of net returns from the investment at the optimal location should be larger than, or equal to the present discounted value of the net returns from the same investment computed for another location.

As regards to consumer goods, it needs to be recognised that the consumers in the backward areas should not be made to pay high prices due to lack of transport facilities. A freight equalisation scheme would however, be beneficial only in the following circumstances:

(i) The essential item under consideration is an important constituent of the consumption basket of an average citizen specially of the weaker sections of population,

(ii) Freight should account for a substantial proportion of the final consumer price in inaccessible areas,

(iii) The item should be subject to perfect market and stable prices so that the benefit of freight equalisation is actually transmitted to the final consumer, and

(iv) The freight equalisation should be administratively feasible.

The last condition is particularly important. If an item is of mass consumption nature, a large part of it will be consumed in villages, and consequently, a substantial part of the freight would be on road transport up to the villages, which can hardly be covered by a centralised freight equalisation scheme. Under such circumstances, freight equalisation can be considered for commodities for which public distribution arrangements exist, or are introduced due to various considerations.

It would be noted from Part II of the report that besides the officially administered freight equalisation funds, freight equalisation is also implemented by a number of industries/manufacturers in their own interest. The incidence of freight on an average, is not necessarily high for the items covered by freight equalisation schemes (i.e., pig-iron, steel, cement and fertilisers) as compared to some other items (e.g., coal and some other items like soda ash, raw rubber, sugarcane); nor the average lead distance for these items is much longer than for the essential items like cotton cloth, tea, soap, soda ash, aluminium and rubber. The analysis also shows that with the exception of, perhaps, cement, freight equalisation scheme appears to be only marginally effective as a device for reducing the comparative disadvantage of unfavourable locations, and that even when the lead is more than 2,000 km the price advantage as a result of freight equalisation varies between 0.3 per cent for machine tools and 2.5 per cent for steel structures. It is only in case of construction costs that the combined effect of freight equalisation on cement and steel reduces the cost by 6 per cent for lead distances of 2,000 km. Moreover, even for cement where a distant consumer gets maximum advantage from freight equalisation,it only 5 per cent of cement consumption that actually paid half of the freight under the freight equalisation scheme, than what would have been paid otherwise. The analysis also points out that there are indications to suggest that, for the freight equalised items, the proportion of production transported by rail has increased since introduction of the schemes and that the average lead distances have also increased during the period. On the other hand, there is some evidence to suggest that the consumption of steel and the production of engineering goods is presently more dispersed than earlier; but a number of factors, besides freight equalisation, would be responsible for such dispersal.

Analysis in Part III of the report suggests that introduction of freight equalisation for raw cotton would not be advisable. The main analytical results which lead to this conclusion are:

(i) The market for cotton textiles is highly imperfect and the marketing margin varies from place to place, from consumer to consumer and from variety to variety.

(ii) Market for raw cotton is high imperfect and is subject to speculations based on expectations of traders, growers and the mills. Thus, prices paid by different mills from the same variety vary widely (up to 50%) and fluctuate from day-to-day (up to 50% in a year).

(iii) Price of cotton is not the only determinant of the cost of cotton per kg of yarn; the other important variants are the cotton mix management efficiency and conditions of machinery. The cost of cotton for the same count of yarn varies up to 30 per cent as between different mills.

(iv) The incidence of freight on movement of cotton is not in excess of 4-5 per cent of the cost of cotton even for long haulages, and less than one per cent in most cases. The freight equalisation can possibly reduce the cost of cotton in far removed areas by 1-2 per cent.

(v) Prices of inputs of textiles other than raw cotton also vary from State to State; there are particularly wide variations in costs of utilities in wage rates.

(vi) Administration of freight equalisation of raw cotton is also likely to pose a number of problems as only 40 per cent of the cotton production is moved by rails. Moreover, as cotton is produced in a large number of specifications, it is subject to criss-cross movements depending on the variety of cloth required to be produced.

Proposals regarding high transportation cost on essential commodities/raw materials used inaccessible/backward areas has been discussed in Part IV of the report. The problem arises when the consumption points are far removed, from the nearest rail head, or are in hilly/inaccessible areas, for which transport is relatively costly or where the transportation costs for certain regions of the country are high due to Government decisions. The solution for such high transportation costs does not lie in introduction of freight equalisation schemes on All-India basis, as only a very small proportion of consumers are involved. Under such circumstances, the high transportation costs need to be subsidised by either (a) Public Exchequer or (b) cess on consumption of the item throughout the country or (c) a surcharge on rail freight or (d) public distribution arrangements. Though the subsidisation of costly transport in limited areas is not one of the terms of reference of the Committee, never the less, the problems has often been raised in the context to freight equalisation. The Committee, has therefore, deemed it fit to bring these problems to the notice of the Government for their consideration.

Three special problems have been referred to in this context. Firstly, it has been suggested that Government might consider extension of transport subsidy to the backward districts, specially those which are not connected by rail. Such a subsidy given on finished goods for resource-based unit, and on raw material for consumer demand based units in backward districts will lead to dispersed growth of industry. Secondly, it has been suggested that the abandoned railway sidings might be reactivised in so far as the backward areas are concerned so as to provide incentives for location and growth of small-scale units in such areas. Thirdly, it has been suggested that the basic necessities of life should be available at almost the same price throughout the country and the extra transportation cost to inaccessible areas might be subsidised. It has also been indicated that in case the oil companies open a depot each in all the tehsils in backward areas, the cost of distribution of kerosene oil could be reduced to the advantage of the consumers in such areas.

The analysis made by the Committee in general tends to suggests that freight equalisation by itself is not in an optimal policy for achieving the objectives of balanced industrial development in a socially optimal manner. In view of this, a rationalised system of location based on comparative advantages of different regions will need to be evolved over a period of time, say, a decade or so. For sponsoring a particular type of industrial activity at specific locations, measures like licensing, and fiscal and other incentives rather than generalised policies on transport subsidy, should be of major consideration. The Committee would not, therefore, recommend an extension of the scheme for freight equalisation to more items of raw materials or other inputs. So far as existing freight equalisation schemes are concerned, in principal, there would be a case for their elimination. However, it has to be recognised that certain investment decisions have already been taken on the basis that such schemes would continue. There is also the problem that sudden abolition of freight equalisation schemes in deficit areas may lead to a substantial increase in prices (not only of quantities despatched from other centres but of the entire quantities consumed in these areas). In view of these considerations. The Committee feels that the existing schemes can be phased out gradually only over a period of time. Wherever total supplies in the country are adequate, and the incidence of freight in the final price is not substantial, freight equalisation schemes could be phased out. In general, the Committee would suggest that the concerned administrative Ministries should periodically review whether existing freight equalisation in relation to individual products needs to be continued.

5

STUDY TEAM ON RURAL EMPLOYMENT – REPORT
July 28, 1975 – November 25, 1975[1]

Chairman Shri R.N. Azad, Jt. Secy. (RD), Department of Rural Development

Members Shri V.B. Easwaran; Shri S.P. Taneja; Shri R. Vengu; A representative of the Planning Commission

Secretary Shri Bhagwan Ram

Alterations

Shri V.B. Easwaran, Joint Secretary (Plan Finance), in the Ministry of Finance, participated in the preliminary meetings of the Study Team before it proceeded on tour to Maharashtra and other States, but could not joint the Team on tours and in subsequent deliberations owing to other pre-occupations. Shri T.C. Dutt, Joint Secretary (F & A), Ministry of Finance (Department of Expenditure), became a member in place of Shri V.B. Easwaran. The Study Team coopted Shri D. Aurora Director (DPAP) and Shri G.C. Mathur, Assistant Commissioner, in the Department of Rural Development, as members.

Appointment

At a meeting of Secretaries held on the 16th July, 1975, to consider some aspects of rural development and employment, it was decided that the Department of Rural Development may, in consultation with the Planning Commission and others concerned, make a quick study

---

1. Ministry of Rural Reconstruction, Government of India, New Delhi, 1979, i + viii + 68 p.

of the problems of rural employment. Accordingly, the Department of Rural Development constituted a Study Team vide Order No. M. 21018/9/75-RME dated the 28th July, 1975.

Terms of Reference

To obtain first-hand information on the implementation of Employment Guarantee Scheme of Maharashtra, its organizational pattern, wage rates, and operational, administrative and financial aspects with a view to suggesting necessary measures for ensuring that at least one adult person in every rural family is provided gainful employment as an unskilled labourer for about 250 days in a year on productive works for the creation of durable community assets within a radius of not more than 4 to 5 km of his village on wages which may be equal to or slightly lower than the average wage for unskilled labour prevailing in that area.

Contents

Foreword; Introduction; Review of Important Rural Employment Schemes; Proposals for Additional Employment Generation; Types of Projects for Rural Works Programme; Selection of Areas; Resource Mobilization; Self Employment and Upgradation of Skills; Implementation and Administrative Machinery; Some General Observations; Annexures from I to V.

Recommendations

1. One of the Team's recommendations is that the employment schemes should be necessarily dovetailed into the on-going plan schemes of the area. Apart from the various state plan schemes, there are a number of centrally sponsored and central sector schemes also operating, e.g., Small and Marginal Farmers Programme, Drought Prone Areas Programme, Tribal and Hill Area Development Programme, Command Areas Development Programmes, etc. Even though these schemes do not have a very large employment content, their objective being primarily geared towards creating infrastructure in the districts for generating continuing employment through development investment, to some extent they do create direct employment opportunities as well. Integration of all employ-

ment programmes within the rural development frame is only possible if well-defined administrative structures are built at the central, state and at the district levels. Quite a few of our schemes have floundered on the rock because of sectoral emphasis and lack of integration and coordination. We, therefore, recommend the following administrative patterns at various levels.

2. **Central level.** The Department of Rural Development in the Ministry of Agriculture and Irrigation could be the nodal department at the centre for schemes which are specially oriented towards rural employment. We recommend this for the reason that it is already in charge of implementation of the SFDA, DPAP and the Hill and Tribal Areas Development Programmes. It also has considerable experience in operating wage employment schemes like the Crash Scheme for Rural Employment and Pilot Intensive Rural Employment Project, etc. The department should, however, have a specific cell created for rural employment not only to oversee the direct implementation of the programme throughout the country but also to ensure dovetailing and coordination with other programmes. The cell should also be in charge of monitoring and evaluation primarily of the concurrent type. The problem of employment, being a continuous one, the cell should also initiate research studies which have a bearing on the impact of employment not only as a direct investment to provide incomes to the rural through productive work but also side effects which may occur on the rural economy through employment programmes and allied areas, e.g., studying shift in employment patterns, etc.

3. **State level.** Since schemes are to be integrated with other rural development programmes, it is essential that there should be one nodal department at the state level as well. We notice that even special programmes like the DPAP, SFDA, TAD, HAD, CAD, etc., are located in different departments in different States of the country and in many States even the DPAP and the SFDA programmes are in two different departments rather than being in one. Therefore, the rural employment schemes have to be located in such a department which will have control over coordination with the other special programmes. We are specifically keen that the employment schemes should not get purely a relief bias. And relief programmes have always been the responsibility of the revenue departments in the states. However, the special employment programmes being a part of the total development process should be located in a development

department mainly concerned with the rural sector. We recommend that efforts should be made to ensure that all special programmes of development in the rural areas which have a major outlay should be located in one ministry department at the state level. Even though the post of the agricultural production commissioner exists in many states, inter-departmental coordination at the state level becomes difficult. It may, therefore, be advisable that this employment programme should be located in the same department which is mainly concerned with schemes relating to rural development and will be implementing special programmes like the DPAP, SFDA, etc.

4. In fact, the Minister for Agriculture and Irrigation, Government of India and addressed the Chief Minister of States and Union Territories suggesting that all schemes which deal with rural development and particularly those which are focused on the rural weak and the rural poor ought to be coordinated and monitored by a nodal department. We learn that the States have welcomed the suggestion and a number of them have already designated a particular department for this purpose. In fact, quite a few States were already having a department of rural development. Many others have now set up such a department. The present Government has re-emphasized the need for integration and in fact it is even proposed to bring all the main programmes of rural development under development under one budget head.

5. Our experience of the rural employment programmes now operating in the States visited is that these schemes, in some areas are not well planned or integrated with the on-going schemes in various sectors. Therefore, we propose a strong Planning Cell located in the nodal department which should be in charge of preparing (a) plans for various programmes within the employment schemes, and (b) linking these programmes and schemes to the overall plan of the district which will also incorporate central sector/centrally sponsored and other special plan schemes. This cell should also be charged with the responsibility of monitoring and concurrent evaluation of the programmes. It is strongly recommended that an economist who is well versed in project formulation and evaluation techniques should be the head of this panning cell and other subject matter specialists, as necessary, may be appointed. Further, it may be mentioned that for the DPAP such cells have been created or have been recommended to the state governments. We, therefore, suggest that such already existing cells employment schemes as well and there should

be no duplication and multiplicity of planning cells for rural programmes.

6. **District level.** The real impact of coordination and integrated planning has to be visible at the district level and, therefore, the administrative structure at this level is of primary importance. As already reiterated our basic premise is that the special employment programme ought to be integrated with other on-going plan schemes and special development schemes sponsored by the central government or by the state government. Therefore, integrated planning is essential which will also require decentralization of decision-making and delegation of authority, administrative as well as financial, from the state level to the district level. It, therefore, becomes important that there should be a single line of authority at the district level which should be in a position to coordinate and integrate the entire development of the rural sector.

7. It was keeping this need in view that special agencies authorities are being established for all the special programmes like the Small and Marginal Farmers Development, Drought Prone Areas Programme, Command Area Development Programmes, Hill and Tribal Areas Development Programmes, etc. These Agencies are well-hinged to the district development set up. We, therefore, recommend that where these agencies/authorities are specific to a district, they should also look after the employment programme to ensure dovetailing with the special programmes. Similar administrative structure should be established in other district which may initially look after the special employment programmes, but over a period of time this should become the district development agency entrusted with the responsibility to plan and integrate all rural development programmes within the district.

8. In states where the zila parishads and taluka or block panchayats have already been delegated powers of planning and implementation and the state governments are satisfied with their performance the existing situation should continue and the employment programmes should also be made the responsibility of these bodies.

9. While suggesting an administrative structure at the district level, onc should also recognize the fact that the heads of departments at the state level also have a crucial part to play. The employment schemes will probably be located with different departmental heads who are at the moment generally operating through their own technical heads at the district level. Relationships of the heads of

departments and their technical heads at the district level with the district administrative organization have got to be clearly identified and also defined. Since the major attempt is at horizontal coordination heads of departments level, we, therefore, recommend that the agency authority established at the district level should have the following functions and responsibilities:

(1) Planning and formulation of projects;
(2) Coordination;
(3) Financing; and
(4) Monitoring and Evaluation.

The district development agency with function defined can effectively plan the programme since all the technical heads of departments will also be members of the agency along with representatives of the people. However, the plan of operation will have to be technically supervised by the heads of department for each sector. Once the plan is approved, it should be the responsibility of the agency to implement it in a phased and also the progress of other schemes which would be inter-dependent on the infrastructure created by the employment programmes.

10. Implementation of the schemes should be with the normal district hierarchies already existing. We do not recommend creation of a separate staff for the agency although in some cases strengthening of the existing machinery may be necessary. The C.D. Block organizations existing in the districts should be fully utilised for this purpose and even strengthened as may be necessary.

11. We suggest that the district collector should be made in charge of the agency as, part from occupying a traditionally prestigious office, he is also in a position to ensure coordination with some of the crucial departments in the district including the revenue department. Even as matters stand today, expect in Maharashtra and Gujarat, the district collector is the head of the agencies set up under special programmes in every state.

12. Considering that the agency is the planning, coordinating and implementing, monitoring and financing body, it should be equipped with staff competent to handle new development concepts and use latest technology. One of our basic observations and use latest technology. One of our basic observations is that even though development has taken enormous strides the district organizations

still continue to be outmoded and traditional in their outlook. We, therefore, suggest that induction of a project economist, a credit planning officer and a person to look after accounts apart from specialists in sectoral programmes would be essential. The employment programmes has necessarily to be tied up, as has been oft-repeated with the on-going development programmes.

Therefore whatever project is taken up has necessarily to fit in not only in the time span but also in the financial frame to create an overall impact on the area. Therefore, it is essential that the staff implementing the programme are trained in modern management techniques apart from training in their specialised fields from time to time to update their knowledge and skills, which will help them in effective and systematic planning both in physical and in financial terms. In fact, training should be a built-in component of the scheme.

13. We also recommend that block should remain the focal point for the sub-district implementation and the community development organizations and panchayati raj institutions should be fully involved in providing a base for people's involvement in the planning and implementation process.

14. Any scheme meant for the rural areas, if it is to succeed, should be such which is acceptable to the people for whom it is designed. The involvement of the rural community, therefore, assumes a very great importance. Wherever, zila parishad exists, it should be obligatory for the agency to present the plan of action to the zila parishad for approval. The members of the zila parishad must have an opportunity to examine each scheme and also to offer their comments on the feasibility and acceptability from the people's point of view. Similarly, the *block samitis* must also be involved in planning at grass-roots level so that implementation becomes easy. Planning here would imply the basic collection of various probable schemes which should be scrutinized from the cost-benefit angle and finally put in the plan of operation of it is economically viable and administratively feasible. The very fact that the samitis would be involved in the first process itself will create a much better impression from the acceptability point of view.

15. In district where either the zila parishads or the block samitis do not exist, it is suggested that the district level or block level committees of select people be formed who should have the opportunity to deliberate upon various schemes and projects and also to give their comments on the viability and usefulness of such schemes.

It may also be ensured that weaker sections in fairly large numbers are represented in block or district committees so as to have an effective voice.

16. Wherever voluntary organizations of known repute exist in the district, they should be actively involved in implementation of the programmes and as far as possible their level and block level committees.

Some General Observations

During the course of the study some other matters came to the notice of the Team which deserve mention:

(i) The problem of rural unemployment does not seem to be in the specific charge of anybody in the State Governments. the State Directorates of Employment are usually concerned only with urban employment or employment matters in the organised sector, mainly through the operation of Employment Exchanges. It is imperative that one specific department is made responsible in the States and UTs in this important area.

(ii) For any meaningful manpower planning it is essential to work out employment potential and employment generation capacity of important development programmes both in the Central and State sectors. For this purpose employment norms must be available. The Study Team has found that either the employment norms are not available in respect of many programmes or the norms available are such that are of little use, being either out of date or uncomparable. Organisations like the Institute of Applied Manpower Research at the Central and similar institutions elsewhere in the country should address themselves on priority basis on this task. Such studies have become all the more necessary with the increasing emphasis on taking up integrated rural development which will necessarily mean a 'mix' of various programmes. Once the norms and potential are available, it will be easier to determine the gaps in employment requirements. In the same context, the Team would like to emphasise that there should be an in-built requirement of any development scheme to clearly spell out the employment potential it is going to generate. This objective has been there in our Planning but by and large it has not been possible to achieve it because of non-availability of sound employment norms.

(iii) In respect of the area like that of Kerala where the problem of unemployment and underemployment is that of educated or semi-educated youth, traditional special works programmes might not be the answer as these youngmen would not be willing to offer themselves for employment on such works. During the Team's visit to Kerala the discussions with the State Chief Minister, other Ministers and senior officers dispelled this impression. It was further confirmed by field visits of the Team where it was seen that a large number of young persons including girls who where matriculates were working as unskilled labourers on road works and other programmes. Though the long range solution of providing gainful and suitable employment to educate youth lies in organising small industries, village crafts, agro-based industries and agro-services on a massive scale till such time it is possible to make a dent by this course of action, the only solution seems to be special works programmes, which of course, as the Team has clearly emphasized in its Interim Report have to be a part of the development strategy for integrated development of the area.

(iv) From the experience gained by the team during discussions as well as field visit to the States, it is felt that the implementation of such programmes as (i) abolition of bonded labour and its rehabilitation (ii) Liquidation of rural indebtedness and arrangements for immediate alternate means of subsistence, and (iii) meaningful enforcement of Minimum Agricultural wages laws can be made effective by viewing them as a part of strategy for providing additional employment opportunities at least to the weaker sections, i.e., bottom 30 per cent of the rural population.

6

STUDY GROUPS ON THE WORKING OF THE LEAD BANK SCHEME IN GUJARAT AND MAHARASHTRA, 1975 – REPORT[1]

Convenor Dr. (Kum.) Meenakshi Tyagarajan

Members *Gujarat*

Shri M.G. Shah, Shri M. Sivagnanam, Shri D.J. Kanvinde, Shri B.M. Shukla, Shri J.J. Choksy, Shri S.S. Hasurkar (replaced Shri L.D. Kataria), Shri P.K. Venkateswaran.

Maharashtra

Shri V.Subramaniam, Shri B.K. Chougule, Shri L. D'Mello, Shri S.B. Kaji (replaced Shri R.D. Rege), Shri A.T. Akolkar, Shri J.S. Hasurkar (replaced Shri L.D. Kataria), Shri P.K. Venkateswaran.

Appointment

At the meeting of Western Regional Consultative Committee presided over by the Union Finance Minister, Shri C. Subramaniam, it was decided that the working of the Lead Bank Scheme in the States of Gujarat and Maharashtra be studied in its various aspect. In persuasion of this decision, the Reserve Bank of India constituted two Study Groups on August 2, 1975.

Terms of Reference

(i) The constitution and working of the District Level Consultative Committees;

(ii) The nature and extent of liaison between financial institu-

---

1. Reserve Bank of India, Bombay, 1975, 33 p.

tions and relationship established with the State Government at various levels; and

(iii) The extent of involvement of banks in the formulation and implementation of area development programmes.

Contents

Introductory; Appointment; Terms of Reference; Genesis of the Scheme; Objects of the Scheme; Allocation of Districts; Branch Expansion Strategy; District Credit Plans in the Two States; District Consultative Committee; Composition of the DCC; Attendance and Participation in DCC Meetings — Government Representatives; Participation by Banks; Representation of RBI; DCC Deliberations — Banks' Involvements in Infrastructural Development Demand for Statistics; Second Phase of the Scheme; Credit Plans; Individual Schemes; Basic Requirements of the Schemes; Project Profiles; Bankable Schemes and District Plans; Allocation of Shares; Forum of Bankers; Possible Difficulties in Implementation; DCC'S Function in Overall Monitoring; DCC — Necessary Features; Identification of Burrows; Motivation; Terms and Conditions of Credit; Defaults in Operation — Role of Lead Bank; Agricultural Lending; Joint Lead Responsibility; Training; Future Branch Expansion; State Level Consultative Committees; Supervision of the Scheme by the Reserve Bank; Conclusion; Acknowledgements; Statements 1&2, Appendix.

Recommendations

Objects of the Scheme

As a first step in the implementation of the "area approach", the various districts in the country were apportioned between all the public sector and a few of the private sector banks. In the districts allotted to it, each bank was designated as the "lead bank" for initiating the spread of banking and accelerating banking development. Even at the time of the allocation, the tasks of the lead bank were broadly outlined. In the circular letter dated December 23, 1969 informing the concerned banks of the distribution of districts under the scheme, the Reserve Bank said "The lead bank will be expected to assume the major role in the development of banking and credit in the allocated districts. At the same time, there is clearly no intention that the lead bank should have a monopoly of banking business in a district. The bank assigned the lead role is thus expected to act as the consortium leader and after identifying through survey, areas requiring branch expansion and areas suffering from credit gasp, it should invoke the co-operation of other banks operating in the district for opening branches as well as for meeting credit needs."

Allocation of Districts

The allocation of districts between the banks was made on the basis of certain criteria, the most important of which were the size of the bank; its resources; geographic contiguity that would yield "clusters' of lead districts and the desirability for each State to have more than one lead bank operating in its territory and for each bank to have lead responsibility in more than one State. Although to the extent possible the role of leadership was assigned to the banks with a relatively good foothold in the district, in several cases the lead bank's own branch net-work was not adequate for its functions (Statement 1). The primary task, therefore, was that of ensuring a swift and wide branch expansion of reaching into rural areas hitherto unexposed, or relatively little exposed to commercial banking.

Branch Expansion Strategy

This task represented the first phase of the operation of the lead bank scheme. Action taken towards its fulfilment had to be speedy, without duplication of effort. The lead banks were asked first to gain familiarity with the salient features of the economy of the districts allotted to them through quick, "impressionistic" surveys in the course of which they were to identify growth centres" holding potential for banking activity. The broad methodology of the surveys and centre identification was explained to the bank officials in charge of the survey work at a meeting convinced by the Reserve Bank in April 1970.

As the initial survey work proceeded, it was clear that there was inadequate appreciation of the objectives of the scheme. For instance, some banks approached the task of identification of growth centres from their own viewpoint and not from that of the entire banking system. Some guidance to the banks was hence considered necessary. Accordingly, late in 1970, a small team consisting of two officers of the Reserve Bank and one from the Department of Banking, Ministry of Finance, had discussions with the Chief Executives and senior officials of each of the banks. The Report of the team laid special stress on the task of centre identification and branch expansion strategy which, at that time, was the objective of most immediate concern. But the Report also discussed the future tasks and requirements of the scheme. For instance, the need for the lead banks to invoke the co-operation of other banks was stressed; it was pointed out "In the minds of bankers, the lead bank scheme had not taken a distinct, operational shape. The fact that the scheme would require the concerted effort of all banks and other institutions in the district, under the leadership of one bank, is not fully appreciated." The team's Report, which was in the nature of guidelines for the operation of the scheme, was circulated among all banks*.

The allotment of centres identified by the lead banks was done through mutual collaboration. To set the pattern, the Reserve Bank initially held meetings at which the identified unbanked centres were distributed between the banks, the accepted principle being that the lead bank would not have any special preference in the choice of centres merely by virtues of its role. This method was subsequently followed by the lead banks who convened similar meetings in respect of the identified centres in their own lead district. Besides establishing the practice of mutual consultation and co-operation, these meetings also considerably speeded up and process of branch expansion. While there have been complaints of some banks failing to fulfil the commitments for opening branches, this has usually arisen out of genuine difficulties such as the lack of some basic facility in the centre, manpower constraint, etc. By and large, therefore, it can be said that the first phase of the lead bank programme was a success both in terms of the number of new offices opened and in the emergence of a pattern of collaborative effort, hitherto unknown to commercial banking. Between end-June 1969 and end-December 1972, a total of 6437 offices were opened in the whole country of which 3831 were in rural areas. By mid-1975, the total of new offices, i.e., offices opened after nationalisation was 8654, which was more than the total number of offices functioning at the time of nationalisation. The branch expansion in Gujarat and Maharashtra is shown in the table on the next page. Both the States have benefited substantially from

---

* For further details of the Report, see "The Lead Bank Scheme: Progress and Perspective", *Reserve Bank of India Bulletin,* November 1970.

the branch expansion since nationalisation. Of the total bank offices opened between July 1969 and June 1975, those opened in Gujarat formed 7.6 per cent and those in Maharashtra 10.2 per cent. In consequence of this expansion, population covered per bank office improved from 34,000 in Gujarat and 44,000 in Maharashtra to 17,000 and 23,000 respectively.

Number of Offices of Scheduled Commercial Banks

	July 19, 1969		June, 1975		Absolute Increase	
	Gujarat	Maharashtra	Gujarat	Maharashtra	Gujarat	Maharashtra
Rural	234	156	607	508	373	352
Semi-urban	290	338	479	540	189	202
Urban	118	199	254	428	136	229
Metropolitan	116	430	212	708	96	278
Total	758	1123	1552	2184	794	1061

District Credit Plans in the Two States

With rapid branch expansion accomplished, the basic infrastructure for banking development was established and the stage was set for the second phase of the lead bank scheme, viz., the formulation and implementation of area development programmes. However, it has to be borne in mind that this phase of the programme, which commenced hardly two years age, presents greater difficulties in implementation, involving as it does collaborative efforts not only between banks but with various levels and types of government agencies as well. The district credit plans completed and in respect of the implementation of which some action has been initiated are Gorakhpur — Uttar Pradesh (State Bank of India); Rai Bareli — Uttar Pradesh (Bank of Baroda); Seoni — Madhya Pradesh (Central Bank of India); Ujjain — Madhya Pradesh (Bank of India). In this regard, progress has been slow both in Gujarat and Maharashtra. In Maharashtra, a district credit plan has been formulated for one district only, viz. Sholapur (Bank of India) and it has recently been formally launched. State Bank of India, which took over only last year, the lead responsibility for the four Marathwada districts originally allotted to its subsidiary, State Bank of Hyderabad, is currently engaged in the formulation of credit plans for each of these district. In Gujarat, State Bank of Saurashtra is engaged in a similar exercise for its lead districts. Apart from this, some "in depth" studies have also been completed. Besides, there has been some progress in banks' involvement in the economies of the two States. Statement 2 shows the relative increase in the shares in banking business of different categories of offices. The increasing activity of rural offices, especially in Gujarat, and of rural and semi-urban offices in Maharashtra is illustrated. Advances to the priority sectors have increased and there have been innovative efforts at reaching sections of the community hitherto totally precluded from commercial banks' operations. However, these have been through the individual actions of the banks, and there are no sizeable schemes of collective action spearheaded by the led banks in either State. Meanwhile, the feeling that banks have "failed" in their responsibility appears to be gaining ground, especially among the State Governments and local authorities and the tendency appears to be to blame the lead bank for this failure. Altogether, there is inadequate appreciation of the scope and content of the lead bank scheme, its limitations and the preconditions for its successful operation. This would apply even to banking circles, especially at the branch level.

District Consultative Committee

At present, the sole evidence of the operative existence of the lead bank scheme is the institution of the District Consultative Committee (DCC), which has been constituted in all the districts of the two States and which is reported to meet with fair regularity in most case. This, in itself marks an achievement since the Committee has provided a forum for bankers and administrators to meet and discuss subjects of common interest and understand each other's viewpoints. Frequently, the exchange of information on lending to specific sectors has prevented duplication of effort. Such discussions also sometimes bear tangible results, as they may expedite administrative decisions, pending which lending to a particular sector or even a particular client cannot proceed. However, in the absence of any concrete development programme for collective action, discussions at the DCC meetings have tended to be of a somewhat general nature, amounting frequently only to an assessment of the progress in lending to the priority sectors. Also, follow-up action is often not taken on points raised at the meetings requiring further discussions with officials and others. As one of the banks having lead responsibility in Gujarat has out it "A feeling is growing that the Consultative Committee meetings are mere rituals, not to be taken seriously. It is this feeling that has created some dissatisfaction as well as disillusionment with Government agencies and the public at large."

There are, no doubt, differences in the experiences of various lead banks in respect of the DCC. These differences apply not only to the deliberations in the meetings but also to the composition of the Committee, the extent of participation by the members and their attitudes and the kind of issues that they raise, relevant to the lead role. A brief examination of these points of difference, based on the special reports prepared by the lead banks in the two States, the reports submitted by the officers of the Reserve Bank's regional offices of the Department of Banking Operations and Development who have attended several DCC meetings, as well as our own field traps and discussions with bankers and officials, would be useful for highlighting the weakness in the present status of the scheme and for pointing out future lines of action.

Composition of the DCC

From the Government side, membership of the DCC generally consists of district level officials, headed by the Collector, officials of the Zilla Parishad and other officials connected with development activity such as the District Development Officer, the Industries and Agricultural Officers and representatives of Regional Development Corporations, where such exist. From the side of the financial institutions, representatives of all the commercial banks operating in the district, co-operative lending institutions and term-lending corporations are included. In a few cases, prominent non-officials, interested in developmental activity or social work are also members of the Committee. The attempt to have a wide and comprehensive representation by including those with only tangential connection or interest in banking development leads to a Committee of unwieldy size. In some cases, the regular members of the Committee included such officials as the representatives of the National Seeds Corporation and Regulated Markets and among non-officials, even journalists. In one district, the DCC consisted of as many as 63 members, while there were "sub-committees" with 35 or more members. While all the members may not attend all the meetings, it is obvious that a large, non-homogeneous composition would not serve much of a purpose beyond perhaps gaining a certain degree of publicity.

Attendance and Participation in DCC Meetings — Government Representatives

The attendance at the DCC meetings so far held in both States has not been uniformly good. This judgement applies not only to the number attending but is based also on the status or importance of those who failed to attend. There have been significant defaults from the side of both the Government and the banks. The absence of the District Collector and other important district officials has been reported several cases, although there appears to be some improvement in this regard in the more recent meetings. Occasionally the Collector sends as his nominee to the meeting a junior official which lowers the quality of the dialogue between banks and the Government. The example set by the Collector is frequently followed by the other officials. However, the formal presence of the officials does not necessarily mean the establishment of a base for purposeful deliberation as they sometimes display apathy or lack of interest in what the banks have to say. One of the banks has said of its experience in one of its lead districts "They (Government officials) are not non-co-operative but they are not active also. They choose their words in such a way that they do not become committal." These features are clearly indicative of the fact that no effective report has been established between the lead bank and the Government at the district level, which is an important prerequisite for the operation of the scheme. The point here is not to apportion blame between the Government and the lead bank but only to underline the fact that unless effective coordination between the Government, as represented by the Collector and other district officials and banks, as represented by the lead bank is established, it would be difficult to formulate workable credit programmes and virtually impossible to implement them.

Participation by Banks

Apathy and indifference in the DCC meetings are not confined to

Government officials alone but are applicable to banks also. The experience not only in Gujarat and Maharashtra but in other States as well shows certain common features in the absenteeism by banks. In the districts where the lead bank is a relatively small bank, or a bank whose roots in the area are more recently established, the larger banks and the banks with older contacts with the area tend to ignore the efforts of the lead bank, or strike a somewhat patronising, observer attitude. Similarly, banks which have a limited representation in the area, with only one or two offices, also tend to avoid the meetings, probably because of a feeling of insignificance. Even among the other banks, the tendency seems to be to avoid any commitment or involvement with the lead bank's activities and to press ahead with their own programmes in the area, even where it might clash with the lead bank's objectives; Several instances have been reported of the "adoption" of villages by some banks in other banks' lead districts or areas of operation, without seeking their prior approval or giving éven a formal indication of intention. While the "lead bank ideology" may be understood at the head offices of banks, the attitude that each bank's responsibility under the scheme is limited to its own lead districts and that in other districts what counts is its own individual effort appears to be wide, prevalent among bank managers and staff at the branch level. Even in the lead districts the idea of "leadership" appears sometimes to be only that of getting ahead of other banks, taking on the best portion of the better schemes possible in the district. Efforts have to be made to correct such tendencies, if the scheme is to make any progress.

Representation of RBI

The regional office of the Reserve Bank's Department of Banking Operations and Development tries to send its representative to all DCC meetings but it has not so far been possible to cover all meetings in all the districts. Some banks feel that the Reserve Bank's representation is necessary at all meetings. For various reasons, the same officers is not able to attend all the meetings of a particular DCC and there are changes in the nomination. It has also been felt by some that continuity should be maintained to the extent possible, so that the understanding of local problems gained by the officer is put to use.

DCC Deliberations — Banks' Involvement in Infrastructural Development

The deliberations in some DCC meetings show certain trends that are not only contradictory to the lead bank scheme but could also undermine the basis of banking operations in the area. A significant example is the failure on the part of Government Officials to appreciate the importance of viability in the schemes that banks can attempt to finance. In some cases, where the District Collectors and other officials evince keen interest in the operations of banks, suggestions are brought up for banks to undertake basically "unbankable" projects. These include the establishment of infrastructural facilities such as roads, bridges, etc., and the provision of support for relief operations in natural calamities such as drought, flood, or famine.

The extension of Government guarantee as a cover or such landings does not, in itself, make them viable. Even where the State officials are appreciative of the difficulties of banks in undertaking such schemes, officials at the district level apply pressure on banks which bankers at the district level find difficult to resist. The functional limitations of banks in this regard have to be recognised.

Demand for Statistics

Other discussions relating to bank lending usually centre centre around priority sector advances and the district officials use the occasion to ascertain the progress in this regard. Particular interest is evinced in Government-sponsored schemes such as the half a million jobs programmes, educated unemployed schemes, etc., and banks are asked to report on the cases pending with them. An offshoot of this interest is the demand for up to date district-wise (and some times even taluk-wise statistics on the progress of banking — on deposits, total allowances and advances to each of the priority sectors. Under the Basic Statistics Returns Scheme, in operation since 1972, the Reserve Bank provides detailed district-wise data on deposits and credit, as of end-June and end-December each year. This is the first time that such comprehensive data are available on the basis of districts and States. These data are compiled from returns received from individual bank branches which now number over 19,000. There is hence an unavoidable time lag of about a year in the compilation and publication of these statistics. However, from the time series that the half yearly BSR publication provide, an idea can be gained of the general trend and progress of banking in each district. In addition, the Department of Banking Operations and Development of the Reserve Bank is arranging to provide district-wise data on priority sector lending at quarterly intervals in all States. It is the genuine fear of the Reserve Bank that excessive and repetitive pressures on bank branches for the supply of data might result in the breakdown of the entire reporting system, which has yet to attain full stability. It is hence in the interest of the system as a whole to keep the demands for district level data at a minimum.

Second Phase of the Scheme

The preceding paragraphs have sought to assess the deficiencies in the operation of the lead bank scheme hitherto. With the preparation of "district credit plans" by some banks, the scheme is entering the crucial second stage. As a leader of the consortium of financial institutions, the lead bank is expected to contribute to the economic development of the districts by preparing bankable schemes to cover viable economic activities, estimating the credit demand arising under these schemes and invoking the co-operation of other financial institutions in meeting this. From an assessment of the trends so far and the insights gained through the field visits and discussions in the two states, it is possible to make some recommendations on the general line of action to be followed hereafter. In a country of the size and diversities of India, it may not be possible to recommend an uniform approach to district credit planning, as the needs of development will very from region to region and much will have to be left to the innovative capacities of each bank. Hence, what can be indicated are only some broad suggestions, which would underline the spirit of the scheme, rather than precise 'directions' to be observed.

Credit Plans

The first suggestion relates to the plans for development financing. Collective action by banks and other financial institutions in the implementation of bankable schemes that would have a definite impact in the area is indeed the crux of the lead bank scheme. The action in the formulation of the schemes now proposed by some lead banks vary in methodology and coverage. The State Bank group is committed to the introduction of a "credit plan" in each of its lead districts, all of which are in the least developed areas of the country. From the first of such credit plans to be completed, that for Gorakhpur district in Uttar Pradesh, it is seen that the plans will be comprehensive and integrated, in that they will cover all the major sectors of the economy (agriculture, allied activities, industries and service sector). The strategy of development ingrained in the plan is based on "depth studies" for representative community development blocks, from which bankable schemes are drawn up to be implemented over a period of five years. This elaborate and comprehensive approach, entailing as it does considerable effort and outlay, may not necessarily be suitable to the stage of development of all districts in the country. Further, individual lead banks will have to take into account their own resources in manpower and funds. The district credit planning methodology will thus have to be tailored to meet the developmental needs of the districts concerned, as also the resources of the individual lead bank. The emphasis should be not so much on methodological excellence in the academic sense, but on expeditious preparation of technologically feasible and economically viable schemes and their collective implementation by all financial institutions.

Even in those banks which have the resources and ability to undertake comprehensive planning and indeed have already set about the task, the credit plan should cover only activities for which bankable schemes can be evolved and not areas which are clearly outside the purview of direct credit extension by banks. For example, one of the credit plans prepared recently for a district elsewhere than in Gujarat and Maharashtra entails an annual outlay of Rs. 110-140 crores, and covers activities such as drainage schemes and drinking water supply programmes, etc. The schemes which comprise the plan will have to be drawn with a sense of realism, taking account of the overall resources of the financial system. It would be helpful if, besides credit demand likely to arise under the bankable schemes, resource mobilisation in the district by all financial institutions is also estimated. It is understood from some banks that the Government officials sometimes express dissatisfaction when the plans outlined by the banks involve a relatively small order of outlay and that more "ambitious" plans are called for. Since what is desired by all is perceptible progress in the pace of development in the short-run, it is essential that targets are pitched at a realistic, if modest, level. Estimates of the financial and organisational resources required for implementing the schemes included in the credit plan should be considered as an integral part of the exercise which also would contribute to a sense of realism and the drawing up of a practical and action-oriented programme. The success of the schemes begun on a modest scale can pave the way for an acceleration of the pace in the future. The banks would gain confidence and enthusiasm from the completion of the schemes while the scope for other development schemes could be opened up through demands from affiliated or linked sectors and through the "demonstration effect" of the success of the completed schemes.

Individual Schemes

It is, therefore, suggested that to start with, banks should set about the task of formulating individual, viable and bankable schemes which can be immediately implemented and completed over a reasonable time span of 3 to 5 years. It is further suggested that these schemes should be in the broad area of the priority sectors — that is in agriculture, small scale industry and small business and self-employed. To the extent possible, the schemes drawn up by the lead bank could be fitted into the major schemes in operation in some districts such as the MFAL, SFDA, DPAP, etc. Schemes need not be drawn up in respect of large and medium industry and trade, whether in the public or private sector, though their incremental credit needs during the period of the credit plan may be broadly estimated with a view to matching the total credit demand arising in the district, with the resources to be generated.

Basic Requirements of the Schemes

In the formulation of the bankable schemes, certain fundamental ground rules may be observed. Firstly, it is necessary that the schemes should be based, as far as possible, on the existing infrastructural facilities available throughout the district. Only if this is assured would the scheme be ready for immediate implementation. In some cases, extra facilities of a secondary nature may be found necessary. These should be pinpointed and taken up with the authorities. But at the same time, care should be taken not to launch programmes dependent on the establishment of facilities in the distant future. To the extent possible, the schemes should be dovetailed with plan programmes being implemented in the district. The priorities indicated in the district plans should be taken into account in framing the schemes. If adequate liaison is established with the district officials, there may even be scope for altering the priorities in order to provide for some investments which might assist the formulation of certain bankable schemes. Further, the "linkages" of various economic activities should also be given due weightage. For example, if agricultural lending for the cultivation of a certain crop is envisaged, care should be taken to provide for the financing of appropriate marketing or processing facilities; again, in the case of schemes of dairy development, it has to be ensured that capacity exists to store/market/process the increased supply of milk that would follow from the extension of credit. Other relevant considerations are the availability of veterinary services, fodder supply, etc.

Project Profiles

The bankable schemes should include details that would assist in the process of actual extension of credit to individual borrowers. In regard to activities covered by the schemes (for example, tailoring, carpentry, poultry, etc.) representative project profiles may be prepared which should give basic economic and technical data. These could serve as a standard check list which would help prospective borrowers in the submission of application forms as well as banks for expeditious appraisal and sanction of the proposals.

Bankable Schemes and District Plans

There are instances where the lead banks have not proceeded with the formulation of schemes because the planning process is slow and the district authorities are unable to indicate any priorities in areas requiring development. The lead banks need not necessarily await the progress of planning for the formulation of bankable schemes. Important data that would be of assistance to banks are sometimes available at the State level. For instance, in Gujarat, the infrastructure corporations such as the Gujarat Industrial Development Corporation, the Gujarat Industrial Investment Corporation and the Gujarat Small Scale Industries Corporation have prepared district profiles which include lists of projects that may be implemented with financial and technical details. Such data should be made use of to the fullest extent possible. This, however, would not obviate the need for separate action on the part of the lead banks. It is suggested that the lead banks make some arrangement at the district or regional level for project formulation and follow-up. To expedite matters, the district authorities could assist the lead banks in identifying areas offering scope for specific schemes. However, it is obvious that the lead banks cannot assume the responsibility for drawing up a district development plan and even a full-fledged "credit plan" is not a substitute for this. Where the process of planning at the district level has yielded a perceptible and progressive pattern, it is of course necessary to ensure that the bankable schemes proposed fit into and supplement the plan programmes, to the extent possible. At present, such "dovetailing" of banks' operations with the district plan is often interpreted in terms of the provision of bank credit to individuals under such programmes as the half-a-million jobs for educated unemployed. Difficulties sometimes arise because the district authorities have in view only one or two specific avenues of employment, e.g., the plying of auto rickshaws or the ownership of milch cattle and offer to banks an excessive number of applications for their financing. Obviously, there is a limit to the spread of any single activity in any area and hence to the extent to which bank finance can be provided for the purpose.

No particular methodology is recommended for the formulation of the schemes and each bank may follow the method best suited to its own resources and the conditions in the district concerned. It is possible that some banks, perhaps out of a sense of inadequacy, might consider handing over the task of formulating a "credit plan" to an outside agency. This was done by a few banks for the preparation of district survey reports and even at that time, it was stressed that such work should be done by the banks themselves, so that a real "feel" of their area of operations could be gained. Since then, all banks have acquired more experience and expertise in survey work and programme formulation. The reliance on outside agencies should hence be avoided. What is important is the adoption of a practical, as against a purely academic, approach. "In depth" studies should not be an end in themselves and it should be ensured that bankable schemes emerge from such studies. On the other hand, the idea of a scheme could lead to a depth study, which should really be a detailed examination of the practical aspects of the scheme and an evaluation of its feasibility.

While the development schemes would have to be formulated in consultation with the district authorities, banks should not await their suggestions or programmes. The establishment of liaison and coordination with district authorities would hence commence at the stage of preparation of the schemes and would increase and strengthen as the programmes gather momentum. While the other banks in the district may have direct contact with the district level authorities only at the DCC meetings, for the lead bank such contacts would have to be far more frequent and at various levels.

Although the total resources available to banks in a district would be an important consideration determining the overall size of the schemes, this need not be an overriding constraint, especially in backward districts, where the existing deposit levels might be low. However, too much dependence on the inflow of funds from the head offices of banks might cause difficulties of an operational nature. External resources provided by such institutions like ARDC and IDBI should be exploited to the fullest extent. The initiative in arranging for these funds for joint projects would have to be assumed by the lead bank.

Allocation of Shares

The first task in implementation of the programme is that of allocation of shares between the commercial and co-operative banks. The schemes drawn up should cover as wide a geographic area as possible in the district, depending on local conditions. Hence in the allocation of the shares, the spread of the branch net-work of individual banks would be an important deciding factor. As far as possible, no bank should be "excused" from participation merely because of its limited representation in the district. The existing level of lending in the district of each bank would also have to be taken into account in allotting shares but where this level is high, the scope for recycling existing funds and altering the pattern of lending in order to accommodate the proposed schemes should be examined.

In some cases a distribution of the credit requirements of the schemes between the participating agencies is spelt out in the credit plan with specific "shares" indicated for each bank/institution. It is certainly not envisaged in the lead bank scheme that the lead bank should take upon itself the task of allocating the credit outlay envisaged in the schemes among the participating agencies. What is important is that the co-operation of other institutions should be invoked and the responsibility for implementation of the plan shared through a process of mutual consultations and consensus.

Forum of Bankers

The allocation of shares for all the participating institutions should be finalised in consultation with each institution. Prior consultation should provide time for the approval of the commitment from the appropriate authorities. It is not necessary that the final, or formal, allocation should be done at the DCC. Actually, some of the banks which have recently finalised credit plans have arrived at a consensus for allocation of shares at special meetings of bankers. In fact, a Committee of bankers as distinct from the DCC, may, if necessary, be formed at the district level for discussion of the technical banking problems arising in the progress of lending which subject may not be of interest to the DCC. Such a forum might also be instrumental in building up greater rapport between bankers and help in sharing information in regard to individual banks' experience in identification of borrowers, recovery, etc.

Possible Difficulties in Implementation

The experience of banks in the second phase of the lead bank scheme has so far extended mainly to the formulation of credit plans and that too in respect of very few districts. Not many banks have yet gone through the process of even partial implementation of a full-fledged programme, involving the participation of other banks and requiring the co-operation of Governmental and other agencies at various levels. As the plans "take off" from the paper to the action stage, various difficulties are bound-to arise. These difficulties would of course vary, in kind as well as in degree, from district to district. But it is possible to envisage at least some of these difficulties, identify the "problem areas" and also indicate possible ways of countering them.

The sharing of the outlay between banks could pose a problem in districts where the pattern of branch expansion is lopsided, with only the lead bank having offices in the interior and the other banks being concentrated in and around the district headquarters. In such cases, the lead bank may have to assume major responsibility for the schemes involving the dispensation of credit in the interior which would include virtually all agricultural lending. Commercial banks operating at urban and semi-urban centres and co-operatives should, however, lend suitable support to the lead bank in the field of agricultural lending, to lighten its burden. Implementation of the programmes would be assisted through proper delegation of powers to branch managers.

A major practical difficulty could arise from the fact that while the decision making in respect of the programmes is done at the district headquarters, the actual work will be spread over the entire district. With the allocation made to individual banks and areas demarcated for specific schemes, the responsibility for achieving the targets is not necessarily pin-pointed. The bank agent or manager of a bank's main office at the district headquarters, who would represent his bank at the DCC and as such might be called upon to explain shortfalls in performance, has no authority or supervisory powers over the agents/managers in the interior of the district. So far as the lead bank's own Districts are concerned, provision is generally made for a special officer for overseeing the bank's own performance, apart from attending to the general work of coordination. Most banks have the equivalent of a lead district officer if not for individual lead districts atleast for a cluster of districts. But this sort of administrative arrangement is hardly possible in areas where a bank has no lead authority. For the success of the lead bank scheme, it is necessary that the progress of the schemes taken up by a bank in areas other than its lead districts is suitable monitored by an appropriate authority in the bank.

DCC's Functions in Overall Monitoring

The task of overall monitoring of the progress of the schemes would have to be that of the DCC. Effectively handled, this could provide collective supervision which is important since a feeling of domination from either the lead bank or the Government would have adverse effects on the psychology of the participating banks.

DCC — Necessary Features

The effective operation of the DCC calls for some prerequisites. It should be compact and comprise only of officials directly connected with the programmes in hand. If found necessary, such non-officials as might have something to contribute to the deliberations of the Committee as also non-member officials connected with some minor aspects of the schemes may be invited to the meetings, depending on the requirements of the agenda. Needless to say, the presence and active participation of the District Collector and other official and all bankers is an essential requirement for the DCC to be an useful forum. To instil a feeling of involvement of the outlying branches and the "man on the spot" carrying out the actual lending, it is suggested that the DCC should hold some meetings at tehsil headquarters and that the branch agents in the area should be invited to such meetings and encouraged to discuss their experiences and problems.

The DCC should meet at regular intervals, at lest once a quarter, and review the progress of the individual schemes. To assist such review, data relating to the lending to the specific schemes included in the credit plan may be called for from individual branches by the lead bank and the consolidated data may be circulated to the members. Since the nature and content of the schemes would vary from district to district, no uniform proforma can be prescribed for general use. A suitable proforma may be devised by the concerned lead bank for each district. It is also necessary at the DCC meetings to define issues which require further action and pin-point the responsibility of follow-up to a particular institution, whether the lead bank, any other bank or financial institution or a particular Government official. A full record of the discussions at each meetings should be prepared and sent to the lead/regional offices of each bank so that where necessary, the appropriate authorities may activise recalcitrant branches. Copies of the minutes should also be sent to every bank branch in the district.

Identification of Borrowers

The translation of specific schemes into action requires clients, willing and able to borrow from banks, fulfilling the minimum conditions of credit-worthiness. Banks often expect and Government departments offer to provide lists of borrowers but it sometimes happens that some persons on the list have no inclination to accept the facilities of the bank and abide by its discipline. More often, while the bank is readily accepted, repayments are not made as scheduled.

These difficulties would serve to illustrate the fact that rapport between the banks and the Government and the involvement of officials with banks' financial programmes should not be restricted to the district headquarters but should percolate to the village branch level. It has been reported that in a district in Maharashtra, progress in the extension of credit to a specific project (setting up of gobar gas plants) was made possible through the combined efforts of the Tahsildar, the Block Development Officer and the concerned lead bank, working together for a few days to screen the applications collected by the Tahsil officials and select borrowers. Similar arrangements for the bank or banks allotted areas for individual schemes would help in speeding up implementation.

It is also desirable that lead banks should be automatically admitted as regular members in SFDA/MFAL Committees. The present constitution of such committees does not appear to provide for such membership, except where a bank is specially invited by the Committee to become a regular member.

Motivation

The lack of interest in banks' lending schemes among the potential borrowers is an important factor limiting the area's absorption capacity. This situation would be especially pronounced in backward and predominantly tribal districts. The problem of motivation is not one that banks can handle by themselves and the usual media of publicity and advertisement may not help much. Perhaps only through some effective demonstration of the service potential of banks can a break-through be achieved. The assistance of private social service organisations and non-official workers should be sought in such areas.

Terms and Conditions of Credit

The financing of the specific schemes drawn up by the lead bank would mean the extension of virtually the same type of credit for the same purpose in different areas by different banks. In the extension of any credit, there are divergences in terms and conditions required by banks, as in the rate of interest, margins, terms of repayment, security, etc. While it would not be desirable or feasible to require the stipulation of identical terms and conditions by all banks, some degree of conformity in the provision of credit under the same scheme in the same area would be expected. Such uniformity or near uniformity is particularly necessary in the scales of finance for crop loans in each area.

Defaults in Operation — Role of Lead Bank

However realistic the assessment of the order of outlay in respect of individual schemes on a total plan, and however fair the allotment of shares between institutions, escalations and shortfalls in fulfilment are likely to occur. It should be an accepted principle that any increase in outlay arising out of a reasonable extent of escalation should be met by the participating institutions. The failure on the part of an individual institution to meet its share may arise either out of wilful neglect, or indifference or unavoidable reasons. In the case of certain institutions such as Land Development Banks, the involvement has an in-built element of chance as they are unable to extend any commitment beyond one year, their resources for future deployment being dependent on the repayments during the year. Delay in administrative sanctions or clearance may result in lags in the programme and the lead bank, with its close liaison with the authorities, should offer its assistance to other banks in overcoming these. Sometimes the difficulties may be deeper and cannot be resolved in the short run. In such cases, as also in instances of unwillingness or inability of some institutions to meet their share despite persuasion or apparels to higher authorities, the whole programme might be jeopardised. In these circumstances, to expect the lead bank to salvage the situation by taking on the share of the defaulters would be neither fair to the lead bank nor in conformity with the spirit of the scheme. Where the lead bank is willing and able to take on the shares of other participants, the tendency to default might spread, resulting in an increase in the burden of the lead bank. This extra demand on the resources of the lead bank would mean that its ability to fulfil its role in other districts where it has no lead responsibility would be affected, thus distorting the overall operation of the scheme. Any tendency on the part of the district authorities to pressurise the lead bank into fulfilling all the schemes at all costs and to expect the lead bank to function as a sort of "lender of the last resort" should be avoided. It is necessary to institute a reviewing authority for the lead bank scheme, to which instances of non-compliance of accepted commitments can be reported by the lead bank.

Agricultural Lending

In the formulation of schemes that would make an impact on the district economy, agriculture has a significant role. In advancing credit to agriculture in areas where the co-operative movement is well developed, which applies to both Gujarat and Maharashtra, hostility and unhealthy competition develop between co-operative and commercial banks. In Maharashtra, the position has been clarified. The recent report of the study team on co-operative agricultural credit institutions in Maharashtra has indicated areas where commercial banks would be free to lend directly to farmers and where lending may be done mainly through primary co-operative societies. The scope for similar action in Gujarat may be examined. It appears possible that apart from financing co-operative societies, commercial banks could share with co-operatives the task of providing credit to this sector through appropriate participation arrangements.

Joint Lead Responsibility

In some districts in the country, lead responsibility has been jointly assigned to two banks. This has been changed in some cases, on the representation of both the banks, but in other cases, joint leadership continues. Aurangabad district in Maharashtra is such an instance where Bank of Maharashtra and Central Bank of India have been designated as joint lead banks. In practice, the "Joint" leadership in not found to be working well. Bank of Maharashtra has a wider spread of branches in the district than Central Bank of India (25 branches as against 5). It is suggested that full leadership be transferred to Bank of Maharashtra. A review of the position in other districts where a similar arrangement prevails may be made and the responsibility given to the bank with the stronger branch base in the district.

Training

The effective operation of the lead bank schemes also requires appropriate training and orientation programmes for the staff of both the banks and the Governments of the district and higher levels. The training programmes for the banks may be provided in the individual banks' colleges and in the Reserve Bank's Bankers' Training College.

The orientation programmes for State Government officials would, however, have to be specially designed and introduced by the concerned lead banks not necessarily in each district but perhaps for the State as a whole. Joint action in this regard by all the banks with lead responsibility in a State may also be considered.

Future Branch Expansion

The question of further branch expansion and the function of the lead bank in this regard also need to be clarified. The extensive spread of the branch net-work of commercial banks achieved since 1969 has yielded a banking infrastructure that is generally adequate. The problem now is mainly that of activising the structure to fulfil its role in area development. The process of further branch expansion will of course continue; but it would seem that the original pioneering role of lead banks in the identification of centres is no longer necessary. Both in the case of banked centres requiring additional bank offices and unbanked centres now grown sufficiently to attract a bank office, the process of further expansion may be left to individual banks, subject to the branch expansion policy of the Reserve Bank. However, the requirements of further bank offices may form one of the topics for discussion at the DCC. In fact even as the development schemes gain momentum, new centres with growth potential including rural centres, would be indicated. In this connection, the view was expressed by the State Government representatives that the area constraint on operations of individual branches has come in the way of lending programmes. It was hence suggested that this factor should be taken into account, to the extent possible, in drawing up branch expansion programmes for the area. The question of providing banking facilities in particular centres may be brought up at the DCC meetings. This could be considered by banks generally and acceptable decisions taken but no special responsibility should be expected from the lead bank. Special consideration would have to be given to the need for banks with long established and flourishing branches limited to district headquarters to spread into the interior of the districts.

State-level Consultative Committees

State-level Consultative Committees are established and functioning in several States. The Committees, or fully authorised sub-committees thereof, should meet as often as necessary, to review not only the progress of the scheme and the problems faced in implementation but other issues relevant to banks' operations in the State. Issues which cannot be resolved in the DCC meeting because they are beyond the powers of the district level officers could be referred by the lead banks to the State-level Consultative Committee.

Supervision of the Scheme by the Reserve Bank

The overall progress of the scheme has to be kept under critical review. For this purpose, it is suggested that an appropriate Standing Committee be constituted in the Reserve Bank. This Committee, apart from reviewing the overall progress, could also study specific problems that might arise in individual districts and suggest measures of overcoming them both to the bonus and to the Government authorities. This Committee could also function as a reviewing authority of the lead bank scheme, referred to in paragraph 44 of the Report.

In needs to be stressed again that the lead bank scheme requires continuous effort on the part of all banks and that equal attention has to be given to those districts where a bank has lead responsibility and to those where it has to act under the leadership of another bank. The latter is perhaps more difficult and for that reason requires more attention. At one of the DCC meeting we attended, the Collector made the point that there was a sad lack of awareness about the lead bank scheme among the general public. The best form of publicity for the scheme would be its successful operation in at least some districts in each State.

The guidelines for the more effective operation of the lead bank scheme, required under the terms of reference, have been drawn from the main conclusions of this report and are given in the Appendix. These may be given wide circulation to improve the understanding of the lead bank scheme.

Conclusion

The lead bank scheme holds out promise of a positive impact on economic development at the district level, but its success is dependent on collaborative effort by all the agencies concerned — commercial banks, co-operatives and the State Governments — and a basic attitudinal change and involvement in the implementation of credit plans or bankable schemes prepared by the lead bank. Hitherto, because of a lack of focus on development and the absence of a clear understanding about the nature and content of the scheme, the potential of the scheme has not been evident. The conclusions reached in this report and the guidelines drawn therefrom seek to spell out the tasks involved in the scheme and their organisational implications. An appropriate monitoring system at the level of the lead bank, the Reserve Bank as well as the State Governments has also been recommended. We are hopeful that with proper implementation of these recommendations the full potential of the scheme will come to be felt.

Statement 1

Branch Net-work of Lead Banks — 1969 and 1975

Sl. No.	Name of the District	Name of the Lead Bank	No. of Offices as on 30-6-1969	No. of Offices as on 30-6-1975
(a) Maharashtra				
1.	Bhir	State Bank of India*	7	13
2.	Nanded	—do—	8	14
3.	Osmanabad	—do—	9	17
4.	Parbhani	—do—	10	17
5.	Akola	Central Bank of India	1	2
6.	Amravati	—do—	1	2
7.	Aurangabad	—do—	2	6
		Bank of Maharashtra	3	26
8.	Buldhana	Central Bank of india	1	4
9.	Dhulia	—do—	1	2
10.	Jalgaon	—do—	2	6
11.	Yeotmal	—do—	1	4
12.	Ahmednagar	—do—	2	18
13.	Bhandara	Bank of India	—	6
14.	Chanda	—do—	—	6
15.	Kolaba	—do—	—	13
16.	Ratnagiri	—do—	—	12
17.	Sangli	—do—	—	10
18.	Sholapur	—do—	2	6
19.	Wardha	—do—	—	7
20.	Kolhapur	—do—	1	18
21.	Nagpur	—do—	4	17
22.	Nasik	Bank of Maharashtra	3	18
23.	Poona	—do—	27	70
24.	Satara	—do—	2	28
25.	Thana	—do—	11	30

* Jointly with State Bank of Hyderabad.

Contd.

(*Contd.*)

Sl. No.	Name of the District	Name of the Lead Bank	No. of Offices as on 30-6-1969	No. of Offices as on 30-6-1975
(b) Gujarat				
1.	Amreli	State Bank of India*	13	21
2.	Bhavnagar	—do—	19	32
3.	Jamnagar	—do—	13	21
4.	Junagadh	—do—	16	42
5.	Rajkot	—do—	15	31
6.	Surendrangar	—do—	13	17
7.	Baroda	Bank of Baroda	22	39
8.	Broach	—do—	6	12
9.	Bulsar	—do—	17	35
10.	Dangs	—do—	—	2
11.	Kaira	—do—	17	34
12.	Panch Mahals	—do—	1	13
13.	Surat	—do—	16	42
14.	Ahmedabad	Dena Bank	18	43
15.	Banaskantha	—do—	1	15
16.	Gandhinagar	—do—	—	4
17.	Kutch	—do—	4	28
18.	Mehsana	—do—	8	31
19.	Sabarkantha	—do—	1	17

* Jointly with State Bank of Saurashtra.

Statement 2

Population Group-wise Distribution of Offices, Deposits and Advances in Gujarat and Maharashtra

(Amount in lakhs of rupees)

Sl. No.	Population Group	Gujarat June 1969 No. of Offices	Gujarat June 1969 Deposits	Gujarat June 1969 Advances	Gujarat June 1974 No. of Offices	Gujarat June 1974 Deposits	Gujarat June 1974 Advances	Maharashtra June 1969 No. of Offices	Maharashtra June 1969 Deposits	Maharashtra June 1969 Advances	Maharashtra June 1974 No. of Offices	Maharashtra June 1974 Deposits	Maharashtra June 1974 Advances
1.	Rural	199 (26.4)	23,83 (5.9)	3,51 (1.8)	578 (40.2)	110,27 (13.4)	33,53 (6.6)	121 (10.9)	8,05 (0.7)	4,58 (0.4)	447 (22.4)	54,77 (2.3)	40,63 (1.9)
2.	Semi-Urban	314 (41.7)	146,02 (36.3)	36,62 (18.7)	454 (31.6)	283,26 (34.5)	115,87 (22.7)	328 (29.4)	81,65 (7.3)	29,58 (2.8)	507 (25.3)	196,92 (8.3)	96,30 (4.6)
3.	Urban	124 (16.5)	131,49 (32.7)	45,90 (23.5)	219 (15.3)	229,38 (27.9)	151,05 (29.8)	239 (21.5)	147,35 (13.1)	96,06 (9.0)	392 (19.7)	312,07 (13.1)	209,36 (9.8)
4.	Metropolitan	116 (15.4)	100,63 (25.1)	109,40 (56.0)	186 (12.9)	198,68 (24.2)	208,27 (40.9)	426 38.2	887,37 (78.9)	940,40 (87.8)	653 (32.6)	1821,34 (76.3)	1780,16 (83.7)
	Total	753 (100)	401,97 (100)	195,43 (100)	1,437 (100)	821,59 (100)	508,72 (100)	1,114 (100)	1124,42 (100)	1070,62 (100)	1,999 (100)	2385,10 (100)	2126,45 (100)

Note : Figures in brackets indicate percentage to total.

APPENDIX

Guidelines for the Operation of the Lead Bank Scheme

General

1. Collective action by banks and other financial institutions in the implementation of bankable schemes that would make a definite impact on the district economy is the aim of the Lead Bank Scheme. The Lead Bank should formulate bankable schemes based on resource potential and felt needs of the people of the district. (Para 22)

2. The establishment of an effective rapport and coordination between the Government at the district level and the lead bank is an important prerequisite for the operation of the scheme. (Para 16)

3. Rapport between the banks and the Government and the involvement of officials with banks financial programmes should not be restricted to the district headquarters but should percolate to the village branch level. (Para 40)

4. The tendency on the part of banks to interpret their own responsibilities under the scheme in terms of efforts in their own lead districts and to consider their role in other districts in terms of individual performance should be corrected through proper inculcation of the spirit of the lead bank scheme, particularly at the branch level. (Para 17)

Formulation of Bankable Schemes

1. The role of the lead bank, as the leader of the consortium of financial institutions, consists in preparing "credit plans" or bankable schemes and invoking the co-operation of other financial institutions in meeting the credit demand arising from the schemes. (Para 21)

2. While the lead bank should bear the responsibility for drawing up the schemes, they should make use of all information available in this regard with the State Governments. (Para 27)

3. No uniform methodology or approach is prescribed in respect of the formulation of the district credit plan. What is important is the expeditious preparation of "bankable" schemes — viz., schemes that are technologically feasible and economically viable —

which can be immediately implemented and completed in a period of 3 to 5 years. The schemes should cover as wide a geographic area as possible in the district. (Paras 21, 22, 24, 31)

4. The schemes should be based on the existing infrastructure facilities available in the district. The schemes should be in the broad area of the priority sectors and to the extent possible fitted into the major schemes in operation such as SFDA, MFAL, etc. Schemes need not be drawn up in respect of large and medium industry though the incremental credit needs of this sector would have to be kept in view. (Paras 24, 25)

5. In the formulation of the schemes the linkages of various economic activities will have to be taken into account. (Para 25)

6. The schemes should be prepared by the banks themselves and reliance on outside agencies for this purpose should be avoided. (Para 28)

7. To the extent possible, the schemes should be dovetailed into the district plan. This may be possible only where the district level planning process is well established. In districts where this not the case, the lead banks need not necessarily await the progress of planning for the formulation of the schemes although the co-operation of the district officials would be necessary for this. It has also to be remembered that no credit plan can be substitute for a district development plan. (Para 27)

8. It is suggested that the lead banks make some arrangement at the district or regional level for project formulation and follow-up. (Para 27)

9. Besides credit demand likely to arise through the bankable schemes, resource mobilisation in the district by all financial institutions may also be estimated. (Para 23)

10. Representative project profiles of activities covered by the schemes giving basic economic and technical data, which would be of assistance in the actual extension of credit, should also be prepared. (Para 26)

Implementation

1. The schemes drawn up should be implemented collectively by the commercial and co-operative banks. In the allocation of shares, the spread of the branch net-work of each institution would be an important deciding factor, but limited representation should

not be a reason for exemption from participation. (Para 31)

2. The allocation of the shares for all participating institutions should not be unilaterally determined by the lead bank but finalised through a process of consultation with each institution. It is not necessary that this should be done by the District Consultative Committee but may be finalised at special meetings of bankers. (Para 33)

3. A Committee of bankers may be formed at the district level if considered necessary for the discussion of banking problems, etc. (Para 33)

4. Where the pattern of branch network is lopsided with only the lead bank having offices in the interior, the major share of some schemes such as those of agricultural development may devolve entirely on the lead bank. In such cases, other commercial banks and co-operatives should also lend suitable support to the lead bank. (Para 35)

5. It should be an accepted principle that any increase in outlay arising out of a reasonable extent of escalation should be met by the participating institutions. (Para 44)

6. In the event of heavy default by other institutions, the lead bank cannot be expected to take on the shares of the defaulters. (Para 44)

7. For the success of the lead bank scheme, it is necessary that the progress of the schemes taken up by a bank in areas other than its lead districts is suitable monitored by an appropriate authority in the bank. The record of discussions of the DCC meetings should be pursued and appropriate action taken to activise recalcitrant branches. Implementation of the programmes should also be supported through proper delegation of powers to branch managers. (Para 35, 36, 39)

The District Consultative Committee

1. The District Consultative Committee should assume the task of overall monitoring of the progress of the schemes. (Para 37)

2. The presence and active participation of the District Collector, other officials and representatives of all banks are essential requirements for the District Consultative Committee to be an useful forum. (Para 38)

3. The membership of the DCC should be limited and the Committee made as compact as possible. Depending on the require-

ments of the agenda, non-members may be specially invited to particular meetings. (Para 38)

4. To instil a feeling of involvement of the outlying branches, some meetings of the DCC may be held at tehsil headquarters. (Para 38)

5. The DCC should meet at regular intervals, at least once a quarter and review the progress of the individual schemes. (Para 39)

6. To assist in such a review, data relating to the lending to the specific schemes (and not to total lending or lending to any other sector) may be called for from individual branches by the lead bank and the consolidated data circulated among the members. A suitable proforma may be devised for this purpose for each district by the concerned lead bank. (Para 39)

7. At the meetings, issues requiring further action may be defined and the responsibility of follow-up may be pin-pointed to a particular institution or Government official. (Para 39)

8. Copies of the full record of discussions should be sent to the lead/regional offices of each bank and to every bank branch in the district. (Para 39)

9. The requirements of further bank offices in the district may also form a topic for discussion in the Committee. (Para 48)

Other Points

1. It is desirable that lead banks should be automatically admitted as regular members in SFDA/MFAL Committees. (Para 41)

2. The financing of the specific schemes would mean extension of virtually the same type of credit for the same purpose in different areas by different banks. While stipulation of identical terms and conditions by all banks may not be feasible, some degree of conformity in the provision of credit under the same scheme would be necessary. (Para 43)

1. Published by Ministry of Education and Social Welfare, 1980, viii, 269 p.

7

RAILWAY ACCIDENT INVESTIGATION REPORT ON FIRE ON LEADING COACH NO. 7606 MOTOR COACH) OF A-41 DOWN BOMBAY VT-AMBERNATH LOCAL TRAIN AT KM 54/5 BETWEEN KALYAN AND VITHALWADI STATIONS OF BOMBAY DIVISION ON CENTRAL RAILWAY ON 29TH SEPTEMBER 1975

September 30, 1975 – January 27, 1976[1]

One Man Commission Shri D.G. Divgi, Additional Commissioner of Railway Safety, Central Circle, Bombay

Officers Present Shri F.C. Bhandari; Shri A.S. Agarwal; Shri C.M. Khosla; Shri R. Ananthakrishnan

Appointment

The Commission was constituted under Rule 4 of the Statutory Investigation into Railway Accidents Rule, 1973 issued by the Ministry of Tourism and Civil Aviation vide their Notification No. RS 13.T(8)/71 dated 19th April 1973.

Terms of Reference

To inquire into the fire on Leading Coach No. 7606 (Motor Coach) of A-41 Down Bombay VT-Ambernath Local Train at km 54/5 between Kalyan and Vithalwadi Stations of Bombay Division on Central Railway on 29th September 1975.

---

1. Ministry of Tourism and Civil Aviation (Commission of Railway Safety), Government of India, New Delhi, 1981, i + 21 p.

Conclusion

51. *Cause*: On full consideration of the factual, material and circumstantial evidence, I have come to the conclusion that the fire on leading Motor Coach No. 7606 of A-41 Down Bombay VT-Ambernath Local Train at E.S. 54/5 between Kalyan and Vithalwadi stations at 20.33 hours on 29th September, 1975, was due to an electric short circuit caused by an external object such as a stray piece of wire between the 1500 Volt Overhead Electrical lines/pantograph and the roof of the coach.

52. *Responsibility*: I do not hold anyone responsible for this accident. The injuries to the passengers, however, would have been avoided if the pantograph had been relocated on the non-passenger carrying portion of the coach.

53. *Relief Measures*: I am satisfied that the medical aid was prompt and the care and attention adequate. The relief measures were satisfactory.

Recommendations

54. The pantographs should be relocated at the earliest so as to be on the roofs of non-passenger compartments. (Para 48)

55. Suitable means of insulation over the roof, particularly in the pantograph zone, should be provided. (Para 49)

56. Means for getting down from the Electric Multiple Unit Trains during emergencies and at out of course stoppages, such as steps, should be provided. (Para 50)

Railway Boards Comments on Various Parts of the Report

Para 54: R.D.S.O. is studying the complete implication of this proposal for all the stock in service. As regards the ICF stock, it is considered feasible to relocate the pantograph above the H.T. Compartment. However, to accommodate the ventilators provided for the resistance compartment and to maintain the moving dimensions within limits, it may be necessary to provide a cut-away lowering the roof and making it flat at this portion. R.D.S.O./I.C.F. are examining the modifications involved.

Para 55: Shalimoid has been discontinued and Densomat having better electrical insulation and fire-retarding properties will be used on the roof by ICF for the time being below the pantograph area on DC EMU stock. The rubber impregnated fibre glass is also proposed to be tried out on a few coaches to get service experience. For EMU stock ceiling, asbestos boards or metal sheeting is provided which should provide protection from sparks or molten metal.

Para 56: Similar recommendations made earlier were considered and it was not found practicable to provide a step ladder at doorways in EMU coaches. In this connection attention is invited to this Ministry's Office Memorandum No. 75/Elec (TRS)/113/7, dated 24-7-1976 conveying Railway Ministry's decision on the subject. However, RDSO is being asked to find a solution to the absence of steps whereby the passengers have some alternative convenient means to get down in cases of emergency.

Para 11 of CRS's Noting: The replacement of the entire DC traction in Bombay area with 25 KVAC system will involve huge investment for sub-stations and overhead equipments, and may result in disuse and consequent scrapping of a large number of assets/stock and lead to high expenditure on modification of DC EMU stock to as to make them suitable for AC operation. Under the present economic conditions, it may not be possible to undertake this expensive conversion.

8

MONEY SUPPLY IN INDIA : CONCEPTS, COMPILATION AND ANALYSIS – REPORT OF THE SECOND WORKING GROUP[1]

Chairman Shri M.L. Ghosh

Members Shri A. Raman; Shri A. Hasib; Dr. N.A. Majumdar; Dr. Meenakshi Tyagarajan; Dr. S.L. Shetty; Shri K.A. Menon

Appointment

The present time series on money supply in India, its components and the factors causing variations in it, which are being regularly published by the Reserve Bank of India, are based mainly on the frame work provided by the Working Group constituted for the purpose in 1961.[1] Since then some modifications and refinements in the presentation of money supply series have been, no doubt, introduced by the Bank, but these could be regarded as embellishments of the basic conceptual and analytical frame provided by the Group. For instance, even the wider concept of money stock, viz., the aggregate of 'money supply' and time deposits with banks – which was actually introduced subsequently in 1964 in the form of "Aggregate Monetary Resources" (AMR) – was originally conceived by that Working Group.[2]

Since the adoption of the 1961 Working Group framework, considerable discussion has taken place among monetary theorists regarding, *inter alia*, the adequacy of the conventional concept of money stock and the various alternative concepts relevant for analysis and policy formulation. In the United States of America, for instance, the Federal Reserve System now employs as many as eight measures of monetary aggregates for analysis and policy formulation; of these, data on five money stock measures (M_1 to M_5) are being regularly

---

1. Bombay, Reserve Bank of India, 1977, vi + 90 p.

published. In the United Kingdom too, five concepts of money stock have come to be accepted as useful for analysis, and three of them (M_1 to M_3) figure in official publications. In Appendix II a brief description is provided of the various money stock measures now being employed in selected countries.

Terms of Reference

To examine the suitability of various concepts and definitions of money supply, suggest methodological changes for compilation so as to bring out the significance and implication of these data for policy formulation and depending on the results of the examination of the various issues involved, prepare a revised time series on money supply as well as factors affecting it .

Contents

Foreword; Introduction; Conceptual Framework; Measurement of Money Stock; Data Base of the Monetary Sector; Sources of Change in Money Supply; Miscellaneous Near-Money Assets and Money Stock Measures; Appendices from I to VIII; Statistical Statements from 1 to 7; Annexure.

Layout of the Report

In this Report, various analytical and conceptual aspects of money stock measures are examined and the factors contributing to the variations in money stock discussed. On the basis of this discussion, a broad conceptual framework for money supply analysis in India has been evolved and in the light of this framework, the new series of money supply data have been compiled and presented, to begin with, for the years 1970-71 to 1975-76.

The Report is divided into five sections. In Section 1, two important issues arising from the terms of reference of the Working Group are examined. First, what are the types of assets which correspond to the theoretical concept of money and which could generally form the basis for analysis and policy formulation, both short-term and long-term? Secondly, is it appropriate to base the compilation and presentation of primary data on money supply in India on theories of money supply determination, which have been evolved in the context of the experiences and the institutional framework of the developed economies? The degree of relevance of such theories to an economy such as that of India and the efficiency of predictive values of concepts based on such theories have also been briefly discussed. In the light of this discussion it has been possible to evolve the conceptual framework in which money supply data could be meaningfully compiled, analysed and interpreted.

In the subsequent sections, this conceptual framework has been sought to be translated into specific issues of compilation of money supply data. To begin with, an attempt has been made in Section 2, to evolve specific measures of money stock: four categories of money stock have been defined. Section 3 discusses the 'gaps' in the present series of money supply data and measures adopted to fill these 'gaps' in order to make the data base of the monetary sector more comprehensive and realistic. In Section 4, the rationale underlying the analytical frame of what has come to be known as factors affecting money supply is examined and certain changes in the methodology of a compilation proposed. Finally, in Section 5, a discussion is presented of some near-money assets which appear to be potential candidates for inclusion in money stock measures but which the Working Group has considered as not eligible for such inclusion. The new series of money supply data compiled in the light of the discussions in the various sections are presented in Statement Nos. 2, 3, 4 and 5.

There is no finality in the area of money supply data. All that the Working Group Report can lay claim to is that it has been possible to introduce a further degree of sophistication in the Indian money supply data: to the extent that some gaps in the present series of data have been filled up, the revised series could be regarded as more comprehensive and realistic than the present series.

SECTION 1

The Conceptual Framework

The main conceptual issues involved in any attempt to meaningfully define and measure 'money' or monetary aggregates are sought to be briefly discussed in this Section. The discussion is presented under three distinct and separate heads. First, the contemporary discussion in monetary theory on the definition and measurement of the stock of money is reviewed. The search for a definition which is both analytically meaningful and operationally useful can only be conducted against the background of such a review. Secondly, it has also become necessary to examine the relevance to money supply of the liabilities of what are called "non-monetary financial institutions", in whatever manner one may choose to define it. Thirdly, the question has also to be posed whether there is any acceptable theory of money supply determination which would be relevant to the Indian situation, so that the kind of format of money supply data, which the Group is expected to a evolve, could be grafted on such theory. On the whole, therefor, the discussion in this Section provides the perspective to the specific recommendations regarding compilation and analysis of money supply data in India, spelt out in the subsequent Sections.

(i) *Approaches to Definition and Measurement of Stock of Money*

The question of an appropriate measure of money stock arose initially out of the basic difference implicit in the two approaches of the 'Quantity Theorists' and the 'Keynesians' to the most distinguishing characteristics of money, that is, the conception of money as a 'medium of exchange' and that as a 'store of value'. The general recognition of the store of value function of money has given rise to the fairly widely accepted phenomenon of substitutability between money, traditionally defined as medium of exchange, and the whole spectrum of other financial assets obtaining in an economy. Therefore, the fundamental aspect of the Keynesian formulation of the demand for money *inter alia* as an asset alternative to other financial assets and consequently, such demand being considered sensitive to interest rates, continues to distinguish it from the approaches of the 'Modern Quantity Theorists' who in their re-formulations of the classical quantity theory, include in principle many rates of interest but empirically find no interest-elasticity of the demand for money with respect to any one asset or group of assets.[3]

This debate regarding the appropriate measure of money stock has been brought into sharp focus in the recent empirical works on the subject of the demand for money. The debate acquired a sharper edge particularly after the 'Modern Quantity Theorists' chose to adopt the unorthodox approach of including in their 'money stock measure' *time deposits* with commercial banks, instead of restricting the scope of the concept to the commonly accepted definition based on money's most distinguishing function as a means of payment, viz., *currency* outside the banking system and *demand deposits* with commercial banks (adjusted for inter-bank deposits). The inclusion of *time deposits* is justified on the ground that these are close substitutes for money. In the process, the 'Modern Quantity Theorists' appear to have clinched the issue in favour of the phenomenon of substitutability between money and other financial assets, and at the same time, their approach has also become open to the charge that "Lumping time deposits together with the money stock obscures movements between them based on changes in the interest rate. Therefore, it is not surprising that an interest rate response cannot be found.[4]

Nevertheless, this debate among monetary theorists has brought forth, in specifying what combination of assets corresponds closely to the theoretical concept of money, different analytical approaches which have even tended to cut across the traditional boundaries of 'quantity theory' (even with reformulation) and 'Keynesianism'. For instance, a contemporary survey of monetary theory and policy distinguishes at least four such approaches.[5] First, there are those who insist on the money's unique function as a medium of exchange and adhere to its conventional definition as currency plus demand deposits with banks (adjusted for inter-bank demand deposits). The second approach is that the 'Modern Quantity Theorists' who conceive of money as something broader than what is visualised in the first approach but, as 'a temporary abode of purchasing power': this approach would include for empirical analysis, time deposits with banks in the measure of money stock. Though the measure of money stock differs in the two approaches, what is interesting is that both find the relationship between income and money (or velocity function) as most stable.

At the other extreme, there are two approaches which adopt a far wider concept of money: here the reference is to the Radcliffe Committee's almost immeasurable[6] concept of 'the whole structure of liquidity', and to the Gurley-Shaw doctrine on the role of non-monetary financial intermediaries in the modern economic process. According to both these approaches, the velocity of money is a meaningless number in the presence of whole gamut of financial assets substitutable for money. The spending decisions by households and corporations are not determined by money, i.e., the quantity representing the means of payment *alone* but by the whole structure of liquidity according to the Radcliffe Committee's thinking and by the totality of financial liabilities of monetary and non-monetary financial intermediaries together, according to the Gurley-Shaw thesis.

There is a difference between the two. The Radcliffe Committee emphasizes the assets side of the intermediaries' balance sheet to the comparative neglect of the liabilities side; non-bank financial intermediaries are important because they lend and even the banks are important not because they create money but because they make loans.[7] On the other hand, the Gurley-Shaw thesis emphasizes the liabilities of non-monetary financial intermediaries so as to bring into sharp focus the financial competition between money created by the monetary system and financial liabilities of other intermediaries. "The more adequate the non-monetary financial assets are as substitutes for money in transactions, precautionary, speculation and . . . diversification balances, the smaller may be the money supply for any designated level of national income. For any level of income, the money supply is indeterminate until one knows the degree of substitutability between money created by banks and financial assets created by other intermediaries."[8] One obvious implication of the Gurley-Shaw thesis is that the 'quantity of money' relevant for monetary theory and policy should include the liabilities of non-monetary financial intermediaries.[9] Their existence in size and diversity also influences the level and structure of interest rates. Therefore, those liabilities and their yields need to be introduced in any 'demand for money' functions. Alternatively, viewed in terms of income-expenditure approach, the aggregate demand in the economic system is not determined by the quantity and velocity of 'money' alone; rather, it is determined by the whole spectrum of liabilities created by the financial system.

In the ultimate analysis, most of these are assertions based on *a priori* observations and hence need to be tested empirically. Even in empirical studies of these issues, there do not seem to be any agreed criteria to arrive at the appropriate definition of money; in fact some well-known quantitative studies have arrived at contradictory results. For instance, Friedman and Meiselman, arguing that money should be defined as that set of financial assets which best explains nominal income, hit upon their now famous duel criteria to select such a set of financial assets. The criteria are: (i) that the sum of assets should have the highest correlation among various aggregates of assets with national income, and (ii) that the correlation with income of the sum of assets should be higher than that of any of its individual components.[10] It was by using these criteria that Friedman and Meiselman defined money to include time deposits (in addition to currency and demand deposits). Employing the same criteria, however, other empirical works have disputed the need to include time deposits![11]

Again, following the Gurley-Shaw thesis, it is argued that money should be a weighted sum of various financial assets, the weights being determined by their respective degrees of moneyness.[12] Accepting this criterion a study has employed elasticities of substitution among financial assets as surrogate to degrees of 'moneyness' and has come to the conclusion with reference to the U.S.A. that money supply should be "a weighted sum of currency, demand deposits, time deposits, deposits in mutual savings banks and liabilities of savings and loan associations".[13]

One purpose of referring to some of these empirical studies was to underline the fact that there are large areas of disagreement even on the basic definitional questions: the degree of disagreement is perhaps greater in respect of the wider issues concerning determinants of the demand for money and influence of money on total expenditure. If these issues have remained unsettled, it is partly because among the hierarchy of financial assets of spending units, from currency to various types of financial assets, there occurs a continuous shift depending upon the underlying economic conditions. Under such circumstances, to depend upon the behaviour of any single measure of money stock for formulation of monetary policy would not be appropriate; instead a wider range of monetary aggregates may have to be taken into account.

It should be emphasised that the absence of any finality in the empirical studies relating to the stock of money does not mean that the policy-makers are operating in a vacuum. All that is sought to be highlighted is that there is no unique approach to either the definition of money or measurement of the stock of money. The concepts and analysis have to be adopted to suit the specific situation. If this is true of the developed economies, it is applicable with greater force in the context of a less developed economy like that of India.

One lesson which can be drawn from this brief discussion is that in building up a sound framework for primary data on money stock, we have to allow for sufficient disagregation so as to permit different combinations of assets to be employed for analysis, depending upon the end-use to which the data are likely to be put.

(ii) *Non-monetary Financial Intermediaries*

In money supply analysis, it is necessary to draw a basic distinction between the monetary system and the rest of the financial system, the one that facilitates the payments mechanism and the other that intermediates between savers and loanable funds and their users. In other words, the monetary system plays a unique role as the 'Administrator of the payments mechanism'.[14] Without going into the controversial question of the extent to which non-monetary financial intermediaries can "create credit", it is possible to identify broadly four characteristics which differentiate their role in this respect from that of commercial banks.[15]

The first characteristic relates to the time period involved in turnover: while the process of commercial bank credit expansion relates to the *payment-turnover* period, that by non-banking intermediaries, involves an *income-turnover period*. The time period for commercial banks' credit expansion is generally very short. Secondly, credit expansion by other intermediaries is subject to substantially more "leakages" than in the case of commercial banks. Except for the currency drain (which also forms a part of the transaction), transaction arising from credit creation by banks within the payments systems pass through them almost entirely, whereas it is not the case with the financial intermediaries. As Warren Smith has rightly observed, "The restoration of reserves to commercial banking system within a few days of the time they are lost through lending is a built-in feature of our payments mechanism, and it is for this reason that their distinctive role as issuers of means of payments gives commercial banks a peculiar ability to expand credit."[16] The leakage in the form of currency, which is rather large in the Indian context, does not alter the basic feature of this uniqueness. Thirdly, the role of credit creation by the two systems has differing economic significance. While the one goes to finance broadly current expenditures over current cash flow, the other helps to channel savings into investment in a wider sense. Lastly, even the non-banking financial intermediaries have to operate their cash receipts and payments through the medium of the commercial banks and the cheque clearance mechanism. They do not maintain liabilities withdrawable on demand with themselves, nor do their loans result in an automatic addition to such liabilities with themselves. The liabilities of these financial institutions cannot be directly used for settling claims without being converted into cheque-able deposits of the banking institutions.

Because of these, and also for the sake of convenience and convention, the whole range of financial institutions is divided into two distinct categories, viz., *monetary institutions* and *non-monetary financial institutions*. As emphasized earlier, the former are distinguished from the latter by their unique role as issuers of the means of payment and settlers of the claims of the spending units mediated through them.[17] This category of institutions includes, besides the monetary authority, those deposit banking institutions which possess liabilities withdrawable on demand and also which are members of the organised clearance mechanism instituted for settling claims against those liabilities.

In view of the fact that the operations of non-monetary financial institutions are qualitatively different from those of the monetary institutions, the liabilities of the former are left out of the money stock measures recommended in this Report. The institutions which are thus outside the purview of the *monetary* orbit are: life and general insurance corporations, development banks, investment and trust companies and the Unit Trust of India.

(iii) *Money Supply Determination*

Lastly, the question needs to be posed whether there is any acceptable theory of money supply determination that could be incorporated into the format used for the presentation of primary data on factors influencing money supply. Even a cursory glance at the enormous number of behavioural, structural and policy-controlled variables underlying the money supply variation process would convince one that no such universally acceptable theory could be identified. Money supply is both an economic as well as a policy-controlled variable. As an economic variable, it is determined by the public's and banks' portfolio behaviour. As a policy-controlled variable, its variation is influenced by what the Monetary Authority thinks the appropriate size of primary as well as secondary money should be. Moreover, the supply of what are called primary and secondary money is not determined within the monetary sector alone; its determinants transgress into the real sector, the current and prospective business conditions as reflected in output and investment trends, the price expectation, and the objectives of monetary policy themselves.[18]

Therefore, we have to devise a format of presentation of factors influencing money supply based on the major sectors of credit use so that the same format could facilitate credit planning and credit projections consistent with the appropriate rate of expansion in 'money supply', independently determined say on the basis of output increases, its sectoral composition, the expected rate of inflation, and the past increases in money supply.

Nevertheless, in building up a sound data base and information system on these monetary aggregates and the factors influencing their variations which is the task of this Working Group, we have found it necessary to present sufficiently diversified information on a regular basis so that further analysis of the same in the form of theoretical and operationally meaningful models relating to financial and real sectors, could be facilitated. The nature and frequency of the information are detailed in the subsequent Sections.

SECTION 2

Measurement of Money Stock

Against the conceptual background sketched in Section 1, an attempt has been made in this Section to evolve specific measures of money stock. The brief review of contemporary developments in monetary theory and empirical research relating to monetary aggregates has shown clearly that the use of a single measure of money stock for monetary analysis and policy would be inadequate and, at times, even misleading. There is no unique measure of monetary aggregate. There is, therefore, a need to take a disaggregated view and employ a variety of monetary aggregates depending upon the end-use to which the data are likely to be put.

Alongside this effort of evolving suitable measures of money stock, there is yet another important exercise, namely, improving the data base of the monetary sector. In fact this aspect of qualitative improvement of the data, in terms of both coverage and sophistication, is as much important as the evolution of suitable measures of money stock. This aspect is taken up for discussion in the next Section.

The Working Group's contribution to monetary data compilation and analysis has therefore to be judged in terms of both the aspects mentioned above.

Reverting to measures of money stock, the hard core of the

monetary aggregates should continue to be basically those assets possessing the quality of "superior liquidity" arising from the conception of money as a medium of exchange. Keeping this in view, four measures of money stock are evolved. Among the four measures evolved, the first and the foremost continues to be, in the words of the 1961 Working Group, "the most liquid and the most generally accepted means of payment available for the mediation of transactions and final settlement of claims."[19] In a sense, the present Working Group has not found it necessary to depart from the concept of the 1961 Group, because, neither the contemporary theoretical debate nor the quantitative research in the field has disputed the uniqueness of some of the financial liabilities created by the monetary system[20] in terms of their superior liquidity and the speed and the automaticity of the process of their creation. Moreover, this approach is nearly universally adopted, as can be seen in Appendix II. The International Monetary Fund (IMF), which has introduced uniform practices of data compilation for its 'Monetary Survey' regularly published in the *International Financial Statistics* (IFS), has also adopted the same concept. In this respect, the main contribution of this Working Group lies in improvement of the data base for compiling the 'money supply with the public'.

The other three money stock measures stem mainly from two factors: first, the growing importance accorded to 'money' as a store of value and second, the need to take into account the probable shifts between liabilities of the monetary system which are means of payment and term liabilities. The four measures of money stock are defined below. Broadly, the main characteristic which separates one measure from the other is the varying degree of its liquidity, the measures being specified in the descending order of liquidity.

M_1 consists of:

(i) Currency notes and coins with the public (excluding cash on hand of all banks);
(ii) Demand deposits (excluding inter-bank deposits) of all commercial and co-operative banks; and
(iii) 'Other deposits' held with the Reserve Bank of India (excluding balances in Account No. 1 of the International Monetary Fund, the Reserve Bank of India Employees' Pension, Provident and Gratuity Funds and *ad hoc* liability items which arise from time to time).

M_2 consists of:

(i) M_1; and
(ii) Savings deposits with Post Office Savings Banks.

M_3 consists of:

(i) M_1; and
(ii) Time deposits of all commercial and co-operative banks (excluding inter-bank time deposits).

M_4 consists of:

(i) M_3; and
(ii) Total deposits with the Post Office Savings Organisation (excluding National Savings Certificates).

Conceptually, the category M_1 is the same as the existing 'money supply with the public', with the term 'public' signifying 'money using' sectors as distinguished from 'money creating' sectors. Since the latter comprise the Government and the banking system, the 'public' in effect means all categories of holders of money other than the banking system and the Government.

The category M_2 presented here, represents a compromise between the need for conceptual neatness and operational feasibility. Ideally it would have been appropriate to include the 'cheque facility accounts' of savings deposits with Post Office Savings Banks in M_1. The rationale underlying such a measure is that the two types of deposits, namely demand liability portion savings deposits with commercial and co-operative banks and chequeable portion of savings deposits with Post Offices belong to the same species though between them, the latter appears to be somewhat less liquid than the former. The measure of M_2 would have then comprised: (i) M_1, (ii) the non-chequeable part of Post Office Savings Banks deposits, and (iii) time liability portion of savings deposits of commercial and co-operative banks. Operationally, however, it is not possible to provide immediately data on such a finer concept because of difficulty involved in obtaining the weekly or monthly figures in regard to chequeable portion of Postal deposits from such a vast network of Post Office Savings Banks in the country. As brought out in Section 3, the size of chequeable portion is also insignificant.

Therefore a separate intermediate measure of M_2 has been evolved which includes, in addition to M_1, the total Post Office Savings Bank Deposits which on the whole are a shade less liquid than demand deposits with banks but more liquid than time deposits.

The category M_3 would correspond again to the existing 'aggregate monetary resources' while M_4 is further expanded variant which includes deposits with the Post Office Savings Organization. Conceptually, both of them correspond to the existing measure of 'aggregate monetary resources' but they would now include a wiader set of financial assets and also cover a larger number of financial institutions.

On the whole, therefore, the new categories of money stock measures may be said to carry forward the process of refinement of Indian monetary data in two distinct areas. Firstly, the new categories provide for a much wider spectrum of monetary aggregates, on the basis of their varying degrees of liquidity. Secondly, the new categories, by extending their coverage, would bring the data closer to reality. The new series, it is hoped, would therefore facilitate a more sophisticated and realistic analysis of monetary trends. The significance of the extension of the coverage would become clearer in Section 3.

SECTION 3

Data Base of the Monetary Sector

In the present series of money supply data, there are several 'gaps' which may be historically attributable to lack of data on certain components of money supply. In part, the 'gaps' may have also been due to the fact that in the past some components of money supply might not have been regarded as important in terms of magnitudes. Whatever may have been the case, such 'gaps' render the present series of monetary data incomplete in their coverage and hence imperfect for realistic analysis and interpretation of monetary trends. It is important to clearly identify such gaps and try to fill them with a view to making the new money supply data series more comprehensive and realistic. As mentioned earlier, this task of improving the coverage and quality of data is as important as the evolution of new measures of money stock.

While the problem of extension of coverage of the monetary data hinges primarily on the co-operative sector and the Post Offices, in terms of refinement of data, the problem of apportioning savings deposit of commercial banks between demand and time deposits, referred to earlier, becomes important. These topics are discussed in this Section. Finally, the new series of money supply data compiled in the light of the discussions in Section 2 and in this Section are provided at the end.

Refinements in the Coverage of Co-operative Sector

One of the substantive changes effected in the new series of money stock measures evolved here is the extended and more refined coverage with respect to the assets and liabilities of the cooperative sector. For lack of timely and regular flow of information from all tiers of co-operative banks, the present practice has been to include the demand deposits of only the scheduled and other State co-operative banks but without excluding the inter-bank constituents thereof. Likewise, in the present 'aggregate monetary resources', their time deposits are inclusive of inter-bank deposits. Now under the Banking Regulation Act, 1949 (as applicable to co-operative societies) and the rules framed thereunder, every category of co-operative bank (spelt out in the following paragraph) is required to submit monthly returns to the Agricultural Credit Department of the Bank. At the instance of this Working Group, the Agricultural Credit Department have devised, on the basis of the monthly returns, methods to compile this information on a systematic basis, so that it would now become possible to first include the assets and liabilities of the other tiers of the co-operative credit institutions and second, to exclude appropriately inter-bank items, within the co-operative sector. This may be elaborated further.

The different categories of credit institutions[21] in the co-operative sector are: State co-operative banks, Central co-operative banks, urban banks, industrial co-operative banks, employees' credit societies, other non-agricultural credit societies, primary agricultural credit societies, and grain banks. Among these, the scheduled State co-operative banks furnish returns under Section 42 of the Reserve Bank of India Act, 1934 (as amended) and up to date information in respect of them is being used for the current series on money supply. The rest of the tiers could be divided into two categories: (i) those that have been designated as 'banking' institutions by bringing them under the purview of the Banking Regulation Act, 1949, and (ii) other societies. The Banking Laws (Applicable to Co-operative Societies) Act, 1965, extended the RBI's statutory control under certain provisions of the Reserve Bank of India Act, 1934 and the Banking Regulation Act, 1949 to State co-operative banks, Central co-operative banks and the primary co-operative banks, defined as primary non-agricultural credit societies transacting banking business and having paid-up share capital and reserves of not less than rupees one lakh. The provisions regarding cash reserves, liquidity reserve requirements, and general control on advances, licensing, opening of branches and issuance of directive have all been extended to them.[22] The special information system, referred to above, is in respect of these institutions designated as 'banks'. These 'banks' which are now proposed to be covered in addition to State co-operative banks, for money supply data compilation under the category of: (a) Central co-operative banks; and (b) Primary co-operative banks consisting of (i) urban co-operative banks; and (ii) salary earners' credit societies (to which the Act applies).

Ideally, even the other non-agricultural credit societies which have not attained the status of 'banks' and the primary agricultural credit societies (including grain banks) which alone, among co-operative institutions, have been permitted to carry on banking business in rural areas, should be covered in the compilation of money stock measures: this is because all of them carry on 'banking' business, generally defined to mean acceptance of deposits withdrawable on demand and used for lending.[23] But these have been kept outside the purview of the legislative provisions and the rules made thereunder regarding the requirements of submitting regular statistical returns, referred to above.[24] Further, on account of the operational difficulties involved in getting regular and timely information in their case, all of these co-operative societies would have to continue to get excluded from monetary data. On an examination of the data for recent years,[25] it is found that all these primary societies (important among them being agricultural credit societies) have negligible amounts of deposit resources, i.e., about five per cent of their total liabilities; a large part of their funds originates from borrowing from the Central co-operative banks in respect of which fuller information is available. Therefore, the magnitude involved in their exclusion from M_1 is negligible.[26]

At present the money supply data series is compiled on a weekly basis (for every Friday) and published with a time-lag of about ten days. On the other hand, information in respect of the co-operative banks, referred to above (namely, the Central co-operative banks, the urban co-operative banks and the salary earners' societies), would flow with a lag of two months or so. This lag, the Group is convinced, is unavoidable; for a period of about six weeks therefore, the available information for the latest month may have to be repeated. The Working Group did explore the possibility of evolving some method and criterion for projecting the weekly data for the intervening weeks for these institutions. No such worthwhile method could be employed for want of any bench-mark weekly series in respect of these institutions.

Even the *pro rata* distribution of variations between months among the intervening weeks was difficult to decide upon, because of the fluctuating nature of the data. In any case, even if it were possible to evolve a *pro rata* distribution method, there is not certainly that such a method would give better results than the 'repeat' method proposed.

An additional point in favour of the 'repeat' method was that the variations between months are not so significant and it is thought the repetition of the month-end figures for a short period of six weeks or so in respect of the lower tiers of co-operative banks, should serve the purpose in view. With a view to having some uniformity in the inclusion of returns of the co-operative sector, it is proposed that the data for the latest month for which returns are received be included in the third Friday of every month and concurrently the revisions for the previous weeks be effected.

Inclusion of the Post Office Deposits

Yet another constituent of 'banking' to which the Group propose to extend the coverage of monetary data is the variety of deposits accepted by the Postal Savings Organization.[27] The 1961 Working Group had argued that the Post Office Savings deposits need to be excluded from 'money supply with the public' because they were "more analogous to time deposits in as much as they originate from the placement of cash with Post Offices and do not act as a basis for credit creation."[28]

It is true that saving deposits with Post Offices are 'primary deposits' in the sense that they originate from the direct placement of cash as distinguished from "secondary deposits" which get created by the granting of credit. But such "primary deposits" are found to be ziaeable even with commercial and co-operative banks (such as the demand portion of saving deposits and even a part of the current account deposits), which get included in M_1. The question is essentially one of the ease with which the Postal Savings Bank deposits can be withdrawn 'on demand'. In this regard, the withdrawal rules have been liberalized since 1965. Withdrawals can now be made either by cheque or by withdrawal slip. Withdrawal by cheque is allowed at present to a depositor who is properly introduced to the Post Office, has a minimum balance of Rs. 50 in his account, is literate and can sign his name. In some of the important metropolitan centres, the Postal Savings Organisation has acquired the membership of the bank clearing houses.

A review of the operations of the Postal Savings Deposits revealed that the chequeable portion of the Postal Savings Deposits is not very significant; further, that even in such deposits the rate of turnover appears to be less than the turnover rate for fixed deposits with commercial banks.[29]

Circle-wise information obtained from the Postal Savings Organisation and presented in Appendix V shows that the amounts of balance in 'cheque facility accounts' formed a negligible proportion of the total balance in Post Office Savings Bank Accounts. This proportion ranged from 0.26 per cent in Gujarat circle to 4.82 per cent in Madhya Pradesh circle; only two circles, viz., Karnataka (15.11 per cent) and West Bengal (7.54 per cent) show higher proportions. Nevertheless, rough estimates show that for the country as a whole, the total balance in chequeable deposits in Post Office Savings Accounts would be about Rs. 40 crores. The figure can be compared with the "money supply with the public" figure of more than Rs. 13,000 crores or demand deposits of commercial and co-operative banks of Rs. 6,000 crores.

Secondly, it would be rather difficult to get information on the total balance in the 'chequeable account', for millions of Postal Savings Accounts spread over lakhs of Postal Savings Bank offices. Thirdly, the fact that Postal Savings Deposits do not form the basis for credit creation cannot be dismissed rather lightly. Lastly, it is also found that these deposits have a lower turnover.

On the other hand, conceptually from the point of view of 'liquidity' these deposits can be compared to demand liability portion of savings deposits with banks. That is why, as stated earlier, it would have been appropriate to include 'chequeable portion' of saving deposits with the Post Office Savings Banks in M_1.

While concept-wise such categorisation seems neat, it raises some operational problems for compiling these data regularly and incorporating them in the money supply series. As has been shown, the chequeable portion of savings deposits varies greatly from region to region; this proportion may also vary over time. Hence, for assessing spatial and temporal variations it would be necessary to conduct periodic studies broadly, on the lines conducted by the Group. This would no doubt be a time-consuming process. Moreover, it would also mean a serious limitation on the frequency with which such data could be published. In view of the analytical significance of Postal Savings Bank deposits as an intermediate stage of liquidity, the Group has prescribed a slightly modified concept of M_2 which, as indicated earlier, includes the total accruals under the Post Office Savings Deposits. In the absence of weekly data on these accruals, it is proposed to publish only a monthly series of this measure.

Another obvious candidate for inclusion in the M_2 category is the so-called 'time liability' portion of savings deposits with banks. At present this portion is actually added on to the time deposits of banks, which seems hardly appropriate. The description "the time liability portion" of saving deposits is itself a misnomer and may be partly explaining by the historical reason that between the "current" and "time" categories, there was no other categories. The very fact that a depositor chooses to deposit money in a saving account, in preference to 'time deposits', shows his asset preference, namely, he would prefer a relatively more liquid asset. The question of the determination of the proportions of current and non-current elements in savings deposits with banks is discussed separately at the end of this Section. In this case also, there is the problem of conducting periodic studies and the question of frequency of publishing the data remains.

So far, the discussion has been confined to the savings deposits with the Post Offices. The aggregate of term deposits could be treated as "quasi money" and hence the Group has proposed that they be included in the extended concept of monetary aggregate, namely, M_4. This extended concept would also include, besides savings deposits, various other deposits with the Post Offices such as Post Office Time Deposits, Post Office Recurring Deposits and Post Office Cumulative Time Deposits. The concept would however, *exclude* different types of National Savings Certificates since special incentives are given to induce holders to hold on to the certificates till maturity. Such certificates are almost analogous to Government bonds with the difference that they are relatively more attractive to individual holders and are non-negotiable instruments. Further, the National Postal Savings Certificates have also been treated as 'approved securities' for the purposes of statutory liquidity requirements laid down for commercial and co-operative banks, under section 24 of the Banking Regulation Act, 1949; hence the certificates have become eligible as collaterals for bank credit.

The category M_3 corresponds broadly to the present category of what is called "Aggregate Monetary Resources", which has been designed essentially to encompass time deposits of the banking system in the broader concept of money. At this stage, the question may be asked: why is it that the deposits with the Post Office — saving and time, etc., referred to above — do not find a place in M_3 itself? Why has it been found necessary to include them in a category at one removed from M_3? There are a few considerations which warrant that deposits of Post Office be treated separately. First, the Postal Savings Organisation can hardly be regarded as belonging to the conventionally defined 'banking system' in which the liabilities become the basis for creation of credit. Yet, it would be improper to ignore these deposits because they do act as some form of substitutes for deposits in the regular banking system and hence, it is necessary to evolve an information system of a hierarchy of monetary aggregates which includes such competitive deposits of the household sector.

Secondly, there is the practical difficulty of obtaining information on a weekly basis. As the amounts involved are large, it is not proper to substitute surrogate estimates. The most appropriate course in this respect, therefore, is to present a separate monthly series of Money Stock, called M_4, which possesses an independent analytical value, analogous to M_3 but not identical with it.

Apportionment of Savings Deposits Balances between Time and Demand Deposits

Finally, the third aspect, namely, the criterion presently employed for apportioning, savings deposit balances with commercial and co-operative banks between demand and time deposit liabilities may be examined. The commercial banks have been advised, at present, to clarify, on the basis of their prescribed withdrawal facilities, that portion of the balance in a Savings Deposit account which is permitted to be withdrawn without notice, as demand deposit and the balance as time deposit. According to the Scheduled Banks' Regulations, 1951 framed by the Reserve Bank of India the actual apportionment of each savings account of a bank branch had to be undertaken twice a year — once for the last Friday of June and again for that of December; the proportion so obtained for all accounts in a branch had to be used for its total savings deposit balances for the following weeks/months.

As for the withdrawal facilities for the savings account-holders, it may be recalled that with the unification of the cash-reserve ratio in September 1962 (at 3 per cent for both time and demand liabilities against 2 per cent and 5 per cent, respectively), the scheduled commercial banks had resorted to competitive liberalisation of their deposits rules since April 1963.[30] Consequently, the demand liability portion of savings deposits of all scheduled commercial banks had risen rather sharply from 64.3 per cent at the end of March 1963 to 86.9 per cent at the end of March 1964 (see data presented in Appendix VI). Subsequently, again with the stipulation that interest rate paid on deposits for periods of less than 15 days should not exceed the rate allowed on current accounts, the short notice deposits were converted into demand deposits.

As a result, and also due to the continuance, though on a small scale, of the competitive liberalisations in saving deposit rules by different banks, there occurred a steady increase in this demand liability portion from 86.9 per cent in March 1964 to 92.2 per cent in March 1968. With a view to putting an end to the divergent practices followed by different banks and for bringing about some uniformity in this regard, the Indian Banks' Association amended, effective April 1, 1968, the rules on the number and amount of withdrawals from savings accounts framed under the then Inter-Bank Agreement on Deposit Rates.[31] This has had the effect of tightening the withdrawal facilities, which was reflected in a steep decline in the proportion of demand liability portion in saving deposits from 93.2 per cent in March 1968 to 84.5 per cent in March 1969. In March 1975 the proportion stood at 85.8 per cent, the fractional increase between March 1969 and March 1975 reflecting probably the shift in favour of small-size deposits.

Thus, what the banks now report as the current and time deposit portion of savings deposits is based on their rules regarding the withdrawal facilities framed by the Indian Banks' Association. Here the basic question is whether the banks do insist on the observance by the depositors of the rules in this regard; for there is a general impression that in practice the savings deposits are operated without any withdrawal restrictions. An analysis of data of the individual banks reveals that the demand liability portion of savings deposit balances reported by them differs widely from bank to bank, ranging from 90 per cent to 68 per cent. A part of the explanation for this is to be found in the bank-wise differences in the size-wise distribution of saving deposits, the proportion of demand liability portion being low in those banks which have a larger proportion of big-size deposits. The Group's discussion with bankers in this regard has revealed neither any conclusive evidence of large scale breach of the withdrawal rules nor any vast inter-bank differences in the practices followed. As it is, the time liability portion, attributable to withdrawal restrictions, forms only about 14 per cent of the total saving deposit balances of all scheduled commercial banks. Although the Working Group has not found any sound basis for disturbing the existing reporting practices in this regard, it would like to emphasise that a sample survey of saving deposits with a view to determining the current and time deposits components should be conducted at an interval of every five years.

In parentheses, it is necessary to refer here to another recent development.

Inclusion of Balances in Non-resident Accounts in Money Stock Measures

The Reserve Bank instituted in 1970 two schemes for attracting savings of non-resident Indians and aliens of Indian origin living abroad. The first scheme called the Non-Resident (External) Rupee Account was instituted, effective from March 1, 1970; in it the unit of account is the Indian rupee and the deposits could be in any type of deposit accounts. The second scheme introduced from November 1, 1975, is called the Foreign Currency (Non-Resident) Accounts which is designated in two convertible currencies namely, pound sterling and U.S. dollars. The balances under the first scheme (with rose from Rs. 6.08 crores on December 31, 1971 to Rs. 22 crores on December 31, 1974), have got merged with the figures of aggregate deposits of domestic origin and various components thereof, as reported by the scheduled commercial banks (authorised to deal in foreign exchange). For cash reserve and statutory liquidity purposes, such balances are treated on a par with the deposits of domestic origin.

However, the balances under the second scheme of foreign currency accounts (which are currently allowed to be maintained in fixed deposits) are being treated on a special footing with concessional provisions with regard to cash reserve and statutory liquidity requirements. Even so, considering the various aspects of these two schemes – their beneficiaries, facilities for local disbursements and for investments in approved areas — the Working Group feels that such balances reflect a potential monetary demand as any of the term deposits kept out of domestic savings. First, the beneficiaries are either Indians employed abroad — in diplomatic missions, in international organisations, or in the private sector — or, aliens of Indian origin, who have a stake in India, and who are likely to spend the balances in India. Secondly, to facilitate such domestic disbursements and/or domestic investments in certain specified areas like units of the Unit Trust of India, Government securities, some national Plan/Saving certificates, and also with some restrictions, shares of companies and in industry generally, liberal provisions have been made under the schemes. Local disbursements could be for purposes including tax payments. For these reasons the deposit balances under the second scheme should also be included under the appropriate money stock measures. This has been facilitated by the recent advice to banks to include such deposits under their time liabilities.

New Series of Money Supply Data

Against the background of the discussion so far, it has been possible for the Working Group to compile, as illustrative of the new series the data for four new measures of money stock, that is, M_1, M_2, M_3 and M_4, for the period beginning with March 1970.

The new series of data are provided in Statements 3 and 4. For obtaining a quick glance at the new series, the outstandings as well as variations in respect of a sample of the new series are presented in Tables 1 and 2 alongside the present series of data.

From these data, it becomes clear that generally speaking the rates of change in individual measures go on rising as one moves along the liquidity spectrum, i.e., from the most basic category M_1 to the more comprehensive category M_4.

SECTION 4

Sources of Change in Money Supply

In this Section the rationale underlying the analytical frame of what has come to be referred to as "Factors Affecting Money Supply" — a frame which forms an integral part of the present series of money supply data is examined. In the process of examination, it has also been possible to rationalise and simplify the compilation of the data relating to some constituent items.

TABLE 1: Money Stock Measures — Present and New

(*Rupees Crores*)

Year/Month/ Week	New Series				Present Series	
	M_1	M_2	M_3	M_4	Money supply with the public	Aggregate monetary resources
	1	2	3	4	5	6
Year						
(Last Friday of March)						
1969-70	6536	7433	9639	10635	6387	9336
1970-71	7321	8311	10958	12142	7140	10588
1971-72	8320	9366	12690	14106	8138	12314
1972-73	9684	10791	15033	16805	9413	14515
1973-74	11172	12424	17571	19843	10848	16952
1974-75	11911	13132	19462	22033	11557	18783
1975-76	13067	14346	22157	25145	12682	21389
Month						
June, 1975	12543	13704	20573	23154	12187	19869
September, 1975	12263	13434	20619	23305	11928	20006
December, 1975	12611	13777	21341	24110	12280	20715
March, 1976	13067	14346	22157	24145	12682	21389
Week						
March 5, 1976	13009		22095		12634	21341
March 12, 1976	13129		22234		12756	21486
March 19, 1976	13078		22133		12702	21382
March 26, 1976	13067		22157		12682	21389

Note: Details are presented in statement 3.

TABLE 2: Variations in Money Stock Measures

(*Rupees Crores*)

Year/Month/Week	New Series								Present Series			
	M_1		M_2		M_3		M_4		Money supply with the public		Aggregate monetary resources	
	Absolute	Percentage	Absolute	Percentage	Absolute	Percentage	Absolute	Percentage	Absolute	Percentage	Absolute	Percentage
1	2	3	4	5	6	7	8	9	10	11	12	13
Year (Last Friday of March)						**OVER THE YEAR**						
1970-71	+785	+12.0	+878	+11.8	+1319	+13.7	+1507	+14.2	+753	+11.8	+1252	+13.4
1971-72	+999	+13.6	+1055	+12.7	+1732	+15.8	+1964	+16.2	+998	+14.0	+1726	+16.3
1972-73	+1364	+16.4	+1425	+15.2	+2343	+18.5	+2699	+19.1	+1275	+15.7	+2201	+17.9
1973-74	+1488	+15.4	+1633	+15.1	+2538	+16.9	+3038	+18.1	+1435	+15.2	+2437	+16.8
1974-75	+739	+6.6	+708	+5.7	+1891	+10.8	+2190	+11.0	+709	+6.5	+1831	+10.8
1975-76	+1159	+9.7	+1214	+9.2	+2695	+13.8	+3112	+14.1	+1125	+9.7	+2606	+13.9
Month						**OVER THE QUARTER**						
June, 1975	+632	+5.3	+572	+4.3	+1111	+5.7	+1121	+5.1	+630	+5.5	+1086	+5.8
September, 1975	−280	−2.2	−270	−2.0	+46	+0.2	+151	+0.7	−259	−2.1	+137	+0.7
December, 1975	+348	+2.8	+343	+2.6	+722	+3.5	+805	+3.5	+352	+3.0	+709	+3.5
March, 1976	+456	+3.6	+569	+4.1	+816	+3.8	+1035	+4.3	+402	+3.3	+674	+3.3
Week						**OVER THE WEEK**						
March 12, 1976	+120	+0.9			+139	+0.6			+122	+1.0	+145	+0.7
March 19, 1976	−51	−0.4			−101	−0.5			−54	−0.4	−104	−0.5
March 26, 1976	−11	−0.1			+24	+0.1			−20	−0.2	+7	—

R.B.I.'s Analytical Frame

The basic approach of the analytical frame is to present the broad sectoral distribution of total domestic credit which, in a sense, may be regarded as the major source of variations in 'money stock'. In other words, such presentation is designed to trace the origin of money supply variations to specific sectors, which draw upon the credit from the banking system. In this sense, the frame is designed to indicate the sources of change in money supply.

This frame is no doubt an accounting identity. It is certainly not claimed that this frame is based on any theory, conventional or otherwise, of money supply determination. The determination of money supply, it should be recognized, is the result of a complex process of interaction between *monetary* and *real* sectors. Therefore, any meaningful theory of the money supply determination has to cut across the monetary sector and include variables also from the real sector. The real factors, for instance in terms of current and prospective output and investment, are as much important in the demand for bank credit as the banks' propensity and capacity to supply credit. In fact, these two aspects could be regarded as the conventional blades of the scissors.

Such a complex process of money supply determination cannot be ingrained into the system of presentation of primary monetary data. The choice of an explanation for the factors influencing money supply in such a system of data presentation has perforce to be made within the monetary sector. Such an explanation is nonetheless meaningful because the monetary sector's transactions with the rest of the economy are a manifestation with the complex interactions, referred to above.

Also the current mode of presentation has substantive operational advantages inasmuch as it facilitates credit planning and forecasting, based on the disaggregation of total domestic credit into major user sectors, consistent with *macro* level projections of the appropriate rate and quantum of increases in money supply. The need for this arises because in the Indian economy, the growth of money stock is not entirely left to the autonomously determined by say a mechanical multiple of some monetary base. In the Indian system, where the Central Bank intervention is more direct and where the sectoral flow of credit for any particular period is determined by the system of credit planning and credit rationing, both the monetary base and the money stock expansion have come to be regulated by the monetary authorities. This point has been forcefully brought out in a study by Bank for International Settlements (Basle) in the following words: "One might say that money supply is a variable that is independent of the behaviour of economic agents during periods of strictly enforced credit ceilings; at such times it would depend only on objectives set by the Central Bank and on the effectiveness of the techniques employed by the latter to achieve them."[32]

Money Multiplier Approach

At this stage the question may be asked: how relevant for the Indian situation is the customary practice of adopting the money-multiplier approach in monetary models? Baldly put this approach takes the so-called high-powered money base as exogenously given, and then attempts to relate the money stock to this base by a multiplier relationship incorporating those behavioural responses affecting the two ratios, viz., the currency/deposit ratio and the reserve/deposit ratio. However, as Goodhart[33] has effectively highlighted, this approach abstracts from the all main operational problems facing the Monetary Authority; the approach fails to take into account the difficulties confronting the Monetary Authority in achieving any desired level of the monetary base itself.

In the Indian situation where credit planning has been adopted in practice for a considerable period, such a mechanistic approach to money supply determination cannot acquire serious operational significance.

In contrast, the Bank's analytical frame which seeks to present a disaggregated picture of credit expansion, indicating sector 'sources' of credit expansion, is more useful for operational purposes. This is certainly not to deny totally the relevance of the multiplier technique of analysis. In fact this approach has been adopted for long-term projections of credit/money supply for, say, the Fourth and the Fifth Plan periods. All that is sought to be emphasized here is that the Bank's analytical frame provides a much better insight for the practical formulation of monetary policy, especially in the short run.

The present Working Group after having given considerable thought to the possibility of any alternative presentation which would be conceptually more satisfying and operationally more useful has come to the conclusion that insofar as the primary data on money supply and factors influencing it are concerned, the current presentation is most appropriate. It is futile to attempt to build into such a frame of the primary data on money supply and factors influencing thereon, any theory of money supply determination if the result is the emergence of a mechanistic formula of little relevance to the realities of the Indian situation. Therefore, it has not been found necessary to depart from the basic frame of presentation of 'Factors affecting money supply', as evolved by the 1961 Working Group.

Briefly, under this framework,[34] the economy has been divided into two sectors:

(a) Government Sector (comprising Central and State Governments); and
(b) Commercial Sector (comprising the rest of the domestic sectors including the rest of the public sector as well as the foreign sector).

Sectoral Disaggregation and Refinement of Data

The transactions of each of the sectors with the banking system (comprising the Reserve Bank of India and the commercial and co-operative banks) are identified in terms of the variations in the banking sector's financial monetary assets and net non-monetary liabilities. The 1961 Working Group had made a special and detailed description of the difficulties in segregating the transactions of the external sector (comprising foreign companies, institutions and non-resident individuals) with the banking sector and hence had rightly suggested the inclusion of those transactions with the domestic commercial sector. Likewise, it was not possible to segregate, from the variations in the foreign assets of the Reserve Bank, the Government sector's purchases and sales of foreign exchange. The variations in the foreign exchange assets of the banking sector are a combined result of its transactions with the Government sector, the domestic commercial sector and the external sector.

Within this conceptual framework evolved by the 1961 Working Group, the present Working Group has proposed some changes in the methods of compilation of factors affecting money supply, which incidentally would facilitate credit planning exercises. These changes broadly fall under two categories: first, enlargement of the coverage of data by the inclusion of those in respect of Central co-operative banks and primary co-operative banks [which has already been discussed in Section (3)] and secondly, refinements in the methodology of compilation. A detailed explanation of these changes is presented in Appendix III. A brief description of major changes proposed and their *rationale* is presented here.

Mechanics of arriving at Bank Credit to Commercial Sector

The mechanics of arriving at 'bank credit to commercial sector' involves now a circuitous method. From the figure of bank credit comprising: (i) loans, cash credit and overdrafts, and (ii) bills purchase and discounted relating to every segment of banking (except the RBI) the sum of a series of inter-bank liabilities *minus* inter-bank assets is netted out. The logic of this was explained by the 1961 Working Group in these words; "Under Item (d) — banks' loans and advances to the private sector[35] — the excess of inter-bank assets over inter-bank liabilities is also included; for, though money at call and short notice is usually regarded as an inter-bank asset, it also arises as a result of advance to the private sector and such advances are represented, by and large, by the *excess* of inter-bank assets over inter-bank liabilities.[36]

Conceptually, all inter-bank assets of the entire banking sector have to be "balanced" by its inter-bank liabilities. If in practice there is no such balance or equivalence, it may be because of the imperfection in data, items-in-transit, exclusion of data in respect of certain banking segments and the like. The circuitous method had some relevance, for instance, when important segments of the co-operative sector such as the Central co-operative banks and primary co-operative banks were not fully covered in money supply. Now, with the fuller coverage, these deficiencies have been overcome. It is also observed from the actual data that for the scheduled commercial banks, the inter-bank liabilities have exceeded inter-bank assets (and not the other way about) which in effect tended to depress their credit to commercial sector (Statement 1). A part of the explanation for this is to be found in the inclusion in their inter-bank liabilities, the commercial banks' borrowings from outside the banking system — from LIC and UTI in the Call Money Market, and from IDBI and ARDC under their refinance scheme (dealt with in detail in a subsequent paragraph).

The excess of inter-bank liabilities over inter-bank assets with the scheduled commercial banks does not find a corresponding amount of inter-bank net assets, in any other segment of the banking sector. Besides, there is rarely any possibility of the figures of bank credit by the scheduled commercial banks being duplicated necessitating adjustment through inter-bank liabilities.

In the circumstances, it is improper to adjust 'bank credit to commercial sector' by the amount representing the *excess* of inter-bank liabilities over inter-bank assets or *vice versa*; it would only result in the distortion of actual bank credit. Such *excess*, if any, should appropriately from part of the net non-monetary liabilities of commercial and co-operative banks which would also contain an element of errors and omissions.[37]

It is, therefore, proposed in the compilation of the new series of data to dispense with the adjustments now being made in regard to inter-bank assets and inter-bank liabilities, for the purpose of working out bank credit to commercial sector.

Secondly, in the present method, borrowings from IDBI and ARDC by commercial and co-operative banks are shown as inter-bank liabilities and hence, as deductible items against the bank credit extended by them. This is done with a view to obviating the double-counting of bank credit to commercial sector. The Reserve Bank's lending to IDBI and ARDC is reckoned in 'RBI credit to commercial sector'. IDBI and ARDC channel a part of the funds through the commercial and co-operative banks to the ultimate borrowers. In order to avoid double-counting of the bank credit figure, this amount should conceptually be reduced from the commercial and co-operative bank credit. However, sources of funds of IDBI and ARDC comprise, in addition to borrowings, paid-up capital and reserves, borrowings from Government, borrowings by way of bonds, etc., which are also used for refinancing eligible loans granted by commercial banks. These sources other than RBI contribute the bulk of their funds. It is, therefore, incorrect to deduct the entire borrowings from IDBI and ARDC. At the same time, it is difficult to segregate, from the banks' total borrowings from IDBI and ARDC, that amount which is attributable to funds provided to the latter by the RBI. Although a small proportion of bank credit will be inevitably reckoned twice, first under RBI credit and then under the other banks' credit, as a matter of operational expediency, it has been proposed not to make any adjustment in respect of the banks' borrowings from IDBI and ARDC.

Lastly, it is found that State Governments lend to the State co-operative banks, which on the face of it has been implications for both 'bank credit to the Government sector' and 'bank credit to the commercial sector'. The figures of 'net bank credit to the Government sector' should, in the normal course, be adjusted by the quantum of such State Government lendings to the State co-operative banks. A closer examination of the nature of these lendings however, how that they are made essentially for performing certain agency functions for and on behalf of the State Governments, such as the monopoly procurement of cotton by the Maharashtra Government, *taccavy* loans of various State Governments and other activities. Hence, it would be inappropriate to make any adjustment in the 'net bank credit to Government'. Besides, as the operations made out of these borrowings by the State co-operative banks are not included in 'bank credit' figure, there is no adjustment needed in 'bank credit to commercial sector' either.

On these lines, the constituent items under other banks' (other than the RBI) credit to the commercial sector would now be: (1) loans, cash credit and overdrafts; (ii) inland and foreign bills purchased and discounted (which together constitute what is commonly called the 'bank credit'); and (iii) investments in approved securities, company and co-operative shares/debentures, etc.

This method is consistently employed in respect of all the categories of banks covered by the money supply data. In respect of the co-operative sector, in view of its three-tier structure, care has been taken to avoid double counting of bank credit. For this purpose, credit extended by each of the tiers only to individuals and other co-operative societies (outside the banking sector) has been taken into account.

A few other changes effected in the presentation of the "Sources of Changes in M_1" which have hitherto been designated as "Factors affecting money supply", are indicated in Appendix III.

Reserve Money: Components and Determinants

Finally, a point about reserve money. At present data on reserve money, its components and factors influencing it are presented only once a year in the Bank's *Report on Currency and Finance*. As these data would be of interest to research workers, it is proposed to publish these data regularly, on a monthly basis, in the Bank's *Bulletin*.

Details regarding the items included in the compilation of the components of reserve money and sources of change in reserve money are presented in Appendix IV of this Report. Data on these are presented in Statement Nos. 6 and 7.

SECTION 5

Miscellaneous Near-Money Assets and Money Stock Measures

In the process of considering different money stock measures, a variety of what might be referred to as near-money assets suggested themselves as "potential candidates" for inclusion in them. A number of them were eventually found to be unacceptable, either because of the basic conceptual intelligibility or operational difficulties. However, the Group felt that it would be useful to place on record the main considerations which led the Working Group to reject their claims for inclusion in different money stock measures. This section takes up for discussion such issues.

The five issue discussed here are a mixed bag: these are Government deposits with the Reserve Bank, cheques in the process of collection, unutilised credit limits, trade credit and deposits with non-banking companies.

Exclusion of Government Deposits from Money Stock Measures

The deposit balances of the Central and State Governments kept with the Reserve Bank of India are now being excluded from money supply with the public. The main reasons for doing so are: first, it is necessary to draw a distinction between money-creating and money-holding sectors. The Central Government has the prerogative of creating money and borrowing on a scale that is not open to subordinate units in the polity,[38] and though there are limits to the borrowing power of the States, there is such a great deal of resources flow between the Centre and States that no meaningful distinction could be made between the two. Secondly, these deposit balances, are the result of the non-commercial, administrative operations of the Government. Lastly, these balances could also be used as instruments of stabilisation of the economy to offset variations in the balances of the public.[39] It is doubtful if, among these, the last argument has any more operational validity. The use of this instrument to achieve monetary policy objectives is possible only if the overall finances of the Government alternate between budgetary surpluses and deficits and in a situation as in India where Government resorts to deficit financing almost persistently, the scope for using these as a monetary instrument does hardly exist. As these balances are maintained at least technically at a cost to the national exchequer because of the interest-bearing nature of the rising Government debt to the Central Bank of the country, these balances are generally kept, as a policy, at a low level.[40]

Even so, when looked at from the angle of Government's indebtedness to the Central Bank which is generally an important source of currency and consequently money supply expansion, it is necessary to make adjustment for their cash balances. The concept of Centre's deficit financing, for instance, is so defined as to exclude cash balances built from the increase in its indebtedness through treasury bills during a given year. The Government's operations here should be distinguished from those of the commercial entities on the important consideration that its purchasing power is not even limited by the quantum of its balances with the Central Bank, that technically such purchasing power is unlimited arising from its prerogative of creating money, and that, therefore, the inclusion of such cash balances would hardly add to any refinement in any money stock measures.[41]

This still leaves the question of Government balances arising from mostly non-commercial administrative operations of the Government. As the 1961 Working Group had noted some constituents of these Government balances with the Reserve Bank emanated from commercial departments of the Government such as the Railways and the Posts and Telegraphs, and these are akin to the deposit balances of any other commercial entities. But it is difficult to disaggregate such balanced into those arising from commercial operations and those from administrative operations, because of the continuous and significant shift of resources between the two constituents. In the budget of the Central Government, revenue and expenditure of the Railways are charged to the 'Consolidated Fund of India', thereby indicating for instance, that the sources and uses of funds of the Central Government and the Railways are interlinked. In the newly prepared manual on Government finance statistics, the International Monetary Fund (IMF) has recommended the suggestion of the commercial (such as the railways) and administrative segments of the Government budget.[42] Once this is done, it should be possible to segregate from Government balances those arising from commercial operations and treat the latter rightly as part of the money stock measures.[43] For the present, operationally, there is no alternative but to continue the existing practice of excluding the entire portion of Government balances from money stock measures.

Another point which becomes clear from the above discussion is that it would be improper to make a distinction between the public and private sector commercial enterprises insofar as the inclusion of their deposit balances in money stock measures is concerned, irrespective of whether those deposits are kept with the Reserve Bank or with the commercial banks. Though there are also transfers from the Government to Public Sector enterprises, such transfers are in the nature of investment in shares and debt obligations of the latter, directly linked to their manufacturing and commercial activities, and rarely in terms of grants or of sharing current revenues.

Irrelevance of Cheques in the Process of Collection for Money Stock Measures

In the United States of America (USA), cheques in the process of collection within the banking system are deducted from the gross demand deposit figures so as to avoid duplication. This is justified on the ground of the practice followed by commercial banks as well as Federal Reserve System in America of giving credit to the payees before cheques are debited into the account of the issuers.[44] In the United Kingdom, too, deduction for the transit items is made on the same ground but it is restricted to those of the deposit banks and also the total of the transit items as are apportioned between bank deposits and advances on the ground that such items tend to double-count deposits and undervalue bank credit, particularly where overdrawn or loans accounts are concerned.[45]

Banking facilities and banking habit are far more developed in countries like the U.S.A. or U.K. than in India. But more than the growth of banking habit and facilities, the relative relevance of cheques in the process of collection to demand deposits lies in the practices adopted by banks in giving prompt credit to the customers. According to the practices adopted by the Indian banks, the scope for such duplication of bank deposits does not exist because, by and large, all the banks — Indian as well as foreign banks operating in India — do not give credit for the payees' accounts before debiting the cheques into accounts of those who issue such cheques. The Banking Commission had, in fact, deplored the inordinate delays in the collection of local cheques by banks which in certain cases took as many as eight days for realisation. "The most frequent complaint against banks relates to the delays in collection of outstation cheques and bills, and prompt return thereof in case of non-payments."[46] It is difficult to state if the situation has improved since then, but it is obvious that no bank has adopted the practice of giving credit to payees' accounts prior to the clearance of the relevant cheques. In this regard, the Banking Commission had made the suggestion that the Banks should consider cheques or drafts realised and proceeds credited to the customer's accounts, if these are not returned unpaid or dishonoured within specified periods.[47]

Where the banks do credit to the payee's account prior to the clearance of the cheque, it is treated as an overdraft facility and hence becomes part of the bank credit. Since this is based on the creditworthiness of the payee such a facility represents additional purchasing power for a temporary period. Therefore, there is no case for deducting such overdrawn amounts at all from the deposit money. There could be cases where some cheques in the process of collection might emanate from overdraft or cash credit facilities.

Status of Unutilised Credit Limits

The existence of substantial ***unused bank credit limits*** is a phenomenon following from "the present cash credit system of lending, where a banker sanctions a maximum limit within which the borrower can draw at his will."[48] "The more important factors responsible for unused credit limits can be enumerated:"[49] the normal leads and lags in the sanctioning of credit limits and their use, the system of determining the bank credit requirements at the peak of the procurement or manufacturing seasons in respect of seasonal industries or sectors, failure to determine the credit requirements rather accurately and hence a built-in tendency for asking limits higher than strictly necessary, experience of past credit squeezes and expectations of future ones inducing borrowers to ask for higher limits and the general tendency of the larger and more influential borrowers to inflate credit requirements and of banks to grant them so as to retain such borrowers. In terms of dimensions, while the extent of unused credit limit is high in cash credit and overdraft facilities (ranging from 38 per cent to 40 per cent), it is the highest in bill finance (about 50 per cent); there is a sizeable element even in demand loans and term loans (about 25 per cent) (see Appendix VII). Such under-utilisation persisted even when there was a commitment charge on the unused portion of the cash credit limits.

The essential question involved here is whether the existence of such unused credit limits 'really hampers the effectiveness of monetary policy'[50] and whether, consequently, such limits should be included in any money stock measure. A closer examination of this phenomenon and the causes responsible for it suggests that the degree of idle credit implied in unused credit limits is generally exaggerated. Take bill finance, for instance, in which the unused credit limit is the highest. Borrowing parties cannot make use of unused credit without the creation of bills or without the existence of book debts against which bills are created. The use is thus conditioned by the actual quantum of physical transactions. It is generally so even with regard to cash credit limits and overdraft facilities, the utilisation of which cannot be resorted to an unlimited extent, for the simple reason that it has to be backed by the requisite quantum of collaterals, and also with a margin.

In other words, a good part of the unutilized portion of credit limits arises from the technical considerations of leads and lags, of the failure of collaterals and transactions to match the credit limits obtained. This is evident from the fact that even during the peak of recent inflationary spiral of 1972 to 1974, the unused portion of total bank credit or of individual types of accounts (for credit other than food procurement) had remained by and large unchanged at around 40 to 45 per cent (Appendix VII). There was no doubt, a sharp decline in the unused portion between June 1974 and December 1974, but this was entirely due to the credit rationing and the consequential reduction in absolute terms in the aggregate of credit limits themselves for Rs. 11930 crores in June 1974 to Rs. 11360 crores in December 1974. This implies that the existence of relatively large limits in the earlier period did not raise the overall utilisation ratio in a period of severe inflation. Nor did the cutting down of the aggregate limits prevent the use of the required quantum of credit.

This does not mean that the size of unused credit limits is not of any consequence to credit policy formulation. It is of utmost importance in determining the 'potential' demand for credit. Even so, what proportion of it represents credit limits beyond the requirements of technical considerations of leads and lags, seasonality, the expectations of prices and policies and the like, is difficult to determine.

Even on statistical grounds, inclusion of a uniform percentage of unused limits in any money supply series will not improve the series. The position of analogous to the findings of a statistical study of selected countries — "that the variability of circulation consequent upon the inclusion of unused overdrafts was so small relative to the commercial velocity of money (excluding unused overdrafts) as to be unimportant."[51] Therefore, the Working Group feels that it is not desirable to include the unused portion of credit limits in any money stock measures.

Trade Credit and Money Stock Measures

An alternative source of liquidity is the availability of trade or commercial credit. Generally speaking, while the granting of trade credit is a normal feature of the trading and commercial activities, its magnitude and average duration get expanded during periods of credit stringency. This destabilising nature of trade credit was noted by the classical economists, but its importance as a threat to monetary policy based on conventional indicators came to be highlighted with the publication of the Radcliffe Committee Report. Subsequent empirical studies on the subject in the developed countries have been conclusive neither in regard to the concept of trade credit (gross or net) nor the extent of their destabilising effects.[52] Nevertheless, in contemporary literature on the subject, there is a general consensus that trade credit is a potential threat to monetary policy based on conventional indicators. The Radcliffe Committee was emphatic that trade credit should not be netted out by deducting commercial credit obtained from credit given; the Committee observed, it is "no more reasonable to net out commercial credit in this way than it would be to net out bank loans and bank deposits."[53] This is as it should be because in a set of combined statistics on the corporate sector (manufacturing and trading) as a whole for instance, trade credit obtained by some firms (and thus included in liabilities) will also appear as trade credit given by others in the group (as assets) except to the extent the transactions based on trade credit take place outside the group. A single firm gets trade credit generally for its purchases of inputs and gives credit for the sale of its finished products, each one thus augmenting demand for independent products. Therefore, the principle of netting out is indefensible on theoretical as well as practical considerations.

On a gross basis, the size of trade credit obtained by the corporate sector in India (both public and private together) is substantial as could be seen from the data in Appendix VIII. The quantum of such trade credit obtained by the corporate sector as a whole has always been on the uptrend consistent with the expanding role of this sector in the initial stages of development. A part of the expansion in such credit is, therefore, more a result of natural growth attributable to the sector's growth itself, than a reaction to the rigour of bank credit policy. Even so, the fact that the rate of expansion in such credit in individual years has varied broadly in correspondence with the degree of stringency or otherwise in commercial bank credit lends credence to the general concensus that trade credit is a method of obviating the rigours of monetary policy. Therefore, the size and direction of such commercial credit deserves to be watched closely.

However, the inclusion of such trade credit data in any money stock measure is operationally beset with many problems, some almost intractable. First, trade credit data can be obtained and compiled only in respect of that received by the corporate sector among the firms engaged in trading and manufacturing activities, while trade credit system is obviously prevalent in all the sectors of the economy. Even within the secondary sector (comprising manufacturing, construction and electricity, gas and water supply), about half of the net domestic product could be said to be originating in unregistered and unorganised sectors for which no such data could be obtained. Secondly, even in respect of the corporate sector, operationally it would be a stupendous task getting regular weekly or monthly or even annual data to correspond to other money stock measures and to be useful for seasonal or short-term credit policy formulations. Obviously, such data have to be culled out from the annual balance sheets of the companies. Lastly, even the figures of combined balance sheets fail to represent those at a single point of time because of the differences in reference periods of company balance sheets. There is also the question of window-dressing and the degree of dependability of the balance sheet data. Hence, there is no alternative but to exclude trade credit from the money stock measures proposed by the Working Group.

Exclusion of Deposits accepted by Non-Banking Intermediaries from Money Stock Measures

The broad theoretical and conceptual considerations relevant for drawing a distinction between monetary and non-monetary financial institutions have been set out in Section 1. This distinction based on their functional differentiation led the Working Group to exclude deposits accepted by non-banking intermediaries from any money stock measures. The group of these non-banking intermediaries covers such a wide range that it would be necessary to review albeit briefly the nature of their liabilities and see if those liabilities have any characteristics similar to the constituent items of money stock measures. In the recent period, the role of all these non-banking intermediaries (NBIs) has been subjected to detailed enquiries by the Banking Commission set up by the Reserve Bank.[54] Among these NBIs, there is a set of financial institutions in the country, viz., development banks (IDBI, ICICI, SFCs and IRCI), insurance companies, and the Unit Trust of India, which work in highly specialized fields. The second set of financial companies, which are enumerated in clause (p) of paragraph 2(1) of the Non-Banking Financial Companies (Reserve Bank) Directions, 1966, and "which mobilise savings of the community by way of deposits or otherwise and utilize them for the purpose of lending or investment;"[55] these include hire-purchase finance companies housing finance companies, investment companies, loan companies, mutual benefit financial companies, chit fund companies and miscellaneous financial companies. There is a great degree of functional specialisation in each of these categories. These non-banking financial intermediaries (NBFIs) do not ordinarily accept demand deposits with the notable exception of the mutual benefit financial companies, called *Nidhis.*[56] Their liabilities are essentially term liabilities. The last set of these non-banking intermediaries belongs to the non-banking non-financial category, mostly trading and manufacturing concerns, which are accepting deposits from the public for use in their own businesses and hence these are not financial intermediaries in the accepted sense of the term.

Broadly, it could be said that the importance of the deposits accepted by the NBIs is rising; the percentage of company deposits to the aggregate deposits of the scheduled commercial banks rose to around 11.0 in March 1975, from about 9.7 at the end of March 1972.

Among these deposits, the share of non-banking non-financial companies constitutes the bulk at about 70 per cent, the remaining 30 per cent belonging to the non-banking financial intermediaries. Within these financial categories, loan companies and hire-purchase companies accounted for 65 per cent of the total deposits of the NBFIs.

In the past, the impetus to the growth of deposits accepted by both financial and non-financial companies has stemmed first, from the existence of the Keynesian "fringe of unsatisfied borrowers". The borrowers also enjoy certain advantages, the most important of them being the freedom from financial discipline either on end-use or on security and margins imposed by the organised commercial or development banks. Thirdly, there is the incentive to depositors in the form of higher interest rates offered.

Without trying to assess in qualitative terms, the role of these NBIs in augmenting aggregate demand, it could be said that:

(a) acceptance of deposits by NBIs entails a pre-emption of the scarce investible resources in the country which in turn engenders an imbalance in the resource allocation,
(b) their operations, however small, have the effect of diluting the Central Bank measures both with regard to the norms of lending and end-use of credit, and with regard to the ceiling on interest rates on deposits accepted by bank, and
(c) their liabilities primarily in term deposits are generally competitive to deposits with the commercial banks.

Notwithstanding the fact that their operations are outside the orbit of monetary institutions, the usefulness of such data on the liabilities of NBIs — both financial and non-financial — is not in question.

It is, therefore, necessary to collect detailed data and information about the size of the liabilities with a view to exercising more effective monetary control on these deposits.

Lastly, reference may be made to some loan companies and *nidhis* which, to quote the Study Group Report "are incipient' banks and there is hardly any distinction in their methods of operations and those of banks."[57] The Study Group had recommended that provisions may be made to enable these types of companies to convert themselves into commercial or co-operative banks. It is also believed that with the suggested enactment of comprehensive legislation to regulate the working of the NBIs, the functioning of these would, in due course, come on a par with that of banks. In such an eventuality, the prescription of regular statistical returns would possibly facilitate the inclusion of liabilities of these institutions in appropriate of money stock measures.

NOTES

1. The Report of that Working Group was published in July and August 1961 issues of the *Reserve Bank of India Bulletin*.
2. The Group wrote thus : "Hence, though time liabilities should not be included in the compilation of money supply data, it is necessary to show separately the total of money supply and time liabilities (including post office savings deposits), as is done in some countries like France, Belgium and Canada. The aggregate of money supply and time liabilities is more meaningful than money supply as such for some analytical purposes related to the formulation of monetary policies." "Analysis of Money Supply in India — I," *Reserve Bank of India Bulletin*, July 1961, p. 1049.
3. For the reformulation of the 'modern quantity theory' see Milton Friedman: "The Quantity Theory of Money — A Restatement" in Milton Friedman (Ed.): *Studies in the Quantity Theory of Money* (The University of Chicago Press, 1956), pp. 3-21. For the empirical results, see Milton Friedman: "The Demand for Money: Some Theoretical and Empirical Results," *Journal of Political Economy*, vol. 67 (August 1959), pp. 327-351. Also other essays in *Studies in the Quantity Theory of Money, op.cit.*
4. Ronalt L. Teigen, "The Demand for and Supply of Money," in W.L. Smith and R.L. Teigen (Ed.) *Readings in Money, National Income and Stabilisation Policy* (Richard D. Irwin, Inc., Homewood, Illionois, 1970), p. 88 Harry G. Johnson writes the same: "But there is no necessary conflict, since Friedman's definition of money includes time deposits and may therefore absorb most of the substitution between demand deposits and currency and interest-bearing assets induced by interest-rate changes." See his "Monetary Theory and Policy" in the American Economic Association and the Royal Economic Society: *Surveys of Economic Theory: Money, Interest and Welfare* — Vol. 1 (Macmillan, 1968, p. 19).
5. This portion draws heavily from the now famous survey article of Harry G. Johnson: "Monetary Theory and Policy" *(ibid)*.
6. 'Immeasurable' because of their vagueness in defining liquidity. To quote their Report: "Though we do not regard the supply of money as an unimportant quantity we view it as only part of wider structure of liquidity . . . it is the whole structure of liquidity that is relevant to spending decisions. A decision to spend depends not simply on whether the would-be spender has cash or money in the bank. There is the alternative of raising funds by selling an asset or by borrowing. . . . The spending is not limited by the amount of money in existence; but it is related to the amount of money people think they can get hold of, whether by receipts of income by disposal of capital assets or by borrowing."

The Report of the Committee on the Working of the Monetary System (London, 1959).

7. John G. Gurley: "The Radcliffe Committee Report and Evidence," *American Economic Review*, Vol. 50 (September 1960), pp. 672-700.
8. John G. Gurley and Edward S. Shaw: "Financial intermediaries and the Saving Investment Process," *Journal of Finance,* Vol. XI (May 1956) pp. 260-261. Also in their principal theoretical work on the subject, they observe thus: "Non-monetary intermediaries are competitors of the Governmental monetary system," *Money in a Theory of Finance,* the Brookings Institutions, Washington, 1960, p. 228.
9. Harry G. Johnson, *op. cit.*, p. 17.
10. Milton Friedman and David Meiselman: "The Relative Stability of Monetary Velocity and the Investment Multiplier in the United States, 1897-1958" in *Commission on Money and Credit: Stabilization Policies* (Englewood Cliffs, New Jersey, 1963). See also Frederick C. Schadrack "An Empirical Approach to the Definitions of Money" in *Monetary Aggregates and Monetary Policy* (Federal Reserve Bank of New York, 1974 pp. 28-34).
11. Timberlake and Fortson conclude that time deposits have a poor explanatory power in predicating income. See R.H. Timberlake and J. Fortson: "Time Deposits in the Definition of Money," *American Economic Review*, Vol. 57, March 1967 pp. 190-193.
12. John G. Gurley: "Liquidity and Financial Institutions in the Post-War Period," *Study of Employment, Growth and Price Levels* (Study Paper No. 14), Joint Economic Committee, 86th Congress (Ist Session), Washington, 1960.
13. V.K. Chetty: "On Measuring the Nearness of Near Moneys," *American Economic Review*, Vol. 59, June 1969, pp. 270-281. See for reviews of these studies, Ronald S. Koot: "A factor Analytic Approach to an Empirical Definition of Money," *The Journal of Finance,* September 1975, pp. 1081-1089.
14. The phrase is from John G. Gurley and Edward S. Shaw: Money in a Theory of Finance, *op. cit.*, p. 192.
15. The first three issues are based on a paper by Warren L. Smith: "Financial Intermediaries and Monetary Controls," *Quarterly Journal of Economics,* Vol. 73 (November 1959), p. 533-553.
16. *Ibid.*, p. 535.
17. To quote the International Monetary Fund's (IMF) practice adopted for its Monetary Survey regularly published in the International Financial Statistics (IFS), "The current IFS practice is to classify as deposit money banks those institutions whose demand deposit liabilities are a predominant part of their total liabilities and to treat as other financial institutions those institutions whose demand deposit liabilities are clearly insignificant." *A mimeographed note on Monetary and Financial Survey* (IMF, 1975).
18. In the context the Working Group gave considerable thought to the most commonly cited notion of high-powered money and money multiplier and was inclined to agree with the following observations made by Goodhart: "For such reasons it is common, indeed customary in monetary models to take the high-powered money base as exogenously given, determined off stage and then to relate the money stock to this base by a multiplier relationship incorporating those behavioural responses affecting the two ratios involved. This approach,

however, abstracts from all the main operational problems facing the authorities. It reveals nothing about the difficulties possibly confronting the authorities in achieving any desired level for the monetary bases. It suggests by itself nothing of the implications for interest rates, markets and financial institutions of the authorities' choice of targets and market procedures. It gives no idea of the underlying forces with which the authorities may have to contend in controlling the money stock. Indeed in making the initial assumption that the monetary base is under their control, all their operational problems are implicitly assumed to have been resolved. Just as the algebra of the banking multiplier effectively obscures the underlying behavioural process of portfolio adjustment in response to relative prices, so the assumption of an exogenously given monetary base effectively obscures consideration of the real problems facing the monetary authorities and their responses to such problems. So a first step is to abandon the assumption that the high-powered money base is given. Instead we may start by proceeding to an examination of the factors determining the outstanding totals of all the various forms of the Government debt extent including the cash liabilities of the public sector. In order to do this, it is helpful to turn to yet another accounting identity taken from the accounts of the flow of funds which describes how the financial deficit (or surplus) of each Sector is financed by flow of funds through the various financial markets." C.A.E. Goodhart: *Money, Information and Uncertainty* — Macmillan London — Also see Section 4 of this Report.

19. 'Analysis of Money Supply in India — I,' *Reserve Bank of India Bulletin,* July 1961, p. 1046.
20. 'Monetary institutions comprise the Central Bank, or monetary authorities, and those banks whose liabilities include deposits payable on demand, often referred to as deposit money banks. Statistics for these two sub-sectors are combined to yield the monetary survey.' IMF : *A Manual on Government Finance Statistics,* (June 1974), p. 32.
21. Non-credit co-operative institutions are obviously to be left out of account because they do not perform banking functions; accepting deposits from the public and lending and maintaining liabilities withdrawable on demand. Likewise, the land development banks both at the state and primary levels belong to the category of development banks, and do not carry on normal banking business.
22. See *Reserve Bank of India's Annual Report for 1965-66* (Bombay, 1966), pp. 29-30.
23. The Government of India's *Banking Commission* (1972) recommended a far wider definition to include the acceptance for deposits whether by a person or body corporate or co-operative society and whether for lending or for investment in one's own business. (Its *Report*, Chapter 19, pp. 469-510). This appears to have been done in the context of the need to protect the depositors' interest. On the other hand, functionally, there is substance in the concept of 'banking' as an institution that accepts deposits withdrawable on demand and used for lending.
24. "Land Mortgage Banks, all primary agricultural credit societies and those primary non-agricultural societies having paid-up capital and reserves of less than rupees one lakh are excluded from the purview of this legislation": See

RBI's *Annual Report* 1965-66, *op. cit.* p. 29.

25. These are available in the Statistical Tables relating to the Co-operative Movement in India, the latest being for 1974-75. (Bombay 1975).
26. In any case, it is recommended that the position be again reviewed after, say, a period of five years.
27. The principle involved here is as described in the IMF's *A Manual on Government Finance Statistics:* "In addition to institutions engaged in ordinary commercial banking activities, the deposit money banks sub-sector includes any demand deposits liabilities of the Treasury or other Government bodies, including the postal checking system" *op. cit.* p. 34.
28. "Analysis of Money Supply in India-I", *op. cit.* p. 1049.
29. Based on discussions with postal authorities. The turnover rate for deposits with commercial banks was as per a survey for 1966, about 2.2 for fixed deposits, 2.5 for saving deposits, 45.0 for current accounts and 13.6 per cent for all deposits together. See *Reserve Bank of India Bulletin,* March 1970.
30. "Various banks have in recent years been progressively classifying savings deposits, . . . as demand deposits following the competitive liberalisation by them of saving deposits rules since April 1963, a process which may have been facilitated by the unification of the cash reserve ratio in September 1962. . . . The other classificatory change follows from the prescription of the Reserve Bank in September 1964 that the rate of interest paid on deposits from periods of less than 15 days should not exceed the rate allowed on current accounts, as a result of which deposits at short notice, have been converted into demand deposits." See *Trend and Progress of Banking in India, 1964 — Reserve Bank of India*, p. 13.
31. See *Indian Banks' Association's Annual Report: 1968,* pp. 13-14. The new rules are: (i) the total number of withdrawals from Savings Bank Account during any quarter will not exceed 25; and (ii) the total amount of one or more withdrawals made by a depositor on any day shall not exceed 10 per cent of the balance in the account or Rs. 1,000 whichever is greater, unless 10 days' advance notice is given.
32. *The Money Supply, Economic Activity and Prices; Bank for International Settlements* — Basle, September 1972.
33. C.A.E. Goodhart, *Money, Information and Uncertainty*, Macmillan, London.
34. For a detailed discussion of this framework, see 'Analysis of Money Supply in India—I", *op. cit.*, pp. 1051-1067.
35. Subsequently amended to be the "Commercial Sector", See Appendix I.
36. "Analysis of Money Supply in India-I", *op. cit.*, p. 1064.
37. The 'errors and omissions' are unavoidable in a compressed version of data compiled from myriad items of assets and liabilities obtained from a multiple of branches of banking institutions.
38. A.G. Chandavarkar: "State Governments' Balance and Money Supply with the Public in India" (An unpublished note).
39. "Analysis of Money Supply in India-I" p. 1046.
40. A.G. Chandavarkar has brought out how " both in unitary and federal States, there are distinct institutional constraints on the use of Government cash balances as a monetary instrument." See his "Government Balances as a Monetary Policy Instrument in the Less Developed Countries," *Economic and*

Political Weekly, August 26, 1972, pp. 1785-1790.

41. In the United Kingdom, the broader M_3 money stock measure includes public sector deposits (public sector comprising Central Government, local authorities and public operations); all of these public sector deposits are excluded from M_1 (which includes only U.K. private sector sterling sight deposits). Besides U.K. has large amounts of non-sterling deposits which are also included in M_3. In India, it is considered improper to make any distinction between the commercial entities in the public sector and those in the private sector and to exclude the deposits of the former kept with commercial banks from M_1 or M_2. Also conceptually the money stock measures M_1 to M_3 should comprise assets generally with a descending order of liquidity. For details on U.K.'s money stock measures, see "The Stock of Money," *Bank of England Quarterly Bulletin*, September 1970, p. 320, and notes on Table 12 (Money Stock) and Table 12 in any regular issues of the *Bulletin*. In the United States, too, a case is being made in certain circles for including Government deposits in M_1 but this is primarily because such deposits are also kept with commercial banks. See Paul S. Anderson and Frank E. Morris: "Defining the Money Supply: The Case of Government Deposits," *New England Economic Review* (Federal Reserve Bank of Boston), March-April 1969 and Boris P. Pesek and Thomas R. Savings: *The Foundations of Money and Banking*" (New York, Macmillan & Co., 1968).
42. IMF: A Manual on Government Finance Statistics, *op. cit.*
43. If they are continued to be kept with the Reserve Bank of India, the Railways' balances will be included in "other deposits with RBI" which is a constituent item of M_1 (and other money stock measures) and in which are included the deposits of development banks (IDBI, IFCI, SFCs, DIC), IMF A/c No. 2, IBRD, foreign central banks and others.
44. The system is described thus: "In computing the demand deposits adjusted component of the money stock measures, cash items in the process of collection and Federal Reserve float are deducted from gross demand deposits. The main reason for these deductions is to avoid the so-called "double counting" of deposit balances that otherwise would occur when checks drawn on money stock deposit accounts at one bank and deposited in money stock deposit accounts in other banks are in the process of collection." See "Revision of Money Stock Measures and Member Bank Reserves and Deposits", *Federal Reserve Bulletin,* February 1973, p. 62. Certain deductions arising from the float which were inappropriate have subsequently been eliminated. *Ibid.* The Federal Reserve *float* is explained in these words: "Deferred availability items arise because the Federal Reserve Banks do not give immediate credit to the deposit account of the collecting bank for all checks deposited with them for collection. The credit is deferred according to a schedule. . . . After such period (a maximum of 2 days) the member banks' reserve account is automatically credited. Since the time actually taken to collect a check may be longer than that allowed in the schedule, this crediting often occurs before the account of the bank on which the check is *drawn is* debited. The difference between the asset account (cash items in process of collection) and the liability account (deferred availability cash items) represents checks that — although not yet collected by the Reserve Banks — have previously been credited to the reserve accounts of

the banks that deposited them."

"... this difference, which is sometimes sizeable is called float." It measures the account of Federal Reserve credit generated by the national check-collection process and available to the member banks", *the Federal Reserve System: Purposes and Functions*, September 1974. (Sixth Edition), p. 34.

45. "The banks' gross figures for deposits and advances are adjusted to allow for sterling transit items. These transit items appear in an individual bank's balance sheet both as credit items (e.g., standing orders) and debit items (e.g., cheques in course of collection). When bank's figures are aggregated these items may give rise to double counting of deposits received from customers outside the banking system or where over drawn or loan accounts are concerned, to the under valuing of total lending made to such customers. In accordance with the treatment adopted for the calculation of reserve ratios. . . it is assumed that 60 per cent of the total value of debit items less credit items affects deposits. This proportion is therefore deducted from gross deposits and the remaining 40 per cent is added to advance. . . . "See *Bank of England Bulletin*, September 1975 (Vol. 15, No. 3), additional notes for Tables 11 and 12."
46. *Report of the Banking Commission* (Government of India, New Delhi, 1972), p. 242-243.
47. *Ibid.*, p. 243.
48. Report of the Study Group to Frame Guidelines for Follow-up of Bank Credit, (Reserve Bank of India Bombay, 1975) p. 17. Besides this Study Group, earlier a National Credit Council Study Group on "the extent to which the Credit Need of Industry and Trade are Likely to be inflated and how such trends could be checked" (RBI, October 1968) dealt with this problem at length.
49. Some of these have been discussed in Anand G. Chandavarkar: "Unused Bank Overdrafts: Their Implications of Monetary Analysis and Policy," *IMF Staff Papers*, November 1968 (Vol. XV, No. 3) pp. 491-528.
50. Anand G. Chandavarkar: *op. cit.*, p. 515.
51. An unpublished study by William H. White on "Interpreting Monetary Statistics when overdrafting is Prevalent", (September 1956) quoted in A.G. Chandavarkar in *IMF Staff Papers, op. cit.*, pp. 518-519. The study included Indian experience.
52. Based on the thinking of the Radcliffe Committee, Sayers considered gross and Breaching and Lipsey net credit; but both of these studies found trade credit reacting to monetary policy, expanding in times of credit squeezes and contracting in times of credit case, but a later study by Coates has not corroborated their findings. See R.S. Sayers: "Monetary Thought and Monetary Policy in England", *Economic Journal*, December, 1960, p. 713: F.P.R. Brechling and R.G. Lipsey: "Trade Credit and Monetary Policy", *Economic Journal*, December 1963. S.B. Laffer: "Trade Credit and Money Market", *Journal of Political Economy*, March-April 1970: and J.B. Coates: "Trade Credit and Monetary Policy", Oxford Economic Papers, March 1967.
53. *Report of the Committee on the Working of the Monetary System* (London, 1959) p. 103.
54. (i) *Report of the Banking Commission* (Government of India, Delhi 1972), pp. 413-435. See also the Report of its Study Group on Non-Banking Financial Intermediaries.

(ii) *Report of the Study Group on Non-Banking Companies* (Reserve Bank of India, Bombay 1975).

55. *Report of the Study Group on the Non-Banking Companies* (RBI, 1975). p. 52.
56. *Ibid*, p. 53 Also Report of the Banking Commission, *op. cit.*, pp. 414-415.
57. See the *Report of the Study Group on Non-Banking Companies*, p. 77.

A view has been expressed that hire-purchase companies in India operate almost on similar lines. However it is felt that conceptually there is little to distinguish the deposits accepted by the hire-purchase companies in India from those by other non-banking non-financial companies. It should be remembered that the Working Group has, throughout this exercise, concentrated primarily on measurement of money or quasi-money stocks, which constitute the liabilities of monetary sector as such, and not on the assessment of dimensions of overall *liquidity* in the economy.

9

COMMITTEE FOR PROMOTION OF URDU, 1975 – REPORT[1]

Chairman Shri K. Gujaral

V. Chairman Begum Hamida Habibullah

Members Shri Mishri Sada; Prof. M. Mujeeb; Prof. Abdul Aleem; Dr. Sarup Singh; Prof. S. Ehtesham Husain; Prof. Gian Chand Jain; Shri Krishan Chander; Shri Malik Ram; Shri Sajjad Zaheer; Shri Abid Ali Khan

Jt. Secy.(I) Ministry of Information and Broadcasting, New Delhi.

Jt. Secy.(CL) Ministry of Home Affairs, New Delhi.

M. Secy. Joint Secretary (Languages), Ministry of Education and Social Welfare, New Delhi.

M. Jt. Secy. Shri S. Ali Jawad Zaidi

Appointment

The Committee for Promotion of Urdu was appointed by the Government of India Resolution No. F.15-25/72-L.I. dated May 5, 1972, notified in Part I, Section I of the *Gazette of India* dated May 20, 1972.

Terms of Reference

To advise the Government on the measures to be adopted for the promotion of Urdu languages and the steps required to be taken to provide adequate facilities for Urdu-speaking people in education, cultural and administrative matters.

Contents

Conclusions

Introductory

1. The Urdu language has played a very significant role in our cultural and political history. Cutting across regional barriers and religious and caste divisions, it developed as a medium of literary expression as far back as the 13th century. In the succeeding centuries, it drew freely upon the literary traditions of Sanskrit, Braj Bhasha, Avadhi, Punjabi, Marathi, Gujarati, Bengali and Telugu on the one hand, and Persian, Arabic, Turkish, Pushto and English on the other. In its developed form, it embodies the best in the languages with which it came into contact, always retaining its own vigorous Indian character and dynamic individually.

2. Both Hindi and Urdu legitimately claim evolution from Khari Boli, a dialect most commonly spoken in and around Delhi. Both share the earliest available specimens of the language. Like all metropolitan languages, Urdu has imbibed the refinement and flourish of urban elite, while preserving in its early literature the simplicity, vigour and sincerity of Indian folk traditions. Its first known poets were Masud Sa'd Salman and Amir Khusrau. Variously described as Hindi, Hindavi, Hindui, Zaban-e-Dehlavi, Deccani and Rekhta, at different points of time the language finally came to be known as Urdu.

3. The magnificent contribution of this language to Indian literature and culture is only partially reflected in Urdu *ghazals*, whose extraordinary popularity has overshadowed the achievements of other literary forms employed to express deeper thoughts and to convey knowledge and information.

4. While Urdu has always been a vehicle of secular thought, it is little known outside the limited circle of scholars that Urdu is also very rich in religious literature of all the principal religions of India. In Islamics, it has covered all the known fields like *Tafsir, Hadith, Figh, Kalam* and *Islamic* history. It is an equally important treasure-

house of books pertaining to other faiths. There are, for instance, at least fourteen versions of Valmiki's *Ramayana* and Tulsidas's *Ramacharitmanas,* four versions of the *Mahabharata,* sixteen versions of abridged editions of *Shrimad Bhagwadgita*. All the four *Vedas*, besides at least three *Puranas* and four versions of *Manusmriti*, are available in Urdu printed form. There are books on *Sankhya* philosophy and *Nyaya Darshan*. Over a dozen books on the reformist Brahmo Samaj, about a hundred on Arya Samaj, a dozen on Radhaswami sect and a couple of books on Deva Samaj and Kabir Panth, besides about thirty books on Jainism and an equal number on Sikhism, including *Shri Adigranth, Jap jee, Janmasakhi*, have already been published. Similarly, there are several versions of the *Bible,* the *Old and New Testament* and also of the Rorah of the Jews. Books on Christianity would easily number over a hundred. There are also works on Bahaism and Theosophy.

5. Many Sanskrit dramas, particularly of *Kalidasa*, and the *Shatakas* of *Bharatri Hari* have been translated into Urdu. Likewise, several versions of *Panchatantra* are available in published form. Works from other languages like Braj Bhasha, Gujarati, Marathi, Punjabi, Telugu, Tamil, Kannada and Malayalam have also been translated. During the last few centuries, many English and French classics have been rendered into Urdu. Famous Indian romances like Sassi-Punno, Sohni-Mahiwal and Nala-Damyanti have attracted the attention of Urdu writers. The impact of Bhakti movement and of the Vedantic philosophy has been deep and wide ranging. This has found expression not only in the mystic ghazals but also in other forms of Muslim religious literature like the *Naat* and *Marsia*.

6. The popularity of the Urdu *ghazal* has inspired poets in other languages to practise this literary form. Works of poets like Ghalib and Mir have been translated into several regional languages.

7. The dynamic secular tradition of the language has been carried from literature to journalism. From the late 19th century onwards, several newspapers and periodicals devoted themselves to the religions and social movements among the Hindus, Muslims, Christians, Sikhs and Jains. Many nineteenth century Urdu papers were the harbingers of secular thinking in India. Dharm Parcharak (1882), owned by Amba Prasad, and edited by Sadiq Husain, took interest in propagating the teachings of all the religions. Similarly, Sat Prakashan (1883) devoted its columns to Hindu and Muslim mysticism alike. *Gau Raksha* (1884) owned by Sindi Khan, advocated

cow protection. The weekly *Sabha*, Kapurthala (1879), owned by Babu Pohlu-Mal and edited by Barkat Ali, preached that every sect and religion were part of the wider human brotherhood.

8. In order to evade the severe curbs on the Indian press, some of our revolutionaries thought of publishing papers from abroad, and arranged their clandestine circulation in the country. Some of the known papers in this category were the *Talwar* or the *Shamsir,* Berlin (1910); the *Hindustani* and later the *Hindustani Akhbar* (1914) San Francisco; the *Yad-e-Watan*, New York (1923); the *Tarjuman-i-Shauq*, Constantinople (1878); the *Sultan-ul-Akhbar*, Turkey (1880); the *Hindustan,* London (1884); the *Aina-i-Saudagari,* London (1887); and the *Hurriyat*, Tashkent (1914). The motivation has changed but the process has gone on and even today Milan group is publishing an Urdu weekly from London.

9. The contribution of Urdu to our national struggle for freedom has also been immense. The torch of liberty was lit by the Urdu papers will before the war of Independence in 1857, when a number of underground movements were organised to overthrow the then British rule. The leaders of the Waliullahi (sometimes wrongly called Wahabi) movement as also revolutionaries like Raja Mahendra Pratap Singh and Maulana Obeidullah Sindhi used Urdu for the propagation of their ideas and produced a rich volume of political literature.

10. With the rise of nationalism, politically conscious writers and poets took up patriotic themes in an organised manner. The names of those who wrote vigorously in support of freedom will easily run into hundreds. Beginning with Munir Shikohabadi who was banished to the Andamans, we come to Hali, Azad, Ismail Meeruti, Munshi Sajjad Hussain, Shambhu Nath 'Mushtaq', Shibli Nomani and Akbar Allahabadi and then to Dr. Mohammad Iqbal, Maharaj Kishan 'Baraq', Brij Narain Chakbast, Maulana Hasrat Mohani and Durga Sahai 'Suroor' Jahanabadi — a galaxy of writers and poets of whom any language would be legitimately proud. Finally, we come to Ram Prasad Bismil, Ashfaquallah Khan, Mela Ram Wafa, Ahmaq Phaphundvi, Prem Chand, Josh Malihabandi, and Jamil Mazhari who sang of liberty. Two of them even laid down their lives fighting for it. Quite a few Urdu writers like Lala Lajpat Rai Maulana Abul Kalam Azad, Hakim Ajmal Khan, Maulana Mohammad Ali Jauhar and Maulana Hasrat Mohani came to occupy important positions in our national life.

11. The Urdu press also played a courageous role in furthering the objectives of the freedom struggle. Maulana Abul Kalam Azad's *Al-Helal* and *Al-Balagh,* were proscribed and the publisher punished with the forfeiture of security several times in 1913. Maulana Mohammad Ali's *Hamdard and Comrada,* Maulana Hasrat Mohani's *Urdu-i-Moalla,* Zafar Ali's *Zamindar,* Shaukat Ali's *Khilafat like the Siasat,* the *Pratap* and the *Milap* of Lahore; *Musheer-i-Bihar* of Patna; *Shan-e-Hind* of Meerut; *Frontier Advocate* of Dera Ismail Khan; *Jhung* of Siyal; *Al Moin* of Amritsar; *Al-Jamiat* of Delhi; *Medina* of Bijnore; *Quami Awaz* of Lucknow; *Rozana Hind* of Calcutta; *Tej* of Delhi; *Haqiqat* of Lucknow and *Payam* of Hyderabad, have earned a lasting place in the history of journalism for their fearless advocacy of the national cause.

12. From the earliest period to the modern times, intellectuals of all communities have served Urdu with their writings. Without a mention of its Hindu, Muslim, Sikh and Christian writers no history of Urdu will be complete. It is not possible to recount even all the important names from the very beginning. We had writers and poets of stature like Chander Bhan Brahman, Raja Ram Narain 'Mauzun'; Jagan Nath 'Khustar', Sarb Sukh, 'Diwana', Bhagwat Rai 'Rahat', Dwarka Prasad 'Ufaq', Ratan Nath 'Sarshar', Brij Narain 'Chakbast', Daya Shankar 'Nasseem', Durga Sahai 'Suroor', Tilok Chand 'Mahrum'. The tradition has been maintained to the present day. Urdu can still be proud of stalwarts like Raghupati Sahai, 'Firaq' Gorakhpuri, Anand Narain 'Mulla' Krishan Chander, Rajinder Singh Bedi and Malik Ram. They tower over many of their Muslim contemporaries.

13. Spoken by some 286 lakh persons, according to the 1971 census figures, Urdu is the sixth largest language of India. If we add to this the number of those who had declared it as their subsidiary language, the figure would cross the three crore mark, only Hindi, Bengali, Marathi, Tamil and Telugu are spoken by large number of persons, Assamese, Gujarati, Kannada, Kashmiri, Malayalam, Oriya and Punjabi, with more compact concentrations in the States, are spoken by lesser number of people. Persons speaking Urdu constitute the second largest language group in Uttar Pradesh, Andhra Pradesh, Bihar Maharashtra, Mysore and Gujarat while they occupy the third place in Haryana, Himachal Pradesh, Punjab, Rajasthan, Chandigarh, Delhi and Goa, Daman and Diu. This vast Urdu speaking population is spread over all the States and Union Territories

with several pockets of concentration, but Urdu does not happen to be the language of the majority in any one State. After the linguistic reorganisation of States, it has acquired the status of a minority language in all the States. Only in Jammu and Kashmir, it has been recognised as the official language of the State. For its future development, therefore, Urdu has to depend heavily on the constitutional and administrative safeguards provided for this purpose from time to time.

14. With its hoary tradition of secularism and of devotion to national ideals and aspirations, and with its roots stretching down deep into our national culture, Urdu has acquired great vitality, and enjoys wide popularity throughout the country. Urdu *mushairas* continue to draw huge crowds, Urdu films and *Qawwalis* are appreciated widely in the North as well as in the South. Urdu *ghazals* sung to the accompaniment of music are equally popular. The number of speakers of Urdu as also of the pupils studying Urdu is on the increase. So is the number of newspapers and periodicals. Many more schools at the primary and secondary levels are now teaching Urdu, while the number of students at the graduate and post-graduate stages is showing a definite upward trend.

15. After independence, our languages were released from the crippling influence of foreign domination. Apart from the official patronage that became available to them, the expansion of education and the growth of genuinely free press provided new impetus to writers. A new generation of young men, well versed in their mother tongue, engaged themselves in creative activity of a high order. Another important factor which accelerated the development of languages was the reorganisation of States on a linguistic basis in 1956. As a consequence, the regional languages concerned were declared the official languages in the States.

16. Outside the areas where these regional languages acquired an official status, they became minority languages and their preservation and development gave rise to new problems. Some of these difficulties has been foreseen and in order to remove them, a scheme of constitutional and administrative safeguards was evolved over the years. Still the hardships inherent in a situation of sudden transition were exploited by some interested elements for purposes other than educational or literary or administrative. Such attempts at the politicalisation of the language issue thrust extraneous considerations to the fore and the focal issue of the promotion of languages was

relegated to the background. It was an unfortunate development indeed for it gave a mischievous twist to linguistic issues and delayed the natural growth and development of all our national languages including Urdu.

17. As a language spoken all over the country, Urdu has some problems of its own apart from those it shared in common with sister languages. Those varied from State to State and area to area. The Government of India have been taking steps in consultation with the State Governments to remove genuine grievances of the speakers of Urdu language and to create conditions congenial to the growth and development of the language. It was felt, however, that lasting solutions to some of the lingering problems could be found only after all these problems had been studied in depth, and a resolution of the difficulties sought through collective deliberation and discussion with all the elements interested in the problem. It was with that end in view that the Committee for the Promotion of Urdu was appointed.

18. The Committee has carefully studied the difficulties and impediments in the way of sustained growth of Urdu, and has tried to offer concrete suggestions for its development at a faster pace and on a firmer basis. These recommendations flow from our firm belief that the preservation and promotion of a language with such rich traditions and enduring beauty, is indeed a matter of national concern. For all those who are deeply interested in the stability of our cultural life and the strengthening of harmonising and integrating trends, the growth and development of the language is of supreme importance. It is widely appreciated that the fulfilment of the just aspirations of the various linguistic minorities in the country must be sought with a sense of urgency.

19. In the course of its visits to various States, the Committee made it a point to contract the respective Chief Ministers and Education Ministers, and was gratified to notice a general climate of goodwill towards the language. The State Chief Minister, were willing to go far enough to meet all the legitimate demands of the speakers of Urdu. In fact, some administrations have already issued instructions to remove certain difficulties that we brought to their notice.

20. Provision of adequate facilities to students belonging to linguistic minorities has been the corner-stone of the scheme of linguistic safeguards evolved by the planners of our national policies. A definite safeguard aimed at enabling the child to receive primary education in his mother-tongue has been provided in the Constitu-

tion. Similarly, each citizen has been assured of his right to present applications and representations in the language of his choice. In addition, a number of administrative safeguards have been provided for education at the primary and higher stages; for prevention of discrimination in the matter of employment on account of lack of knowledge of a regional language and the availability of acts, notifications, etc., in the minority languages. In the course of implementation, a number of lacunae have been noticed, causing hardship to speakers of Urdu as also to some other linguistic minorities. There is demand not only for the removal of these difficulties but also for extension of facilities. In making the recommendations, the Committee has endeavoured to ensure that the agreed scheme of safeguards is fully implemented and deviation or distortion occurring at lower administrative levels is ended. The arrangements made in some States are, by and large satisfactory, while in several other States they leave much to be desired. Urdu speaking people have been experiencing difficulties, mainly due to the non-implementation or inadequate implementation of the agreed safeguards. We are convinced that things would change for the better if the implementing machinery were activised and reinforced where necessary. Non-implementation of agreed national policies and schemes creates a credibility gap which is difficult to overlook and affects the morale of the people. A serious effort must be made to ensure full and speedy implementation.

21. The survey conducted by us has revealed that, despite the difficulties, there is continuing increase in the number of students learning Urdu. The number of Urdu medium institutions and Urdu teachers has also gone up. Arrangements for the training of Urdu teachers, however, require improvement.

22. In the post-Independence period, Urdu newspapers and periodicals have registered a spectacular rise both in their numbers as well as in their circulation. Off-set printing has helped considerably in improving their get-up. These improvements, however, fall short of the requirements and the majority of newspapers and periodicals suffer from lack of resources and reluctance to take to modern techniques.

23. Since Independence, the number of books printed has been constantly on the increase and there is a much greater variety in subjects covered now. Many of the popular Urdu works have been printed in Devanagari script also and have run into very large editions. Similarly, many more translations from other Indian languages

into Urdu have appeared in recent years. The Committee has taken note of these welcome developments as also of the shortcomings in implementation of safeguards and the needs of a growing language.

24. In making the recommendations, the Committee has been guided by the sole objective of ensuring that the safeguards enshrined in our Constitution are fully implemented and that the National policy of preservation and encouragement of Urdu as one of the national languages is carried out in letter as well as in spirit. The Committee feels that Urdu as a language is a valuable national asset and, as such, it observes full encouragement and patronage.

25. Our recommendations cover the constitutional administrative, educational, literary and journalistic fields. The greatest emphasis has been placed on the full and faithful implementation of the various schemes evolved by the Central and State Governments for the preservation and promotion of Urdu. To eliminate doubts and to ensure proper understanding of the basic official formulations in respect of the language, it has been proposed that the State Language Acts should spell out clearly the areas and purposes for which a language is to be used, in addition to the official language. The Andhra Pradesh Language Act, which draws its authority from Article 345 of the Constitution, may from the pattern with such amplification as has been indicated in this Report. The Centre has to ensure effective implementation of the safeguards for the linguistic minorities in the matter of the use of the language as a medium of (a) education and communication; (b) work and employment; and (c) administration and justice.

26. In the educational field, the 10 : 40 and 15 : 60 formulae for provision of facilities at the primary and secondary levels respectively have failed to give satisfaction to the linguistic minorities. On the contrary, these have given rise to a number of new problems. As a result, complaints of inadequate provision of educational facilities have remained over the years, despite the instructions for advance registration of linguistic minority pupils. The maintenance of registers is erratic and the stipulation of numbers creates problems in cases of drop-outs. Simultaneous registration of the required number on particular dated has been found to be difficult of achievement in-actual practice. It has, therefore, been suggested that concentration of linguistic minority population of ten per cent or more in any area be taken as the basis for the provision of primary education through the mother tongue in that area. One-third of the total number of

pupils, studying through the minority language at the primary level, should be taken as moving on to the next stage of education and this proportion should form the basis for provision of educational facilities at the secondary level. The existing 10 : 40 and 15 : 60 formulae should be abandoned.

27. The problem of lack of trained Urdu teachers is acute. Immediate action by the Central and State Government is required to train sufficient number of Urdu teachers. Meanwhile, untrained but otherwise qualified persons may be appointed on the condition that they would get trained within a specified period. As it may not be possible for the States to bear the entire additional financial burden of the training of Urdu teachers, the Central Government should open a few more centres for the training of Urdu teachers on the lines of the centre recently established at Solan for the Himachal Pradesh Government.

28. The Three-language Formula has already been varied and modified by most of the States in different ways. At several places, the formula has created difficulties for the students offering Urdu as a special subject. We have attempted to work out a formula which gives due importance to the national and regional languages in addition to the mother tongue.

29. In evolving our basic approach to educational safeguards, we have felt the need for having mixed schools were the medium of instructions could be the regional language as also the mother tongue. The Committee has laid stress on the opening of parallel classes for imparting instruction in the mother tongue in order to avoid segregation.

30. The need for the implementation of the constitutional provisions for the acceptance of petitions and applications, etc., in any language of the citizen's choice, and other administrative arrangements for the translation of important acts, notifications, etc., has been emphasised. Following the pattern set by the Conference of the Chief Ministers held in 1961, the Committee has recommended the setting up of translation bureax at the State and district headquarters in areas which conform to the population test indicated under our recommendations regarding Education. It has also been suggested that it should be considered an educational qualification for an administrator if he knows the major languages of the area in which he is posted. Officers learning more languages, it is recommended, may be given incentives in the form of advance increments, cash awards, etc.

31. For Urdu newspapers and periodicals, which mostly come under the category of small and medium-sized newspapers, the Committee has recommended a more liberal treatment in the matter or release of advertisements, purchase of machinery and equipment, etc.

32. For the promotion of higher research and literature, the Committee has made a number of suggestions including the establishment of two research institutes — one at Hyderabad in the South and the other in the North at Aligarh, Rampur, Lucknow or Delhi in that order of preference. The holding of writers' workshops and the establishment of a writer's cooperative to undertake publication of Urdu books have also been recommended.

33. Given a fair trial, these recommendations will not only remove the difficulties about which complaints were received but may well offer a pattern for the solution of similar problems facing other linguistic minorities. The following is a summary of our main recommendations under the appropriate headings. The figures in brackets at the end of each recommendation indicate the chapter and the number of the para for example 1.26 stands for Chapter I and para 26.

Recommendations

34. *Constitutional Safeguards*

(i) The Committee recognises the genuineness of the desire for effective implementation of the constitutional and administrative safeguards to the speakers of Urdu. However, it feels that the pattern of providing safeguards, for the linguistic minorities in the State Acts on official language has been set by the Andhra Pradesh Official Language Act, which draws authority from Article 345 of the Constitution. The Committee commends it to the States and Union Territories for similar action with the further proviso that the areas and purposes (educational, administrative, judicial, etc.) for which the State decides to allow the use of the language should be comprehensively specified in the Act itself. Andhra Pradesh should also take further action on the lines indicated above.

(ii) The Centre should ensure effective implementation of the safeguards for the linguistic minorities, by the States and

Union Territories. The functional importance of a language lies in its use (a) as a medium of communication and education; (b) in the spheres of employment and occupation; (c) in administration and judiciary; and the scheme of implementation has to cover all these aspects. (3.60)[2]

35. There is a clear divergence of view among constitutional experts regarding the interpretation of Article 347 of the Constitution. These differences cannot be resolved by the Committee by attempting to pronounce a judgement on the legal validity of one or the other of the conflicting interpretations. We are, therefore, not in a position to make a definite recommendation on the exact of Article 347. (3.52)[2]

Education

Urdu Medium in Primary Education

36. Having considered the evidence and relevant facts and figures in the States and Union Territories, the Committee has arrived at the conclusion that while arrangements for teaching Urdu at the primary stage of education have been made by some States, they are inadequate, taking the country as a whole. Article 350-A of the Constitution has cast a duty on every local authority within the State to provide facilities for instruction in the mother tongue at the primary stage of education for children belonging to the linguistic minority groups. It is, therefore, recommended that the Education Departments of the States, Union Territories and local authorities should make necessary arrangements for teaching of Urdu at the primary stage for the benefit of those who claim it as their mother tongue.

37. There are specific problems in some of the States and the Committee has recommended the steps detailed below separately in respect of each State.

(ai) Andhra Pradesh: It was complained that a practice had developed in some parts of Andhra Pradesh when Urdu

---

2. Relevant para(s) of the Report.

speakers were being asked for financial contribution to secure permission to start Urdu medium classes. The condition applied to all languages like but Urdu institutions being economically weaker may be feeling the impact a little more. The State Government may like to examine this aspect of the problem and advise the local bodies accordingly. (4.57)[2]

(aii) Delhi: It was stated that the Delhi Administration has already acquired a large number of dilapidated buildings like Kalan Mahal, Zeenat Mahal, Old Bulbulikhana, Sirki Walan School, etc., it should not be difficult, therefore, for the Delhi Administration to construct building for Urdu medium schools in these areas. The Committee understands that it has now been decided that at least one Urdu teacher would be appointed in each school in Delhi and the existing paucity of Urdu trained teachers would be overcome by appointing untrained teachers who were otherwise qualified for appointment. Such teachers should be given adequate in-service training. Once these teachers have been appointed, the Ministry of Education should arrange for their expeditious training. (4.70 and 4.73)[2]

(aiii) Jammu and Kashmir: In Jammu and Kashmir, it was brought to the notice of the Committee that the learning of both the Urdu and Devnagari scripts was not compulsory and the result was that while in the Valley and Ladakh area, most people were learning through the Urdu script, in Jammu area the general preference seemed to be for the Devanagari script. Care has to be taken that the formula adopted there in this respect does not lead to segregation.

(aiv) Punjab: Arrangements exist in Punjab for the teaching of Urdu at higher academic levels but the non-availability of facilities at the roots makes this incongruous. While there may not be need for opening Urdu medium schools at many placed, opening of Urdu medium sections wherever necessary may be considered. (4.102) 10: 40 Formula.

38. At present facilities for education through the medium of Urdu at the primary stage are provided in institutions where there are 10 students in a class or 40 in the school as a whole. The Statewise review of the working of this formula has revealed a number of bottlenecks. These have led to numerous complain from several quarters. The formula has been found inadequate to meet the needs

of the Urdu speaking people. It is, therefore, recommended that:

(i) Where in an urban or rural area, such as village, town or municipal ward, Urdu speakers constitute ten per cent of the total population, at least one Urdu medium primary school should be set up. Wherever necessary, the number of such schools may be increased. These schools should not be exclusively of one medium. Efforts should be made to keep Urdu and non-Urdu medium students at the same school to avoid segregation.

(ii) In areas at the village or the municipal ward level where Urdu speakers form less than ten per cent of the population, there should be provision of Urdu teachers in such schools as are likely to get a minimum of ten students. This likelihood shall be determined on the basis of the population of the children of Urdu speaking persons of school going age in a particular locality.

(iii) To tide over the immediate difficulty that will arise by a sudden demand for such a large number of teachers, appointment of bilingual teachers in the schools mentioned in category (ii) above should be undertaken. The existing staff may also be given incentives to learn Urdu and the incentive may take the form of an allowance or an advance increment or a lump sum reward. (4.132)

Urdu Medium at Secondary Stage

39. As we have already recommended Urdu speakers constituting ten per cent of the population should be the criterion for providing facilities in the case of primary education. We can further stipulate the provision of secondary and higher secondary education in the Urdu medium on a scale related to the number of primary school leavers. For classes VI to VIII where the constitutional directive envisages that all children should receive compulsory education, we will have to make a special provision for such instruction wherever education has been introduced compulsorily for these classes. On the basis of estimates made, it may be presumed that two-thirds of the students leaving primary schools would be desirous of moving on to the next stage of education. Urdu medium sections in the existing schools should be provided on this basis and Urdu knowing teachers ap-

pointed in anticipation of students offering Urdu as a medium. We feel that the opening of such sections will give the Urdu speaking students an opportunity to mix freely in the school and on the playground with students whose mother tongue is not Urdu and will make for greater emotional integration. In our view the emphasis should be on such mixed schools. However, new Urdu medium schools should also be opened wherever necessary. In such Urdu medium schools also there should be provision for parallel sections with the regional language as the medium. As we have indicated in our separate recommendation for Uttar Pradesh, the opening of one Urdu medium higher secondary school for every group of eight to ten primary schools may provide a workable basis for determining the requirements of Urdu medium higher secondary schools in cities with concentrations of Urdu speakers. (4.202)[2]

40. The standard of teaching Urdu in the Urdu medium higher secondary schools, mostly run by the linguistic minorities themselves, needs to be raised. The Government should help these institutions to enable them to provide better teaching facilities so that the students coming out from these institutions are able to compete with their counterparts coming out from other institutions. (4.197)[2]

41. The procedure for obtaining permission to open Urdu medium higher secondary schools and sections has been made so complicated that it has become almost impossible for the linguistic minorities to set up new schools. Urdu speakers usually come from weaker sections of society and, therefore, the pre-conditions, if any, for giving such permission should be relaxed in their favour and the procedure so simplified that it becomes possible for organisers of the schools and sections to implement their plans within two months of the date of application. (4.198)[2]

42. In addition to these general recommendations universally applicable to all States, the Committee has made the following recommendations in the light of the specific requirements of the States mentioned below:

(ai) Andhra Pradesh: The Committee feels that it is important for the Government of Andhra Pradesh to make arrangements at all levels of education for teaching Urdu, and also starting Urdu medium schools or classes on the basis of population as recommended in this report. (4.153)[2]

(aii) Bihar: It was pointed out that in Bihar most of the schools imparting education through the Urdu medium in the secondary schools or having Urdu medium sections were run by the linguistic minorities itself. No such facility was available in the Government, district board or municipal board schools. This neglected sector should be better looked after the facilities provided as recommended by us elsewhere. (4.158)[2]

(aiii) Delhi: The Committee strongly urges upon the Delhi Administration and the Ministry of Education to provide within a period of two years facilities for teaching through the Urdu medium at the secondary stage in the Union Territory on the basis of the formula now recommended. (4.162)[2]

(aiv) Haryana: The Haryana Government should make arrangements for teaching of Urdu on an expanded scale. Urdu medium schools should be started particularly in Mewat area. (4.163)[2]

(av) Madhya Pradesh: The Government of Madhya Pradesh should open Urdu medium schools on the new basis within a period of two years. Provision should also be made for appointing an Urdu teacher in higher secondary schools where Urdu is taught. (4.173)[2]

(avi) Punjab: According to the decision taken by the Senate of the Panjab University in August 1971, English, Hindi or Urdu may be the medium of instruction and examination in any affiliated college or recognised institution. In view of this change, there is a strong case for provision of facilities for the teaching of Urdu at the secondary level by the Government. (4.180)[2]

(avii) Uttar Pradesh: In order to satisfy the persistent demands of the Urdu speakers in Uttar Pradesh, we recommend that: (i) on the basis of the general population formula and the pattern for the higher secondary schools on the basis of the projected strength of students opting for Urdu medium at the secondary schools, our recommendations should be implemented forthwith; (ii) in many pockets of Urdu speakers in Uttar Pradesh where the above formula may not be applicable, arrangements for teaching of Urdu should be made by starting Urdu sections in Hindi medium schools; (iii) since Urdu speakers are generally spread all over the State, it is important to ensure that at least one Urdu teachers is available in every school so that the facilities for teaching Urdu as a subject become readily available as soon as Urdu speaking students are brought on roots; and (iv) the suggestion of the Anjuman Taraqqi Urdu for the opening of Urdu medium higher secondary school for every group of ten Urdu medium primary schools may offer a workable basis for determining the requirements of Urdu medium higher secondary schools in cities with concentrations of Urdu speakers. (4.191)

Three-Language Formula

43. The Three-Language Formula enunciated in the National Policy Resolution of 1968 provided that; (a) in Hindi speaking areas, the Three-Language Formula should be Hindi, English and a modern Indian language (preferably one of the Southern languages); and (b) in non-Hindi speaking areas, Hindi, English and the regional language. Several permutations, and combinations have been introduced by the various States at the implementation stage. It has created many difficulties for Urdu speakers. It is, therefore considered necessary that in any formula that is worked out is should be ensured that students are able to study their mother tongue as well as the official language of the State. The Committee has, accordingly, suggested that the modified Three-Language Formula should provide:

(i) in Hindi-speaking States

(a) Hindi (with Sanskrit as part of a composite course);
(b) Urdu or any other modern Indian language excluding (a); and
(c) English or any other modern European language.

(ii) in non-Hindi-speaking States

(a) Regional language;
(b) Hindi;
(c) Urdu or any other modern Indian language excluding (a) and (b); and
(d) English or any other modern European language. (4.240)

44. The Three-Language Formula, at present in vogue in Andhra Pradesh with a degree of success, may also be adopted as an alternative by the non-Hindi speaking States for Urdu speaking

population. The formula is:

(a) Urdu and Hindi (a composite course);
(b) Regional language;
(c) English or any other modern European language.

Care should be taken to ensure that the Hindi course in the Hindi speaking States, and the regional language course in the non-Hindi speaking States are somewhat different and sampler from the course for those whose mother tongue is Hindi in the former and the regional language in the latter. Likewise for those whose mother tongue is other than Urdu. A similar formula could be made applicable to other linguistic minorities by substituting in the above formula the mother tongue of the linguistic minorities concerned in place of Urdu. (4.241)[2]

45. We feel that studying languages other than the mother tongue should not be regarded as a burden on the students. In fact, such study helps in bringing people speaking different language in close contact with each other and thus promotes social cohesion and national integration. We are, therefore, keen that the students whose mother tongue is Urdu should learn Hindi and those whose mother tongue is Hindi should get an opportunity to learn Urdu. (4.242)[2]

46. In order to encourage learning of additional languages, we suggest that in the Hindi-speaking states provision may be made for a student to offer an additional language as a subject, and in the non-Hindi speaking States, any one of the four languages mentioned earlier may be treated as an additional language. Marks obtained in the additional subject over 30% may be added to the aggregate of the student to improve his division/grade. Failure in the additional subject should not affect the students result. The Committee noticed that the National Policy Resolution is not being followed in the Centre's own schools, viz., the Kendriya Vidyalayas or in schools affiliated to the Central Board of Secondary Education. We feel that it would be unwise to continue with the non-implementation of the Centre's own directives in its own schools and would recommend that non-adherence to the concept of the Three-Language Formula in the Central Schools on the plea of transferability of pupils should not be allowed to continue any longer. We feel that if the Central Government is itself not able to enforce the Three-Language Formula, it cannot possibly exercise any normal influence over the States. It

would therefore, be necessary in all Central Schools also to apply the Three-Language Formula strictly, as laid down in the National Policy Resolution. (4.243 and 4.244)[2]

Training of Urdu Teachers

47. As a result of the general expansion of education and also in view of the announcements made by some States like Bihar and Uttar Pradesh of their decision to appoint Urdu teachers in primary and secondary schools, there is bound to be an immediate demand for a large number of trained Urdu teachers. Some of the States are trying to get over the difficulty by appointing untrained teachers on the condition that they get trained within a specified period. This presupposes the existence of the necessary training facilities on round, which in reality do not exist. In order to surmount the difficulty, we recommend as follows:

(i) Immediate and effective steps should be taken to ensure expansion of training facilities in various States to cope with the demand.

(ii) Keeping in mind the present paucity of trained Urdu teachers, States Like Andhra Pradesh, Bihar, Gujarat, Karnataka, Madhya Pradesh, Maharashtra, Rajasthan, Uttar Pradesh and West Bengal should set up centres for giving concentrated short-term courses for Urdu teachers as has already been done by the Central Government at Solan in Himachal Pradesh from the academic year 1973-74. These special courses should be sponsored and financed by the Central Government.

(iii) In the remaining States, where facilities for teaching Urdu are to be provided, the number of Urdu teachers required is comparatively small and does not justify separate centres. Therefore, in these States Urdu medium sections should be opened in some of the training centres. The Central Government may also set up centres for such States collectively at suitable places.

(iv) All the State Governments should conduct a quick survey throughout their States to assess the requirements of Urdu teachers for different stages of education and the number of Urdu teachers that are available to teach Urdu and other subject through Urdu medium. A Committee of educationists including Urdu teachers from schools and colleges, should be associated with the survey. While assessing the present need, it should also attempt a projection of the future needs. (4.286)

48. The problems of Urdu medium teachers are different from those of teachers of the Urdu language. For an average Urdu knowing person it would be difficult to teach general subjects through that medium if he did not know Urdu as well as the relevant subjects to be able to explain them clearly and cogently. It was on that ground that the demand for the training of Urdu medium teachers was being backed. While, as an ultimate objective, one may continue to support the argument, some make-do arrangement for training in the existing colleges has also to be entertained in the transitional period. That is what has been done in respect of most of the regional languages and this can be done in the case of Urdu as well. But, where Urdu-knowing persons fail to gain admittance to training colleges, the problem assumes another dimension. We would recommend to the States to ensure that the prospective pupil-teachers from the linguistic minority are assured of admission to the training institutions. (4.276)[2]

49. As regards training of Urdu teachers, the State-wise position has been reviewed and the recommendations made by the Committee are summed up as under:

(i) There may not be a case for opening a separate training school or college for Urdu teachers in Rajasthan but some sections should be opened in the existing institutions to give training to Urdu teacher to overcome the present paucity of such teachers. (4.270)[2]

(ii) The decision of the Government of Uttar Pradesh not to appoint a teachers in any Urdu medium school unless he is suitably qualified in Urdu and has a working knowledge of Hindi, would seem to be incongruous. This decision was taken following the recommendations of the Kripalani Language Committee. A necessary corollary to the acceptance of the recommendations should have been to make adequate arrangements for the teaching of Urdu teachers and not to withdraw even the existing facilities. (4.274)[2]

(iii) We recommend to the Government of West Bengal to augment the training facilities, and relax the ban on the appointment of untrained Urdu teachers till such time as these facilities are made available. (4.284)

Text Books

50. There have been persistent complaints from Urdu speakers about the non-availability of Urdu text books in several States. Even where Urdu text books had been published, they were not readily available in the market or became available so late that the students in sheer desperation changed over to other media. The publication of text books after the academic session has begun is self-defeating. The State Governments must ensure that all Urdu textbooks are not only printed but are also made available in the market well before the beginning of the academic session. (4.323)[2]

51. The distribution machinery for Urdu textbooks will also need considerable toning up. Where no such machinery exists, it will have to be created to ensure that the complaints do not recur. (4.324)[2]

52. The price of paper has risen steeply and since most of the new textbooks in Urdu are printed by the offset process, the cost of production has also gone up. For an average student, particularly if he belongs to a weaker section of the society, it is now extremely difficulty to afford such textbooks. The Government may, therefore, consider subsidising the production of Urdu textbooks. (4.325)[2]

53. Apart from the quality of production, the quality of translation as also of the contents requires attention. There were complaints that translations were being entrusted to people who were not fully competent to undertake the job. It was also brought to our notice that the textbooks obtained from other States did not contain material of local interest, particularly for the primary and secondary students. There were also deviations from the syllabi prescribed by the borrowing States. It would, therefore, be necessary to examine carefully the books produced by private publishers as also by other States to see if they fully satisfy the requirements of the State concerned. (4.326).

54. A number of States have established bureaux to publish textbooks. In the State of Karnataka it has been found difficult to do so in respect of Urdu textbooks. There should certainly be a body of experts to supervise translations and to spot out good translators.

This body could be constituted as an advisory board, consisting of eminent educationists and writers, which could meet from time to time for the purposes indicated above. (4.312)[2]

Grades of Urdu Teachers

55. From Madhya Pradesh, Rajasthan and Uttar Pradesh complaints were heard that Urdu teachers were not being given proper grades. In Rajasthan, for instance, the Committee was informed that a primary school Urdu teacher got only Rs. 105 per month, with no allowance or increments. Naturally, there was a demand for equal pay irrespective of the subjects a teacher taught. The Committee feels that the grades of pay of Urdu teachers in the schools run by Government or local bodies should be the same as those of teachers with equivalent qualifications in other subjects. (4.327)[2]

Insecting Staff

56. We are of the view that the one Joint Director (Urdu) should be appointed in States with a sizable Urdu speaking population like Uttar Pradesh, Bihar, Madhya Pradesh, Rajasthan, Maharashtra, Andhra Pradesh, Karnataka and the Union Territory of Delhi to look after the educational problems of the linguistic minority of Urdu speakers. They should essentially be Urdu knowing. The raised status of the head of the inspectorate would help quicker solution of problems and removal of difficulties. In states other than those mentioned above, an Urdu knowing officer of appropriate status should be entrusted with the job. (4.329)[2]

Adult Education

57. Witnesses from Andhra Pradesh, Haryana, Maharashtra and Uttar Pradesh complained that the adult education centres run by the States Government or local bodies did not provide facilities for the teaching of Urdu. This prevented Urdu speakers from joining these centres. The Committee recommends that in States with a sizable Urdu speaking population where there are centres for adult education, classes for teaching Urdu should be opened. (4.330)[2]

Correspondence Courses

58. The States authorities should persuade at least one university in each of the States of Andhra Pradesh, Bihar, Haryana, Himachal Pradesh, Karnataka, Madhya Pradesh, Maharashtra, Punjab and West Bengal to start correspondence courses in Urdu. (4.332)[2]

Libraries

59. The Committee is of the view that Urdu students should get their due share of library facilities provided in schools and colleges having arrangements for teaching Urdu. In school and college libraries, arrangements should be made to maintain the books properly and a catalogue should be prepared and Urdu knowing staff should be appointed to look after the Urdu sections of the libraries. In schools having only sections for Urdu knowing students, assistance of the Urdu teachers concerned may be sought in this regard and they may be given incentive for doing the extra work. (4.336)[2]

60. The States Governments should evolve a formula under which substantial allocations should be made to purchase Urdu books for schools and college libraries. (4.337)[2]

61. The universities and States authorities should ensure that at least the libraries in the universities and the States libraries in the States with a sizeable Urdu speaking population are properly maintained and, where none exists in such States, new ones are started with modern and updated collections of Urdu books. The staff in the libraries should also have a complement of Urdu knowing persons. (4.338)[2]

Teaching of Urdu in Colleges

62. Many universities and colleges situated in areas with a concentration of Urdu speakers, did not have full-fleded departments of Urdu. The right of pupils of linguistic minorities to study their mother tongue right up to graduate and post-graduate levels is concerned by all and for the realisation of that right, facilities for teaching of Urdu need to be provided in the universities and colleges located in areas with a sizeable population of Urdu speakers. (4.340)[2]

63. Witnesses from Punjab emphasised that there was no

prejudice against Urdu in Punjab and the people there wanted to learn it. The Panjab Universities courses, however, had been framed in such a way as to prevent students of B.A. and B.Sc. from offering Urdu as a subject. This should be remedied. (4.350)[2]

Urdu Research Institutes

64. To promote higher research in Urdu literature and language, with particular reference to allied classical and modern Indian languages and dialects, two Urdu research institutions, one in the North and another in the South should be established. The institute in the South should be located at Hyderabad and be affiliated to the proposed Central University or the Osmania University. In the North, the choice will be among Aligarh, Bhopal, Lucknow and Delhi in that order. (4.357)[2]

65. Fellowships should be created at each research institute on the pattern of those in similar institutes in the country. (4.359)[2]

66. Serious research work cannot be carried on without the availability of adequate research material. It will, therefore, be necessary to strengthen simultaneously a Central research library at each of the two places, by adding rare books, manuscripts, microfilms and photostats within the region and outside. For example, at Hyderabad, Idara-e-Adbiyat-e-Urdu will form the nucleus of the research institute there. (4.360)[2]

67. At present three colleges, two in Hyderabad and one in Maharashtra, in addition to the Jamia Millia Islamia, are imparting institution in humanities and social sciences through the Urdu medium. Jamia Millia Islamia has all along been imparting education through the medium of Urdu and its examinations are recognised by the Central and State Governments under Section 3 of the U.G.C. Act. It has been given the status of a "deemed university". In view of the past role of the institution and its potentialities for the future, we recommend that financial assistance and other facilities should be provided to it for graduate and post-graduate studies through Urdu medium. (4.368)[2]

Urdu Medium Colleges

68. We also recommend that at least one college should be set up in a State for making Urdu a medium of instruction up to the

graduate level. (4.369)[2]

Bureau for Promotion of Urdu

69. Some sitnesses suggested the creation of a Central Urdu Directorate to be run and maintained by the Union Ministry of Education. The Directorate, they suggested, should work for the promotion and development of Urdu and for coordinating the work being done in the various States. The Committee notes in this connection that the Bureau for Promotion of Urdu, which has recently been set up, functions directly under the Union Ministry of Education and Social Welfare. The Committee feels that the Bureau should be suitably strengthened and assigned the task of coordinating and monitoring the work of promotion and development of Urdu and at the Centre and in the States in the field of education. (4.370)[2]

Administration

Use of Urdu for Official Purposes

70. The Union Government and the States Chief Ministers have agreed to provide facilities to linguistic pockets having a population of fifteen per cent or more. A more liberal attitude will, however, be amply justified in the case of a language like Urdu which has no compact concentration of speakers in any one States but has a substantial population in a number of States. In the Committee's view, there is strong case for an extension of facilities to wider areas. The agreed facilities should be provided in the administrative sphere for all concentrations of ten per cent and above, down to tehsil, taluk and in the case of municipalities, the war level. (5.55)[2]

71. The problem of facilities to be provided in a municipal area was considered by an Ad Hoc Committee of Delhi Municipal Corporation under the chairmanship of Shri Ramcharan Aggarwal in 1961. It is hoped that the Commissioner would continue to implement the recommendations of the Committee ir letter and spirit.

Translation of Laws and Regulations

72. One of the main hurdles in the implementation of the decisions taken by the Chief Ministers and Education Ministers with

regard to translation of rules and regulations has been the non-existence of translation cells/bureaux at the State and district head-quarters most of the States. Some States like Andhra Pradesh, Uttar Pradesh and Bihar have set up nuclei at the State headquarters and the Maharashtra Government has provided a skeleton staff even at the lower levels. But there is no evidence of these bureaux of cells having started translation of laws, notifications, etc., into Urdu. The staff provided is either too inadequate or is yet to be appointed. We would urge upon the concerned States to take immediate steps to activate these organisations and to set up new ones where needed. These cells and bureaux could undertake the work of translation of petitions, etc., and send replies to representations received in Urdu. A few new posts of urdu translators and supervisors should be created at the State headquarters and in the districts. However, the burden on the exchequer can be minimised considerably by offering incentives to the existing staff to learn Urdu also in addition to the official language of the State. (5.77)[2]

73. The Bihar Government has pointed out the difficulties in providing adequate machinery including staff to them for implementing the programme. This position cannot be accepted as irremediable. Until the Government is in a position to appoint the requisite staff, it may well try to get the work done on a job basis from non-official translators. (5.60)[2]

74. For the districts, in the State of Gujarat, the collectors have been authorised to get laws, etc., translated into minority languages without the provisions of necessary financial resources or the physical facilities required. This needs to be looked into and necessary action taken to remedy the position. The Committee recommends that where a local body has a sizeable population of Urdu speakers in any ward, it should get its notifications, bye-laws, etc., translated into Urdu also. (5.61)[2]

75. In both Punjab and Haryana, where a large section of population still carries on its work in Urdu, the Government may consider the advisability of widening the scope of the present instructions to extent the benefit to this section as well. (5.63)[2]

76. The Government of Madhya Pradesh has informed the Commissioner for Linguistic Minorities that the translations of local Acts, etc., were being issued in Urdu. The witnesses contended that was not the case. The Committee recommends early fulfilment of the assurances given. (5.65)[2]

77. Under its Directorate of Languages, the Maharashtra Government established regional offices at Bombay, Poona, Nagpur and Aurangabad to undertake translation work and promised that all efforts would be made to provide regional offices with personnel conversant with the minority languages to translate speedily Government notices, rules, etc. Arrangements for the translation of texts of notifications, voters' lists and other notices, etc., issued by the local bodies into Urdu, in areas with a population of 10 to 15 per cent of Urdu speakers should be made early. (5.66)[2]

78. The preparation of the lists of areas with concentration of Urdu speakers had not been finalised in Orissa. This needs to be expedited on the basis of the new census. The State Government should made adequate arrangements to make available locally at the district, sub-divisional, or taluka levels, the laws, rules and regulations of statewise character as well as those applicable locally, to the public in Urdu also, where concentrations of Urdu speakers exist. (5.67 and 5.68)[2]

79. The limiting of the scope of issuance of translation in Punjab to non-statutory notifications alone is an abridgement of the agreed safeguards, which should be implemented in full. (5.69)[2]

80. The Government of Rajasthan had agreed as a special case, to publish such laws, rules, etc., in Urdu as were of special interest to Muslims. Publication of these rules and laws in Urdu should not be restricted in this manner and should be broadened to cover other rules and laws as well which are of interest to all citizens. (5.70)[2]

81. The translation bureau of the State of Uttar Pradesh was not equipped to undertake translation of laws and notifications and nothing tangible could be expected of it. It is recommended that it should be strengthened suitably to undertake translation of laws, etc., without further loss of time. (5.75)[2]

Representations in Urdu

82. The Committee feels that the right of the linguistic minorities enunciated in Article 350 is absolute and should be fully respected. The right to receive a reply in the same language in which a letter is addressed to the Government has also been administratively recognised. It has been suggested that Urdu cells should be set up in the Government offices at all levels where the population is ten per cent or more. The officers manning the cells should be well con-

versant with Urdu, Hindi and the regional language. It should also not be very difficult for most of the State Governments to provide translation bureaux/cells at the district as well as State headquarters. (5.98)[2]

83. While a great deal of emphasis has been laid on the provision of translation facilities at various levels of administration, and also at the State Government secretariat level, the main approach of this Committee is that these translation bureaux and set-ups can be very useful where the State language is other than Hindi or for the specific purposes of translating laws, etc. But, in those States where the State language is Hindi, the difference between Hindi and Urdu obviously is mainly the difference of script and vocabulary. If those officials who have to deal with the people of the area know both the languages and scripts, it will really make the administration more efficient and the problems of the public will be better understood by the Government. The Committee, therefore, feels that in Hindi States, knowledge of Urdu should be made compulsory for those who have to administer at various levels. (5.99)[2]

84. It was represented to the Committee that there were still difficulties in States like Madhya Pradesh, Maharashtra and Haryana in regard to the acceptance of petitions, etc., in Urdu and the replies being sent in that language. These have been dealt with in detail in the report. The Committee has made suggestions for expeditious provision of agreed facilities.

85. The orders passed by the Uttar Pradesh Government in regard to representations, etc., stated that there would be no objection to accepting representations "written in Persian or other scripts." The name of the language was, however, not mentioned. It created the impression that the script only and not the language would be acceptable. Pointing out the lacuna, the Commissioner for Linguistic Minorities has requested that facilities should be available to the speakers of different languages also. The Committee feels that the ambiguity has arisen because of faulty drafting and it would not be difficult for the State Governments to rectify the error by issuing the necessary clarification. The Planning Secretary, Government of Uttar Pradesh told the Committee that no record of the number of letters or representations received in Urdu was available with the Government. He also said that sending replies in Urdu depended on the availability of Urdu-knowing staff in a particular office. In the absence of any assessment of the staff required or availability of the

staff or the volume of work, one can understand the slow progress made in this respect. The Committee recommends that pending such detailed assessments at least a nucleus should be created at the various levels. (5.94 and 5.95)[2]

Learning of Urdu by Officials

86. It is a well accepted concept of administration in democratic society that the administrators have complete understanding of the grievances and the problems of the people. A script or a language barrier can well defeat this purpose. Ultimately, it would be an easier and more effective method to deal with the problem if the employees were encouraged to learn one or more minority languages. As there has been no effort on the part of the administrators to learn minority languages spoken in their spheres of work, communication gap has developed. The gap should be bridged by providing adequate translation facilities, in the offices and by giving incentives to officials to learn at least one minority language of the State. In the Hindi-speaking belt, officers could be persuaded to acquire knowledge of Urdu also. For a person well versed in Hindi, it should be quite easy to pick up urdu with a little effort. (5.100 and 5.101)[2]

87. In order to encourage Government servants to acquire knowledge of Urdu, it was proposed that persons having knowledge of both Urdu and Hindi should be given incentives either in the form of additional salary or advance increments. Some states have done this in the case of tribal languages by providing lump sum incentives. (5.111)[2]

Government Service and Urdu

88. The Committee recommends that the State Governments should reassure the linguistic minorities that entry into the services will not be denied on account of lack of knowledge of the official language but that the candidates will have to acquire proficiency and pass a departmental test in the State official language before confirmation. As regards the standard of the departmental examinations in the official language of the State conducted before the completion of probation, effort should be made to keep it at the level of proficiency. (5.152)[2]

89. The Chief Ministers' Conference in 1961 had restricted the

option to English and Hindi as media of examination. The Committee feels that this does not meet the situation fully. Although the number of candidates who are not likely to have full knowledge of the State language is continuously on the decline, the Committee is of the view that to mitigate the hardship likely to arise in the case of linguistic minority minority candidates, the option of the minority languages should be available. The stipulation should invariably be that the candidate after selection and before expiry of the period of probation must qualify in the official language of the State. This will be fully in conformity with the thinking of the State Reorganisation Commission as also of the stipulation of Government of India in their Memorandum of 1956. The Committee appreciates the 1967 decision of the Government of India whereby the Union Public Service Commission permits a candidate to take these examinations for all-India Services and Central Services Class I in any of the Eighth Schedule languages. The Committee feels that this facility should be further extended to the States services as well. (5.108)[2]

90. In the Home Ministry Memorandum of 1956, it was stipulated that where a State or a district has 15 to 20 per cent population speaking a language other than the official language, such a minority language would also be recognised as a medium of examination held for recruitment to the State or district level services as the case may be. The Committee endorses the stipulation in the Home Ministry G.O. of 1956 with the modification that the prescribed limit for eligibility should be brought down to ten per cent of the population in the States for State cadres and in the district for districts cadres. (5.109)[2]

91. The Madhya Pradesh Government has waived the condition of the regional language being compulsory for the State services and has stated that proficiency in Hindi is insisted upon in some services at the time of recruitment. The details of these posts have not been communicated to the Commissioner for Linguistic Minorities. In all fairness to prospective candidates the State Government should publicise the categories of posts for which proficiency in Hindi is a compulsory pre-requisite. (5.131 and 5.132)[2]

92. Punjabi of the matriculation standard is the minimum requirement for most of the State services in Punjab and only of the eighth standard for some technical services. The Commissioner has taken up the question of holding the proficiency examination after selection and before termination of probation and the Committee

feels that the State Government will have no difficulty in agreeing to the suggestion. (5.138)[2]

93. At present, possession of knowledge of Bengali is considered essential for some of the State services in the State of West Bengal. The Commissioner for Linguistic Minorities has taken up this question with the State Government which is re-examining the whole position in consultation with its departments and in the light of the position obtaining in other States. The Committee is sure that the State Government will keep the interest of the linguistic minorities in view at the time of taking a final decision so that the employment opportunities available to them are not affected adversely. (5.148)[2]

94. In the Andaman and Nicobar-Islands, the Administration has prescribed the knowledge of Hindi is one of the qualifications in the recruitment rules to various posts. The linguistic minorities objected to it on the ground of the rules being in conflict with the decision of the Chief Ministers' Conference, and requested the Administration to hold a proficiency test after the selection and before the end of the probationary period. The demand is reasonable. (5.149a)[2]

95. In Chandigarh, the area is regarded as bilingual and knowledge of both Hindi and Punjabi are pre-requisite for employment, following the pattern that was prevalent in the erstwhile Punjab. Since Urdu is a recognised language of the territory, it should also be available as an option. (5.149b)[2]

96. In Delhi, knowledge of the regional language, Hindi is not a pre-requisite for recruitment to the posts of lower division clerks. Delhi, being the capital, should ensure that it is not made a pre-requisite for other categories of posts also. Some witnesses complained that linguistic minorities did not fare well in the recruitment. This needs to be looked into. (5.149c)[2]

Urdu Typists and Typewriters

97. Great difficulty is being experienced by the States of Jammu and Kashmir, Uttar Pradesh, Andhra Pradesh and at the Centre because of lack of arrangements for the training of Urdu typists and procurement of Urdu typewriters. As there is bound to be a demand for Urdu/Arabic typewriters in a number of West Asian and Far Eastern countries, it is suggested that the Government of India in the Ministry of Commerce and Heavy Industries may like to examine, on

a priority basis, how best the question of the manufacture of Urdu typewriters can be undertaken. It might become a foreign exchange earner. (5.102)[2]

98. To meet the immediate demands of the Jammu and Kashmir and Uttar Pradesh Government, newspapers and cultural and literary organisations for Urdu typewriters, import licences should be given liberally. (5.104)[2]

99. This also leads us to the question of training of Urdu typists and stenographers. Although a centre for the training of Urdu typists has been started at Delhi, there is demand from other States also. These States should set up or subsidise centres for training in Urdu reporting and stenography. Where need is felt, provision may be made for the appointment of Urdu stenographers and typists. (5.105)[2]

Urdu in Courts

100. Another problem pertains to the publication of court notices in Devnagari script in Urdu papers. The publication of these notices in a language or script which the readers of the newspaper are not expected to know, defeats the very purpose of publication. It was pointed out that the language used in the notices was the same as was prevalent in pre-Independence days. If true, its transliteration into Urdu script at the time of sending it to the newspaper should not present any particular difficulty. As there is still a complement of bilingual staff in the civil courts and collectorates, the rectification of the position should not present much difficulty. In any case, the text could be got rendered easily into Urdu script through authorised scribes. The Committee recommends accordingly. (5.160)[2]

101. The Committee has noted that the work of translating of acts, etc., into Urdu has been entrusted to Jammu and Kashmir Government. The Committee recommends that the work of translation of acts, etc., into Urdu should be finalised and the translating agency set up by the Jammu and Kashmir Government should be enabled to finish the job quickly by allotment of adequate funds. Once these proposals are completed, these translated laws will be available to everyone, including the litigants throughout the country. (5.162)[2]

102. The documents are sometimes filed by a party in his own language and the authorities insist that its authenticated translated

copies should also be attached. The Committee has been informed that in some places the translation facilities are not available and this causes a great deal of hardship to the parties. The Committee, therefore, recommends that adequate translation facilities should be made available against normal payment, particularly at district and lower levels. The Committee also at the same time feels that sometimes the party may be so poor as to find it hard to pay an additional sum for getting the documents translated. It will meet the ends of justice if in such cases, the financial burden of translation is borne by the authorities and not by the party. (5.163)[2]

103. Some of the States, particularly Uttar Pradesh and Haryana, were issuing copies in Devnagari script of the documents written in Urdu. Witnesses pointed out that such transliteration resulted in may errors of spelling and mispronounciation, sometimes making it difficult to place complete reliance on the copy, particularly for official and judicial purposes. Copies should be made available in the script in which the original is written. If necessary, outsiders my be engaged for copying against payment on job basis. (5.164)[2]

104. Although Telugu has been declared the official language in Andhra Pradesh, the use of English is also being continued for administrative reasons. There seems to be sufficient reasons for allowing continuance of Urdu in the Telengana region in the judicial field as well in the view of the fact that Urdu was being used by the courts in the past. A situation has already arisen in that State where Urdu knowing judges find themselves transferred to another region although they do not possess adequate knowledge of Telugu. A way out has been found by the Uttar Pradesh Government who have made it compulsory for judicial officers to learn Urdu in addition to the official language. The policy is in keeping with our general recommendations that the officers should be encouraged to get acquainted with the minority language. The Committee commends the Uttar Pradesh Government's decision to other States with a sizable population of Urdu speakers. (5.167)[2]

105. The Committee has been told that the Uttar Pradesh Government has now decided that a document written in the Urdu script can be accepted without attaching to it a true copy in Hindi. This is an example which other Hindi speaking States may well emulate. (5.171)[2]

Urdu in Legislatures

106. The use of Urdu by the legislators and the publication of agenda papers, etc., in Urdu are matters on which an all-India policy will have to be laid as it involves the rights and privileges of the legislators. The Committee would, therefore, suggest to the Central Government to discuss the matter with the Chief Ministers and Speakers of the various legislatures to be able to formulate an acceptable guideline. (5.175)[2]

Electoral Rolls

107. In keeping with the Committee's general recommendation, the facility of printing electoral rolls in Urdu should be extended to all areas having an Urdu speaking population of ten per cent. (5.179)[2]

Union Public Service Commission

108. In pursuance of the resolution adopted by the Parliament in December 1967, the Union Public Service Commission allowed the use of any language included in the Eighth Schedule and English as a medium for answering the papers in general knowledge and essay. Two years later it included an optional paper on any one of the fifteen languages. The next logical step in pursuance of the resolution adopted by Parliament will be to permit candidates to answer optional papers in any of the languages included in the Eighth Schedule. The Commission has set up a Committee to examine the question of accelerated adoption of languages of the Eighth Schedule as media of examination for all-India and Central services. It is hoped that the Committee will consider all aspects of the problem while taking a decision. (5.185)[2]

Posts and Telegraphs

109. It was represented to the Committee that the Posts and Telegraphs Department should issue all notices and publish all the forms and postal stamps for public use in Urdu also. Registered letters, money order forms and VPPS written in Urdu should be accepted and letters with addresses in Urdu handled with due care in transit and at the time of delivery. As Urdu has been recognised as a

State official language only in Jammu and Kashmir State, necessary steps are being taken by the Posts and Telegraphs Department to print money order forms in Hindi, English and Urdu for this State only. The Committee feels that once in India, where there is, say, a population of ten per cent or more of Urdu knowing people. Without adding much to the costs, it will give great relief to the Urdu-knowing public. Nor would the question of supply of Urdu forms already printed to Urdu speakers require further reference to the Cabinet. In any case, whatever may be the technical or procedural hurdles, these should be overcome and the Posts and Telegraphs forms including money order forms should be printed in Urdu in substantially large quantities to meet the demand from Urdu speakers all over the country in areas with an Urdu speaking population of ten per cent and above. (5.186 — 5.188)[2]

110. At present public notices are being issued in Hindi and English only. However, important notices and circulars, which are meant for use in a particular region or circle, are being issued in regional languages, including Urdu, by the circles concerned. In conformity with the principles laid down by the Ministry of Home Affairs for the translation of notices, etc., for pockets with a concentration of linguistic minority and in accordance with the norms suggested by this Committee, the Posts and Telegraphs Department should make similar arrangements. It would sound odd that while States are asked to fall in line with the all-India pattern, Central Government departments should be following a divergent policy. (5.189)[2]

111. The absence of a clear and unambiguous policy seems to make it difficult for the Posts and Telegraphs authorities to take concrete steps to supply public notices to the concerned departments in Urdu also. The Committee would recommend to the Posts and Telegraphs departments to accommodate in their pattern of work the requirements or linguistic minorities as well. (5.190)[2]

112. The Committee feels that the policy of the Department to encourage the staff to learn more languages should be pursued more vigorously in the case of postmen, sorters and those who have direct dealings with the public. In making the suggestion, the Committee does not have in mind the case of Urdu alone. Departmental promotions, rewards or advance increments could be some of the ways of encouraging the staff. (5.192)[2]

Railways

113. The names of stations should be displayed in Urdu also, especially in States like Andhra Pradesh, Uttar Pradesh, Bihar, Jammu and Kashmir, Rajasthan, Madhya Pradesh, Himachal Pradesh, Haryana, Punjab and the Union Territory of Delhi. (5.195)[2]

114. The Committee appreciates that it may not be possible to print the name of the station and the fare on a ticket in all the recognised languages. It was, however, suggested that if the stations from where the journey begins are in areas where Urdu happens to be the second largest language after the regional language, the fare and the name of the station may be printed in Urdu also. This formula should be applied to other scheduled languages as well. (5.196)[2]

115. The present policy of the Railways is to confine the printing of the time tables to Hindi and English. It would, however, be open to private individuals or organisations to print the time-table in Urdu if they so desire and the Railway Board would cooperate in giving them the necessary material. (5.197)[2]

Sign Boards and Name Plates

116. There was also a demand that mile-stones, roads, streets, lanes, etc., should bear names in Urdu in addition to English, Hindi and the regional language. Similarly name plates of officers and doctors should be in Urdu script also. It would be placing the Urdu-knowing minority at a disadvantage if these minor facilities were not made available to them. The same facilities were required from municipalities, town areas and other local authorities where a sizable number of Urdu speakers lived. Notices meant for display on public notice boards were also required to be in Urdu. The Committee would like to avoid a sweeping recommendation but commends these suggestions to the authorities concerned for sympathetic considerations. (5.199)[2]

Media of Mass Communication

(i) *All India Radio*

117. Having reviewed the present frequency and duration of Urdu programmes at various stations, the Committee feels that the

criteria evolved by All India Radio, namely, (a) population; (b) local interest; and (c) the availability of talent are by and large satisfactory, but in some respects they are somewhat vague and also inadequate. The additional factors to be reckoned with are the importance of place and its linguistic traditions. From this point of view, the frequency of Urdu programmes at Jullundur, Lucknow and Patna needs to be stepped up. The frequency of Urdu programmes at Simla, Calcutta, Bombay, Nagpur, Ranchi, Rampur, Bangalore-Dharwar, and Mathura is very low and calls for an upward revision in the matter of allocation of time, and broadcasts of developmental features, national programmes and special programmes. (5.210)[2]

118. Urdu speakers constitute the second largest group of listeners in both Lucknow and Hyderabad. The time allotted to the Urdu programmes there is very inadequate. The duration of Urdu programmes at Rampur had not been indicated to us but as Rampur has an overwhelming percentage of Urdu speakers and can serve a part of the Western and Central Uttar Pradesh, where also there are large pockets of Urdu speakers, a strong Urdu Unit should be established there. (5.211)[2]

119. An increasing tendency has been noticed on the part of Indian language broadcasters and news readers, etc., to use uncommon and ornamental words in preference to simple and commonly spoken words. While it is appreciated that most of the translations are done in a great hurry, the language of the broadcasts can be improved and brought closer to the spoken language if a periodical review of the broadcasts talks and news in undertaken – at least once every quarter. For this purpose a small committee of Urdu experts, including outsiders should be formed to undertake such a review. (5.213)[2]

120. Increase in the time allocation for Urdu broadcasts will necessitate the appointment of Urdu producers/assistant producers/ and the ancillary staff like copywriters at all these places. In selecting the staff, the present emphasis on poets must change. Young and energetic talent from among writers and journalists should be also be inducted to give greater variety and verve to our programmes. (5.220)[2]

121. The Committee strongly recommends that the stations located in areas with a sizeable population of Urdu speakers should appoint Urdu producers/assistant producers. They should work in close coordination with their Hindi counterparts. (5.214)[2]

122. There is also need for introducing changes in the pattern of

Urdu programmes from the point of view of originality as also of wider acceptability to different sections of population. Urdu speakers belong to different communities and regions and this fact should be kept in mind while drawing up the programmes. There is little justification for not giving sufficient attention to Muslim, Parsi and Christian festivals in the Hindi programmes and to Hindu, Sikh, Christian and Parsi festivals in the Urdu programmes. (5.215)[2]

123. There was considerable demand for broadcasting developmental features and national programmes in Urdu. This should be accepted. (5.216)[2]

124. It has been stated that the representation given to Urdu in the matter of plays is too inadequate Urdu has a long history and a rich talent in the field of plays. The Committee recommends that in the national programmes of plays and features, Urdu plays and features may be included on a more liberal scale. (5.217)[2]

125. In drawing up the schedule for the Urdu programmes, Urdu should figure more frequently in the programmes for women, children, youth labour and kisans also. (5.218)[2]

126. A complaint was made regarding the repeated relaying of old poetic symposia. This was obviously being done to save expenditure. Excessive resort to repetitive relays should be avoided at all costs. As the *Mushairas* are very popular, they should form one of the important items of the Urdu programmes. It would be worthwhile to tape the *Mushairas* organised at other important regional centres by private organisations. This will give an opportunity to budding talent in various parts of the country to be heard outside their immediate circle. (5.219)[2]

127. At Bombay there were complaints of faulty pronunciation and non-relaying of Urdu news broadcasts from Delhi. A noted Urdu poet complained that the news bulletins were often translated in highly artificial language. This needs looking into. (5.223)[2]

128. At Bhopal it was suggested by the Local Urdu newspapers that slow speed news bulletin in Urdu should be started. This may be accepted. (5.224)[2]

129. In Television, the name of the writer/poet should be exhibited in Urdu also when he is shown reciting Urdu poetry or participating in a literary discussion. This would, however be in addition to Hindi or the regional language as the case may be. (5.221)[2]

(ii) *Press Information Bureau*

130. The Committee has noticed that almost entire work of this organisation in Urdu consists of translation apart from the scrutiny of newspapers. In very few cases has the organisation attempted to initiate publicity originally in Urdu. Effectiveness will be seriously eroded if effort is not made to tailor publicity material produced to suit the special needs of the Urdu-speaking audience. (5.226)[2]

131. There appears to be a lurking tendency to associate the language with Muslims and as such to issue only items relating to them in the special publicity features. Even now there is a large number of newspapers owned by non-Muslims. Some of the most widely circulated dailies and periodicals fall in this category. It is, therefore, necessary to issue material of interest to other religious groups also on special occasions. As things stand today, Urdu still provides a potent forum for putting across secular and progressive ideas and it should be fully utilised for promoting these ideas. Unlike newspapers in other languages, which represent economically affluent sections, Urdu newspapers are generally not in a position to commission special features, articles, etc. Independently written and well documented material, therefore, will be welcomed by the Urdu press. The extra expenditure incurred on recruitment of additional staff for production or original features will be more than fully justified. (5.227).

132. The Press Information Bureau could make available to Urdu newspapers and journals translations of suitable material on foreign affairs appearing in the Indian and foreign reviews and scripts of the informative talks broadcast from All India Radio. (5.228)[2]

(iii) *Publications Division*

133. The number of books brought out in Urdu forms only a small proportion of the books published. In 1972-73, only two Urdu books were published as against a total of 52, released in all the languages. This seems to be the normal pattern of production, the only exception being 1971-72, when eleven books were brought out. We recommend that the matter be looked into. (5.229)[2]

134. It would be worthwhile trying to publish a journal in Urdu which would consolidate information scattered over many journals brought out by the various Ministries. This should be attempted in

other languages also. (5.230)[2]

135. The Government of India may consider whether it is desirable to maintain the present multiplicity of publications issued by the various Ministries and Departments. Perhaps some sort of coordinated approach would help not only in effecting economy but in making it possible for various sections of the population to have information on more than one subject consolidated into one journal. The Committee does not aim at discouraging specialised journals altogether but it is certainly in favour of a stricter scrutiny to effect economy and to avoid duplication of effort. The savings in staff and expenditure effected as a result of such scrutiny could be diverted partly to meet the expenditure of consolidated journals proposed to be brought out in different languages. (5.231)[2]

136. There has been a pressing demand for the publication of the Urdu version of "*Yojana*", the journals issued on behalf of the Planning Commission. We understand that the Government had already agreed to the proposal in principle. Publication of the Urdu edition of the *Yojàna* should be undertaken preferably in a place like Delhi or Hyderabad to ensure quick and simultaneous distribution all over the country and also a good standard of production. (5.233)[2]

137. Some of the witnesses wanted cheaper editions of Urdu literary books to be brought out by the Publications Division. This work, though important, does not fall within the purview of the Division. The proper organisation to handle this job should be the National Book Trust and the Committee commends the suggestion to them. (5.234)[2]

138. There was a suggestion that the Publications Division should bring out a book on Urdu literatures, journalists and poets who participated in the Indian Freedom Movement. This should be carried out. (5.235)[2]

(iv) *Distribution of Plan Literature*

139. There was some criticism of the faulty distribution of plan publicity and other literature issued by the Central Government in Urdu. This applies not only to Urdu but also to other publications. The recent experiment of opening a shop in Super Bazar, Delhi, to sell all official publications seems to have been successful. Such shops should be opened elsewhere also. Counters may be started, in particular, in various universities which could be managed by students'

cooperatives. Such shops and centres could also handle the literature produced by the State Governments. (5.236)[2]

(v) *Films*

140. The Films Division produces documentaries, etc., in all the languages listed in this Eighth Schedule, including Urdu. The major contribution of films is that they have not allowed any barriers to grow between Urdu and Hindi. The Committee has noted that the linguistic integration of the country has been considerably assisted by the films produced in the country. There is need to produce more films in a popular language on subjects in which Urdu speakers may be specially interested. (5.237)[2]

(vi) *Directorate of Advertising and Visual Publicity*

141. It was suggested that every year exhibitions of scientific and informative books in urdu should be organised in various parts of the country. The idea is plausible and may be examined. While it may not be possible to have a separate exhibition for Urdu, other languages may also be associated with it. The periodicity should be decided by the D.A.V.P. (5.238)[2]

142. A few recommendations are given below for the consideration of the State Governments:

(i) Government Gazette: In response to popular demand the Uttar Pradesh Government has decided to publish the whole Gazette in Urdu. The Andhra Pradesh Government is also doing the same. These are very welcome decisions and some other States with a sizable population of Urdu speakers may well emulate the example. (5.240)[2]

(ii) Publicity Materials: In a number of States with concentrations of Urdu speakers, there is only a skeleton staff provided for the preparation of publicity material in Urdu. The editors of newspapers from Srinagar and Jammu complained that only the English version of press releases was being supplied to newspapers there. The Information Secretary who appeared before us assured the Committee that the State Government had expanded their Urdu section. As soon as the staff is recruited, the supply of material in Urdu would commence.

The Committee hopes that the assurance has been implemented. (5.242)

143. A number of witnesses complained of the absence of an Urdu section in the public relations department of the Maharashtra Government. In view of the fact that a large number of Urdu dailies is being published from Maharashtra, the State Government, which has been known for its liberal language policy, should look into the matter. (5.243)[2]

144. The Committee was told in Uttar Pradesh of the non-availability of literature on the Five-Year Plan and developmental projects in Urdu. It is hoped that this deficiency will be looked into and remedied early. Suitable augmentation of Urdu knowing staff in the information/publicity departments of the State is recommended. (5.244 and 5.246)[2]

Implementation of Safeguards

145. The Committee expresses its displeasure at a manner in which some of the authorities at lower levels were trying to take constitutional and other safeguards lightly. The Committee hopes that all concerned would realise that their failure has created a state of emotional tension and dissatisfaction. (5.249)[2]

146. Officers charged with the tasks of implementing constitutional and other guarantees must understand clearly that these guarantees are to be fulfilled. Any laxity or the part of the implementing machinery should be interpreted as its failure to carry out the specific mandates of the Constitution. There has been a demand for the creation in the State Governments of some dependable machinery to deal with the questions pertaining to linguistic minorities. The Commissioner for Linguistic Minorities has been pressing the States to nominate an officer to deal with problems of linguistic minorities. (5.250-5.252)[2]

147. There were persistent complaints that the orders issued and policy announcements made by the State Governments from time to time were not being implemented or were only partially observed. Sometimes, difficulties were created through misinterpretation. Such a situation tends to shake the confidence of the linguistic minorities in the sincerity of assurances given. It also creates administrative difficulties. Misgivings about official intentions on the part of the

general public will be removed once it is made clear that non-compliance of orders will earn State displeasure. (5.253). The Committee accordingly recommends that:

(i) In order to ensure full implementation, the States should identify officers responsible for the implementation of safeguards for linguistic minorities without further delay. These officers should be of a sufficiently high status to be able to coordinate effectively with the various departments and ministries. The appointment of such an officer should be notified to the public through the press and the official gazette, so that individuals and organisations may know whom to approach in case of need. (5.254)[2]

(ii) A demand was voiced in Andhra Pradesh for the appointment of an advisory body consisting of officials and non-officials under the chairmanship of the Education Minister of the State Government to look into the grievances of Urdu speakers and to make recommendations. The Committee feels that in the light of recommendations of the Conference of the Committee of Vice-Chairman of Zonal Councils held in November, 1961, State level committees should be appointed in the States for this purpose under the chairmanship of the Chief Ministers. This would, among other things, look into complaints in respect of primary schools as well. (4.56)[2]

(iii) Similar arrangements should exist in the Union Ministry of Home Affairs, which may earmark an officer specially for the work relating to linguistic, minorities it will be his job to coordinate with other Ministries and departments also (5.254).

(iv) Cells should be created in the States and in the Ministry of Home Affairs to assist the officers referred to in paras (i) and (iii) above. (5.254)[2]

(v) The Linguistic Minorities Commissioner has repeatedly mentioned in his reports that complete statistics and full information was not being supplied to him regularly. This does hamper the effective functioning of the Commissioner and also deprives Parliament of an opportunity to discuss the reports fully. The Committee would strongly urge upon the States and Union Territories/Administrations to ensure the submission of timely and complete statistics to the Commissioner. (5.254)

Journalism

Financial Assistance

148. The Central Government may advice the nationalised banks and other financial institutions to give sympathetic consideration to the needs of the Urdu press in view of its financial backwardness and instability. (6.87)[2]

149. Most of the Urdu papers and periodicals are individually owned and majority of them do not have enough enough resources. There is a strong case for encouraging the formation of cooperatives to run the papers. It would entitle them to loans and all the concessions available for cooperatives. (6.89)[2]

150. While a few newspapers and periodicals are printed in their own presses, many more are printed outside. This is truer of the medium and small newspapers. It adds to the cost of production and diverts their already meagre resources from other more important items. The remedy lies in at least the dailies and weeklies having their own printing presses to run on modern lines. The difficulties of procuring the printing machinery will case considerably only after significant expansion in the indigenous production of the printing machinery has been achieved. In the meanwhile, Urdu papers should be allowed to import machinery not manufactured locally, on a liberal scale. (6.94 and 6.95)[2]

Newsprint

151. It was represented to the Committee that Urdu newspapers faced a number of difficulties in obtaining newsprint in turn and in sufficient quantity. The complexion of the whole problem has changed since the question was first raised before the Committee. The supply position has become much more acute and the prices have shot up much higher. It is against this backgrounds that the demand for the simplification of the procedure for obtaining newsprint and elimination of delays in its supply is to be viewed. Complicated procedures and delays sometimes forced the small newspapers to go to the black market. This procedures have been considerably simplified after the report of the Small Newspapers Enquiry Committee was presented. Government may consider the possibility of further streamlining them. (6.109)[2]

152. A new factor has been introduced by the recent decision of the Supreme Court rejecting restrictions on the allocation of newsprint to any category of papers. We, however, feel that some way should be found for a favourable revision of allocation to smaller newspapers, including Urdu ones. (6.114)[2]

153. The possibility of evolving a new distribution policy in respect of the newsprint in the country to give some relief to the smaller newspapers with a circulation up to 15,000 should be explored. (6.114).

154. To facilitate the distribution of newsprint to smaller newspapers and to Urdu papers, it is necessary that State Governments make arrangements either through cooperative banks or finance corporations to lift the bulk newsprint requirements of their area and distribute it to the newspapers in their States on the basis of their allocations. This will considerably mitigate the present hardships faced by smaller newspapers who have to take delivery of the newsprint from main port towns and then arrange transportation to the destination themselves. (6.116)[2]

Advertisements

155. At present the Directorate of Advertising and Visual Publicity does not give advertisements to newspapers and periodicals unless they have been in existence for more than six months and have attained an average circulation of 1,000 copies. In this connection, we would specially like to plead for exemption to papers and journals professing to serve the intelligentsia. This section, though small, functions as opinion maker and deserves special consideration. It will, however, be the discretion of the Directorate of Advertising and Visual Publicity to decide the quantum or the nature of advertisements that should be released to such newspapers and periodicals. (6.1211 and 6.122)[2]

156. Mass campaigns: As regards mass campaign advertisements, at least 60 per cent of such advertisements should go to the small and medium newspapers, including those of Urdu, particularly in the rural and semi-urban areas. In view of the general economic backwardness, the existence of large pockets of Urdu knowing people in most of the linguistic regions, as also the under-developed state of the Urdu press, some special consideration should be shown to them at the time of allocation of advertising funds for general and display

advertisements. (6.125 and 6.126)[2]

157. Announcements and Notifications: The display advertisements should be reduced in size in order to accommodate a larger number of small newspapers and periodicals within the available allocation. (6.129)[2]

158. Public and Private Sector Advertisements: In view of the existence of large pockets of Urdu knowing people in most of the linguistic regions, some consideration should be shown to Urdu papers at the time of allocation of advertising funds for the public sector undertakings. Private sector should also be persuaded to release some advertisements to Urdu media. (6.131)[2]

159. Centralised Release of Advertisements: The Union and State Governments should strictly enforce the policy of centralising advertising in the Directorate of Advertising and Visual Publicity or the corresponding organisations in the State directorates of information/public relations. Fears, even if unfounded, should be removed by laying down definite guidelines to ensure that advertisements are given on merit, that is circulation, class appeal and the area served. These centralised agencies would be able to rotate advertisements to the smaller and medium newspapers in a manner that no section or region remains uncovered and that papers catering to special interest like education, health, women, children, science, labour, etc., are not neglected. (6.132 and 6.143)[2]

160. It would be necessary to ensure that Urdu papers get their due share in classified advertisements. (6.133)[2]

161. There are a number of States which do not publish any newspaper in English though they give advertisements to English papers on the strength of their circulation. The same rule should apply to Urdu newspapers. (6.140)[2]

162. The Committee is of the view that the determination of rates for advertisements by D.A.V.P. must follow the normal commercial practice. However, smaller and medium newspapers must not be allowed to entertain the feeling that their insecure financial position is being taken advantage of in awarding lower rates. (6.149)[2]

163. Payment of Bills: Urdu newspapers, with their instable finances, cannot afford to wait long for payments. Expeditious clearance of bills should be ensured not only in their case but in the case of all other medium and small scale newspapers. (6.151)[2]

164. Through joint consultation with professional bodies like A.I.N.E.C. and I.F.W.T. some procedure could, perhaps, be worked

out for the economically weaker sections of the press to ensure accreditation. Even limited accreditation for certain functions could be thought of. (6.160)[2]

Postal Rates

165. The disproportionate rise in postal charges has affected the price structure of the periodicals. A downward revision of the postal rates in the case of magazines and periodicals has been urged by several editors and publishers and there is some justification in their submissions. The present postal rates for periodicals are high and the incidence falls on the consumer whose purchasing power is already low. The committee strongly urges the Government to give substantial concession to periodicals and other publications in regard to postal rates. (6.82)[2]

Small Newspapers Consultancy Service

166. The Urdu newspapers and periodicals, which have been categorised mostly as small, needs assistance in the matter of selection of printing machinery, in the resolution of other day-to-day problems, in the maintenance of proper accounts, sales promotion, organisation of circulation and advertisement revenue and in the general measures for economies in expenditure. It would be worthwhile to set up a small consultancy cell in the Press Information Bureau to advise the Urdu press in these matters. (6.96)[2]

Training in Journalism

167. With the coming up of the Indian Institute of Mass Communication, it should not be difficult to organise refresher courses of short duration for the benefit of the small newspapers. (6.165)[2]

168. Punjab still being a virile and thriving centre of Urdu journalism, there is full justification for the Panjab University starting a course in Urdu journalism also. We feel that, with a little persuasion, the Panjab University should be agreeable to run courses in Urdu journalism. (6.167)[2]

169. State Press Units: Small Urdu units, capable of handling the work of press relations and communication and headed by an experienced journalist at least of the level of a State Information Officer should be established in all the States from where Urdu

newspapers and periodicals are published. (6.173)[2]

170. These units could take up translation of all the press releases and even summaries of important enactments, ordinances, five year plans, etc., to ensure fuller appreciation of governmental policies and active participation of the people in developmental activities. (6.174)[2]

171. There should be adequate arrangements for the scrutiny of newspapers to provide feed-back to Government on the basis of what is appearing in the Urdu press. (6.175)[2]

Katibs

172. With the expansion of education, as also of journalism, the demand for katibs is likely to grow manifold. Earlier, the traditional madrasas used to provide good katibs. It appears that even they have ceased to attach importance to calligraphy. The Committee has, therefore, recommended that some of the established madrasas like the ones at Deoband and Lucknow may be advised to start classes in calligraphy and kitabat. (6.181)[2]

Press Advisory Service

173. A press advisory machinery should be in existence at the State and, wherever possible, at the district level also, to scrutinise cases of violation of journalistic ethics or press laws. If such a course is adopted, many of the complaints from the press vanish, on the press advisory Boards, Urdu newspapers should also be adequately represented. (6.185)[2]

Literature

Urdu Academies

174. The Committee notices with satisfaction that the States of Uttar Pradesh and Bihar have set up separate academies for Urdu, while the State of Jammu and Kashmir looks after the promotion of Urdu literature through its Academy of Arts, Culture and Languages. There are other State level sahitya parishads or academies in Andhra Pradesh and Madhya Pradesh. We are sure that the claims of Urdu will receive due recognition soon in Andhra Pradesh, Chandigarh, Delhi, Haryana, Himachal Pradesh, Karnataka, Madhya Pradesh.

Maharashtra, Punjab, Rajasthan, Tamil Nadu and West Bengal. Pending the establishment of such academies there, the State Governments/Administrations should ensure that Urdu writers and scholars within their territories are represented on the existing academies and parishads and are given the same incentives as are available to fellow writers in the official or other regional languages of the States and Union Territories. In some State academies, the representation of Urdu writers is nominal. This should be remedied by providing due representation to them. (7.69)[2]

175. The role and effective functioning of the academies has become important in the context of rapid developments taking place on the cultural and literary fronts. Much can be done by the academies to stimulate original writing and research through subsidies or grants. They could offer greater incentives for the writing and publication of books on social and physical sciences and for other functional literature which could prove helpful to readers in the choice of professions and in earning a livelihood. (7.70)[2]

176. Indeed, there is a genuine need for general reading material on topics of vital interest to society. Writers must aim at producing literature which will broaden the outlook of the readers and modernise their approach to life in general. The ministries/departments of education and culture at the Centre and in the States, as also the various academies set up all over India, should make it a point to earmark a substantial proportion of their budget for promoting production of specialised literature in various fields. (7.56)[2]

177. State academies should also promote the compilation of reference works like bibliographies, biographical dictionaries, encyclopaedias, directories, etc., in Urdu and help in the cultivation of closer links between urdu and other regional languages. We would strongly urge upon the Union Ministry of Education and Social Welfare and the concerned State departments to reshape the role of the academies on the above lines. (7.71)[2]

Incentives to Writers

178. In the absence of a clear-cut policy, directive or even a regular scheme of assistance to writers, the ministries and departments both at the Centre and in the States have been working on an ad hoc basis. It is high time that a regular scheme of incentives is drawn up. The Education Ministry may initiate discussion with the

States on the subject with a view to chalking out a coordinated programme. (7.72)[2]

Financial Assistance

179. Writers and authors should receive some subsidy from the Central and the State Governments to enable them to publish their own works. Some of the banks could also advance loans to such writers against the publication itself. (7.74)[2]

Distribution of Awards

180. There have been complaints of nepotism and favouritism in the distribution of awards, prizes and even assistance. The motivation for such complaints is not always impersonal. But, it must be admitted that there is considerable room for improvement in the procedure adopted at present. We would like to make a few suggestions for the serious consideration of the Governments and the academies:

(i) The composition of the Committee appointed to select awardees should be broad-based and representative not only of the talent available in the reaching profession but also of scholars and writers outside this circle.
(ii) The heads of various language departments usually get represented in the selection committees on the basis of protocol, while good scholars and writers at the lower levels are not considered fully eligible for representation on these committees. The composition should, as a general rule, reflect merit and scholarship and not seniority in service.
(iii) No person should be allowed to remain on such selection committees for a term of more than two years. Rotation would eliminate many causes of complaint.
(iv) One of the prime responsibilities of academies which deal with more than one language is to ensure that patron age is equitably distributed and no linguistic group suffers from a sense of injury. Therefore, the academies should err, if at all, on the side of liberality towards linguistic minorities. (7.75)

Assignments of Translations

181. Some witnesses complained that very few translations from

other languages into Urdu have been undertaken by the Sahitya Akademi. This respectable body has a clean record of fair play and justice and any inference to the contrary will be really unjust but, because of its very stature, a heavy duty is cast on it to see that obstacles, if any, obstructing speedy execution or Urdu translation and publication programme are removed. (7.76)[2]

182. It has been alleged that translations have been entrusted to a very small circle of writers, who have in a few cases got it done through others, adversely affecting quality. At least the Sahitya Akademi must ensure that translations executed under its supervision are of top quality. (7.77)[2]

Coordination among Government Agencies

183. There is multiplicity of agencies directly or indirectly controlled by the Government of India which are doing more or less the same job. For example, Publications Divisions, National Book Trust, Taraqqi-e-Urdu Board and Sahitya Akademi, besides several State Government organisations are publishing books. One comes across several instances of duplication and overlapping. The Government of India should devise means of bringing about coordination between the various official and semi-official organisations in the matter of selecting titles and writers. (7.108)[2]

Research and Reference Works

184. In the absence of organized research work, much of the effort centres around individuals behind the project. This leads to overlapping for neither the individuals nor the academies and the other sponsoring bodies are aware of the similar work being done elsewhere. Interests of the language and of research work will be well served by the constitution of a central coordination committee consisting of representatives of all the various official and non-official organisations engaged in or concerned with research. Governments could be represented through the representatives of the University Grants Commission, the Sahitya Akademi, the Taraqqi-e-Urdu Board, the urdu academies of Bihar and Uttar Pradesh, Madhya Pradesh Sahitya Parishad and the Jammu and Kashmir Academi of Art, Culture and Languages and similar bodies. They could jointly chalk out a programme of research. The Sahitya Akademi should

take the initiative in convening a preliminary meeting of experts to formulate the scheme for each major language including Urdu in its basic outlines. (7.80)[2]

185. Similarly, there is need for coordinating the production of reference work. We are told that more than one agency has plans for compiling dictionaries, encyclopaedias, etc. This work also does not admit of duplication. The coordination Committee discussed above, could re-plan and re-schedule their work also. (7.81)[2]

Old Age Stipends

186. The amount of old-age stipends given to Urdu writers by the Centre and the States needs to be raised substantially. The present limit of Rs. 150 is too low, considering the phenomenal rise in the price of commodities that has occurred during the past few years. (7.79)[2]

Scholars Empritus

187. There are a number of eminent Urdu scholars whose services deserve to be utilized even in their old age. There should be a scheme of having Scholars Empritus who should be given a substantial scholarship pursue their researches and writings. The amount of scholarship given should be adequate to cover all their expenses as also the expenses on such helpers as calligraphists, typists and research assistants they might require. (7.114)[2]

Vocabulary and Terminology

188. Urdu writers must borrow freely from other languages and thus come closer to the sister languages of India, especially Hindi which differs from it only in the use of script and vocabulary. The desire to enrich Urdu vocabulary by drawing upon other languages, however, has to be tempered with caution. Judicious selection has to be done not by outside or official agencies but by the writers themselves, in the interest of the rapid advancement and growth of the language. (7.49)[2]

189. Whether in the matter of accepting terminology for the modern sciences or assimilating more and more words in common use in the various regions of India, Urdu writers must show the same

foresight and responsiveness which made for the speedy growth of the language in the earlier years of its history. The Committee is glad to record that the vast majority of writers, poets, critics and scholars of Urdu, with whom it had occasion to exchange views, was found to be in sympathy with these basic objectives. (7.50)[2]

190. To make Urdu a medium of instruction at the higher stages of learning it is essential that it treasure house is enriched with books on technical and scientific subjects. The absence of Urdu medium instruction in the higher stages of learning on the one hand, and the paucity of experienced writers in Urdu on the other, have together formed a vicious circle. Keeping in mind the numerous branches of modern science and technology it is essential that international terminology is retained and adapted to the extent possible, for technical and scientific subjects. Any rigid stand on terminology, which rejects all-India and inter-regional considerations will recoil on the growth prospects of the language itself. The Chief Ministers of the States were right in deciding, at their meeting in August 1961, that the technical and scientific terminology should be based on international usage and should be common to all the Indian languages. The decision, so far as Committee's knowledge goes, has been accepted by all the States. The Committee, therefore, commends this criterion with regard to the coining of terminology in Urdu for scientific and technical subjects. Inadequacy, if any, should be carefully looked into and connected in the light of the principles already referred to. A line of demarcation may, however, be drawn between the humanities and the scientific subjects. Subjects like philosophy, logic, sociology and economics can be studied even with independent terminology developed in Urdu but not the scientific and technical subjects. (7.58, 7.59 and 7.65)[2]

Urdu Books in Devnagari Script

191. The Committee feels that the script and language usually go hand in hand and together they make a composite personality. It has, therefore, not recommended any change of script for Urdu or any other language for that matter. It has, however, noted that the close proximity of interests between Urdu and Hindi has already stimulated publication of Urdu works in Devnagari script also. There is strong case for publishing Urdu books in Devnagari script, in addition to the Urdu script. The diwans of Urdu poets and the

anthropologies of Urdu poetry in Devnagari script have sold in thousands. In our opinion, the experiment should be extended to cover fiction and humour also. This will blunt the edge of controversy that has marred the recent history of both the languages. They will stand to gain by coming closer and by thinking in unison. We would also suggest publication of Hindi fiction and humour and satire, as also popular Hindi poems in the Urdu script and would strongly recommend the Government of India earmarking some funds for the purpose and entrusting the job to some semi-official organisation. (7.40, 7.41 and 7.42)[2]

Inter-lingual Exchanges

192. The Committee has endorsed the suggestion that the history of Hindi literature should be incorporated in the history of urdu literature and vice versa. (7.51)[2]

193. The Committee welcomes the suggestion that Hindi scholars should be invited by the university departments of Urdu to give lectures on the latest trends in and problems faced by Hindi. Urdu scholars should be requested to deliver similar lectures to Hindi students on Urdu and its problems and we commend it to our universities for immediate implementation. (7.52)[2]

Writer's Workshops

194. Writing is a craft as well as an art. While the talent to write is inborn, the technique of writing is acquired through a process of trial and error, which involves great waste of time and labour. The Committee is convinced that there is a positive need for organising writers' workshops to enable the writer to understand the craft better. These workshops could conduct a course in commercial writing which would help open the doors of the film, radio and television media to the Urdu writers and also enable them to enter the advertising, publicity and public relations professions. (7.104)[2]

195. These workshops could also conduct a course in book trade. This would help the new entrant to this field of writing to be equipped not only with a knowledge of book production, printing, advertising, etc., but also with business management. (7.105)[2]

196. The Institute of Mass Communication is doing partly this type of job but it is not language based. The Institute may make a

beginning in that direction by opening Hindi and Urdu Sections, to be followed in due course by sections for other languages also. (7.106)[2]

197. The expenditure on the workshops will have to be borne partly by the Central Government and partly by some States having concentrations of Urdu speakers like Andhra Pradesh, Bihar, Karnataka, Maharashtra and Uttar Pradesh. (7.107)[2]

Copyright

198. For the growth of healthy practices in the publishing business, the signing of a copyright and royalty contract between the writers and the publishers should be made obligatory and such contract should be duly registered with the appropriate governmental authority so that they could be enforced legally by either of the parties, if ever need arises. Appropriate changes should be incorporated in the copyright law. (7.80)[2]

Piracy

199. The problem of piracy in publishing has assumed menacing proportions in Urdu. Piracy deprives the rightful authors and the publishers of their genuine profits and dumps on the market unauthorized and badly produced versions. The Committee feels that the Government should institute a probe into the whole matter in order to uncover and break the racket once and for all. To check the evil, all publishers should be asked to get themselves registered with the appropriate governmental authority. (7.90)[2]

200. There is obviously need for legislation to protect the author as well as the book lover and the general tax payer from unethical practices of piracy and misuse of copyright. (7.97)[2]

Calligraphy

201. Difficulty in finding suitable katibs has been worrying writers and publishers alike. As publishing in Urdu is still largely geared to the litho process, the very survival of the trade is threatened if a solution to the problem is not found soon. For the purpose of literature, Urdu academies in the States, the Lalit Kala Akademi at the Centre and similar other organisations should give serious thought to the

preservation of kitabat and calligraphy as a valuable art form. This effort should be in addition to what has been recommended in the chapter on Journalism. (7.44 and 7.45)[2]

Use of Type for Printing

202. Irrespective of what may be done to save that art of calligraphy and kitabat, the future of Urdu seems to be linked with type. We would do well to start preparing for the inevitable. (7.46)[2]

Publishers' Problems

203. The partition of the country was responsible for the loss of a very active publishing centre of Urdu in Lahore. It also resulted in the migration of some of the established Indian publishers to Pakistan. The loss was only partially set off by the publishers who came over to India because they did not stay long in the business of publishing Urdu books. Only a few new publishers have entered into the business of printing Urdu books recently. During the last decade, printing costs have shot up. These factors inhibited the rapid expansion of the Urdu publishing trade. There is obviously need for new and well organised publishing houses to come up and undertake this work on a large scale. They have also to organise a system for a large scale production of books to bring down costs and to improve standards. The channels of distribution of Urdu books are even less scientifically organized than book production. For a vast country like ours, there should be an all-India net-work of book-sellers or book agents for all the languages of the country. Such network of booksellers and book agents including news agents can be built up mainly through cooperative effort. It could take care of the sale of Urdu books as well as newspapers and periodicals. If an all-languages sales organisation takes longer to materialise, we may expedite the setting up of one such network exclusively for Urdu. (7.82, 7.83, 7.85 and 7.86)[2]

204. The high cost of production of the akademi books and inadequate sales arrangements have also come in for criticism. The tendency on the part of each Central or State academy to undertake sales separately without an adequate sales organisation restricts sales and increases handling costs. A coordinated approach is recommended. (7.78)[2]

205. The State academies which are producing their own books may consider the desirability of entrusting the work of publication to some established publishers who may be subsidized by them, if necessary, when the proposed writers' cooperative, which we shall discuss later in detail is set up, this work could profitably be given to it (7.78)[2]

206. As there is no regular journal to carry notices of new book arrivals in Urdu, giving a short description, including names of publishers and prices, the Anjuman Taraqqi Urdu or some such organisation should consider publishing such a journal. (7.87)[2]

Cheap Editions

207. There has been a tremendous rise in the cost of production and, as a result, the prices of books have shot up. To spread the reading habit amongst the people, low priced books like paper-backs require to be made available to the public all over the country, wherever demand for Urdu books exists. This will be difficult to achieve without the active support of the Government. A special allocation of low-priced printing paper should be made to such publishers as are prepared to bring out cheap editions of quality books. There should also be a phased programme for the production of low-priced printing paper on a large scale, keeping in view the future demand. (7.91)[2]

Loans from Banks and Import Facilities

208. Banks should advance loans at reasonable rates to publishers/printing presses to enable them to put up modern presses and to expand or renovate the existing presses. The Government should help by giving facilities for the import of such machinery as is not manufactured indigenously. But to serve the long-term needs of the growth of the industry, then Government of India must launch a project for manufacturing offset presses within the country as soon as possible. (7.92)[2]

Calligraphers' Ink

209. The Katibs use a special kind of ink for writing. It has been stated that there is only one company in the country which holds vir-

tual monopoly of this item. No research had so far been conducted either to improve its quality or to find a substitute for it. This needs to be looked into. (7.93)[2]

Railway Stalls

210. The railway books stalls used to provide the biggest outlet for Urdu books and journals but of late there have been complaints from the publishers and general readers alike that the facility has been virtually withdrawn. The Railway Ministry should see to it that the Urdu books are also displayed properly at the railway books stalls. (7.94)[2]

Refresher Courses

211. As the publishing trade in Urdu is disorganised and still in its infancy in so far as modern techniques are concerned, periodical exposure of the enterprising publishers to the latest methods being adopted by more progressive publishers will be useful. It is, therefore, suggested that the Indian Institute of Mass Communication, New Delhi or the School of Printing at Allahabad may be asked to evolve a refresher course for them. (7.95)[2]

The Cooperative Concept

212. The logical steps for the urdu writers, in the face of many difficulties, is to organise a cooperative publishing venture of their own. An excellent example of this type of endeavour to develop a language and to protect the authors' rights is provided by the Sahitya Parvarthaka Cooperative Society Limited for Kottayam, Kerala. There is no reason to suspect that Urdu writers cannot emulate the success story of their Malayalam counterparts. The Committee feels that an Urdu Writers' Cooperative Society should be set up with Government assistance to publish and sell Urdu books. While the broad aim should be to ensure a fair deal to writers and to provide the types of literature vital for the growth of the language, the society must run on strictly commercial lines. (7.97, 7.99)[2]

213. The selection of books on manuscripts for publication by the Society should be made by an independent selection committee on which the majority of members should be established literatures not connected with the Society. The Government, which would own a

majority of shares, should nominate the Chairman of the Society, who must be fully conversant with Urdu and all production techniques. It may also be necessary to stipulate that books or manuscripts written by the members of the selection committee itself would not be eligible for selection, unless approved by a separate panel appointed by the Society. (7.100)[2]

Sales Organisation

214. The above-mentioned Society would not be able to function properly without a sales-organisation and a sales network spread over all the regions where Urdu is read and spoken to a considerable extent. The research and evaluation wing of the Society should be able to devise scientific criteria for the opening of sales-points. Broadly speaking, every city of district, which has about one lakh Urdu-knowing persons, should have a sales-point of the Society. The emphasis on a district is relevant because the census figures reveal that about 60 per cent persons who returned Urdu as their mother tongue reside in rural areas. We could utilise the existing sales channels also. (7.102-7.103)[2]

Export of Books

215. Urdu is being taught in several universities of Europe and America. Their Urdu departments have libraries which purchase Urdu books annually in bulk from India. Moreover there is a large number of Urdu-knowing people in Pakistan, Great Britain, Canada, U.S.A., U.S.S.R., and other countries. We could develop an export trade if proper attention were paid to it. The Government should make a study of this export market either through our diplomatic missions abroad or otherwise and take steps to encourage export of quality Urdu books. (7.109)[2]

National Bibliography

216. Very few books published in Urdu were being received and fewer still brought on the registers of the National Library, Calcutta, for want of staff. This situation is very unsatisfactory. The members of the Committee, who visited the Library were surprised to find that even some of the most popular titles and works of well-known writers

were not available there. Notices of new publications appear in some Urdu literary journals, specially the Kitab Numa and the Farogh-e-Urdu. It is important from the writers' point of view also to ensure that their works are sent to the National Library under registered cover. (7.110)[2]

217. The staff for Urdu in the library needs to be strengthened immediately. It should function under an officer who is well conversant with Urdu literature so that he can keep a watch on new arrivals in the market. (7.111)[2]

218. The National Library, at the end of each year, should publish a register, giving short description of all the titles in Urdu. The list containing Urdu books should be published in Urdu also and should be supplied to booksellers, universities, etc., in India and abroad. (7.112)[2]

Grants for Libraries

219. The question of providing grants to libraries specially in the educational institutions, deserves attention. There should be adequate provision for the purchase of Urdu books on a regular basis. Private Urdu libraries should be given grants at par with those in other languages. (7.113)[2]

Grants for Conferences

220. Government should provide suitable grants for holding literary conferences and seminars. Literary trusts engaged in similar activities should also receive such grants. (7.115)[2]

CHAIRMAN INDEX OF COMMITTEES & COMMISSIONS IN INDIA 1947-75 Volumes 1 to 13